THE WAYWARD SHERIFFS Of WITCH COUNTY

TRUE MISADVENTURES OF OPERATING AMERICA'S OLDEST JAIL AND COURTHOUSE.

by

Robert Ellis Cahill

Former High Sheriff & Jail Keep

Albie Marrs
9 Pickering Way
Salem, Ma.

ISBN 0-975877-80-1

Cover designed by Erik Rodenhiser

Published by:
Old Pine Tree Publishing House
P.O. Box 470083
Kissimee, Florida 34747

FORWARD

Knowing that some day I would write a book on my experiences as High Sheriff of Essex County, Massachusetts, I spent a few minutes almost every day while on the job documenting what was going on around me. When I finally sat down at the typewriter, some twenty years later, I found I still needed more information from my old deputies about incidents I had forgotten, or was never told about while in charge of the courts and jails of Essex County. Therefore, I must give a thanks to the following for their invaluable contributions to these chapters: Deputies Terry Marks, Bill Ryan, Jim St. Pierre, Billy Cox, Dugie Russell, George MacKinnon, Loretta Rainville, Bob Curran, and Harry Healy. For photographs I must thank Arthur Reynolds, Norman Dugie Russell, *The Salem Evening News*, and *The Beverly Times*. A thanks for typing and correcting my terrible spelling to Loretta Rainville and Beth Thompson.

Finally, I must thank John Sarrouf, the editor of this book, not only for keeping the manuscript flowing properly in the right direction, but for deciphering my unintelligible scribbling.

This book is true in every aspect, and only in a few instances have names been changed to protect the innocent . . . and the guilty.

The antique Sheriff's House (left) and Old Salem Jail, both built in 1811, as seen from Howard Street Cemetery, where accused witch Giles Corey was crushed to death in 1692. (Photo by Dugie Russell)

This book is dedicated to the following former deputy sheriffs of Essex County, Massachusetts. Some have passed on, others have retired, and at the publication of this book in 2004, only a few remain active in the sheriff's department.

Thanks to all of you for the memories

— Bob Cahill

✳ Steve Archer — Beverly	✳ Charlie Geary — Newbury	✳ Larry Puleo — Salem
✳ Sal Bartolo — Winthrop	✳ Dick Geary — Danvers	✳ Henry Quirk — Salem
✳ Ray Beals Jr. — Beverly	✳ Bob Ginsburg — Beverly	✳ Ron Raffenello — Ipswich
✳ Tom Beaulieu — Salem	✳ Roger Guerette — Danvers	✳ Loretta Rainville — Salem
✳ Warren Bethune — Beverly	✳ Paul Guy — Salem	✳ Charlie Reardon — Salem
✳ John Blaisdell — Marblehead	✳ John Haley — Beverly	✳ Arthur Reynolds — Swampscott
✳ John Bowes — Barnstable	✳ Warren Harding — Saugus	✳ Jake Ricci — Beverly
✳ Leon Breckenridge — Peabody	✳ Charlie Hardy — Rowley	✳ Adam Ricci — Beverly
✳ Robert Brown — Methuen	✳ George Hashem — Salem	✳ Don Richard — Peabody
✳ Mike Burke — Lynn	✳ Harry Healey — Marblehead	✳ John Riley — Salem
✳ J. Mike Cahill — Salem	✳ Bill Hart — Haverhill	✳ George Rioux — Hamilton
✳ Charlie Canto — Methuen	✳ John Hocter — Middleton	✳ George Riordan — Lynn
✳ Joe Caraccio — Methuen	✳ Phil Holt — Gloucester	✳ Lester Roberts — Danvers
✳ Jim Carter — Lawrence	✳ George Hollum — Amesbury	✳ John Ross — Lynn
✳ Joe Carter — Lawrence	✳ Evelyn Hunt — Peabody	✳ Joe Ross — Lynn
✳ George Cashman — Newburyport	✳ Jack Jerdan — Hamilton	✳ Norman Russell — Beverly
✳ Norman Cassola — Beverly	✳ John Kuczun — Salem	✳ Peter Russell — Marblehead
✳ Frank Castanzo — Salem	✳ Mario Landolfi — Beverly	✳ Bill Ryan — Haverhill
✳ Phil Corriveau — Methuen	✳ Bill Lees — Lawrence	✳ Jimmy Ryan — Haverhill
✳ Ernie Comeau — Danvers	✳ Sam Lena — Marblehead	✳ John Rock — Byfield
✳ Billy Cox — Newburyport	✳ Dick Lombaro — Beverly	✳ Frank Roberge — Methuen
✳ Joe Cronin — Lawrence	✳ Dave Lonergan — Salem	✳ Jim St. Pierre — Salem
✳ Frank Ciulla — Gloucester	✳ Paul Lydon — Beverly	✳ Steve Salvo — Salem
✳ Bob Curran — Salem	✳ George MacKinnon — Salem	✳ Al Sears — Amesbury
✳ Tony D'Agnese — Swampscott	✳ Walter McGrath — Ipswich	✳ Dick Silver — Salem
✳ George Delano — N.Andover	✳ Carl Majeskey — Danvers	✳ John Smedile — Salem
✳ Francis Delano — Swampscott	✳ Charlie Manuel — Boxford	✳ Travis Smith — Peabody
✳ Paul DeJoie — Lynn	✳ Manya Manzi — Methuen	✳ Ted Solovicos — Salem
✳ Joe Deshaies — Lawrence	✳ Terry Marks — Lynn	✳ Nick Spaneas — Peabody
✳ Cynthia Diamond — Peabody	✳ Cliff Marshall — Dedham	✳ Ed Sweeney — Ipswich
✳ George Dobson — Saugus	✳ Bob Marshall — Salem	✳ Bob Talbot — Danvers
✳ John Duffy — Lynn	✳ Earl McCurdy — Byfield	✳ Marshall Teemley — Salem
✳ Romeo Emilio — Haverhill	✳ Tom McGovern — Lynn	✳ Bill Terry — Beverly
✳ Larry Fossa — Peabody	✳ Albie Marrs — Salem	✳ Dick Tracy — Haverhill
✳ Paul Ferguson — Newburyport	✳ Ed Mees — Swampscott	✳ Gus Toomey — Salem
✳ Ronald Ford — Lawrence	✳ Al Morneau — Salem	✳ Emin Topalli — Lynn
✳ Henry Fournier — Amesbury	✳ Frank Murphy — Lawrence	✳ Leo Vaillancourt — Beverly
✳ Hank Gagnon — Salem	✳ Dick Macdonald — Salem	✳ Jim Walsh — Salem
✳ Helen Gallo — Danvers	✳ Dick Paverada — Danvers	✳ Sal Zavaglia — Salem
✳ Paul Gaudet — Nahant	✳ Al Poulin — Newburyport	✳ Shirley Zucaro — Salem

Deputy Sheriffs on parade in Newburyport: Top Row, Left to Right: Roberts, Healey, Haley, Tracy, Mees, W. Ryan, Hart, Joe Ross, Fourth Row: Lees, Cronin, Quirk, Smith, Paverada, Reynolds, Third Row: Walsh, Lonergan, Cox, Beals, Terry, Curran; Second Row: J. Ricci, Sweeney, Lyden, G. Delano, Poulin, Canto, Cassola; Front Row: Reardon and Sheriff Cahill.

TABLE OF CONTENTS

Bob Cahill, the new Sheriff of Essex County in 1975, presents Deputy Adam Ricci his badge at the swearing-in ceremonies at Salem Courthouse. (Photo by Arthur Reynolds)

INTRODUCTION

The Salem Jail and House of Correction was the oldest continuously operating penal institution in the United States when I became high sheriff back in 1975. Construction began on this granite bastille in 1811 and was completed for occupancy in the winter of 1813. Awaiting its completion, thieves, debtors, and drunks shared bunkspace with captured British soldiers and sailors in two prison ships anchored offshore: one in Salem Harbor, and the other in the North River, less than 100 yards from where the new jail was being built. In his journal, patriot Paul Revere mentions trotting by the new jail "being constructed," some 36 years after his famous ride. From its earliest days, the jail site was steeped in and surrounded by some of history's great dramas. Within shouting distance was the drawbridge that spanned the North River, where in February of 1775, American colonists first officially took up arms against British troops, spilling the first blood of the American Revolution. Some 300 Redcoats, under the command of Colonel Leslie, had arrived on the scene to confiscate cannons that had been hidden in the North Fields by the colonists. The bridge was drawn, blocking the British advance into North Salem, giving the Minutemen time to assemble and prepare for battle. The British decided to attempt to cross the river by boat, but the only two rowboats on the south bank of the river were smashed in by Colonists before the Redcoats could get to them. To add to the British frustration, one of the boat wreckers, a mulatto ironically named Joe Whitcher, began mocking the soldiers, one of who then stabbed the colonist in the chest with a bayonet. He wasn't badly hurt, but the bloodletting was enough to convince Colonel Leslie that unless he backed off, war would commence. The incident is known to this day as "Leslie's Retreat," and for a few weeks, delayed the inevitable beginning of the war at another North Bridge in Concord, Massachusetts.

Less than 100 yards down the river from the jail, Salem's founder, Roger Conant, and eight other fishermen and their families built houses and settled what was America's first incorporated town in 1626. It was only four years later that over 1,000 people came from England to settle at Salem, led by Governor John Winthrop and America's first sheriff, Richard Saltonstall. By 1630, Salem was already twice the size and population of Plimouth Plantation, which was settled ten years earlier.

Old records reveal that the Salem Goal in 1636 was "a mere dwelling near the North River." In November of 1666, a cage was erected at Salem "as a prison, on the westerly side of the meeting house." Winter was unbearable in this makeshift prison, where temperatures routinely remained below freezing for weeks, and prompted the construction of a "new goal" in 1669, "completed by carpenter Samuel Archer for 37 pounds silver." Ben Felton was a neighbor to and the keeper of the jail, where "prisoners could leave the prison to work for him on his own account—and some ran away." A string of escapes pressed the need for improvements in the jail's security. On June 28, 1670, "John Baker, inmate, twitched the prison lock and escaped." He was caught before he traveled too far and "was whipped ten times." Five years later, almost to the day of the first escape, James Booth, alias James Garritt, escaped. A "Negro named John, chained by one leg," escaped from Salem Jail in May of 1679. "He escaped with the chain," records reveal, and in November of the same year, John Haskins also escaped. Testimony by the jail keeper to the selectmen of the town in December was that "the prison is insufficient and any man can go out as he pleases."

A new, more secure, wooden jail, with a granite dungeon in the basement to hold the more dangerous criminals, was constructed in 1684. Within nine years it would become the most notorious jail in America, known as "The Witch Jail". It was here that those accused of witchcraft were held in 1692, awaiting execution at nearby Gallows Hill. During the one-year Witch Hysteria of Essex County, also known as "the Salem Witch Trials," 19 men and women were hanged, one old man was crushed to death with stones by order of the sheriff, and at least two died from torture and exposure in the Witch Jail. When the hysteria ended in early 1693, after the "afflicted" teenage girls went too far by accusing the Governor's wife of being a witch, about 160 innocent victims were released from Salem Jail and other local holding pens. Some had gone insane, including five-year-old Dorcas Good, who was held in jail for almost a year after her mother was hanged as a witch. There are many well-documented stories of the torture that took place in the dungeon beneath the jail at the hands of Sheriff George Corwin and his deputies, but none as horrific as the crushing of old Giles Corey in the field beside the jail. In the attempt to make Corey plead either innocence or guilt to witchcraft, Sheriff Corwin crushed the life out of him with heavy stones. Robert Calef, who witnessed the torture, wrote, "In the pressing, Giles Corey's tongue was pressed out of his mouth; the sheriff, with his cane, forced it in again." The old man's last words were, "I curse you, Sheriff, and I curse Salem." 121 years later, possibly right on the spot where Corey expired, "the new granite goal" stood like an impregnable fortress, surrounded by a twelve-foot wooden fence and a guard-turret. It was exactly 162 years later that I was sitting in the same fortress as High Sheriff of Essex County, and there had hardly been one improvement in the place since it was built in 1813.

✳ ✳ ✳

I was born and raised in Salem, and during most of my adult life, I lived across the North River from the jail in an old saltbox house built in 1807. Like most Salemites, I never gave the jail much thought. Although I passed by it almost every day, I hardly ever wondered what went on inside its gloomy granite walls. One of my earliest memories of the jail was the summer I was ten years old and camping out at Forest River Park in Salem with four of my pals. We had pitched the tents and were settling in around the fire when over our portable radio came the announcement that a dangerous criminal had escaped from the Salem Jail. His name was Winsocki—or something like that—for I remember the five us started singing joyously: "Buckle down

Winsocki, buckle down. You can win Winsocki if you'll only buckle down." Our excitement and jubilation soon turned to fear, however, when we realized how close we were to the jail and how that forest made an ideal criminal hideout. So we ended up leaving our tent in the park and going to Paul O'Leary's house to finish out the night on his parents' living room floor.

✳ ✳ ✳

Since as far back as I could remember, a Wells had been the Sheriff of Essex County. Roger Wells, only a few years older than I, had been sheriff for ten years. His father had been sheriff before him, and two uncles before that. They were all Republicans. In fact, every sheriff ever elected by the 34 cities and towns that made up Essex County had always been a Republican. Although the state had become over-whelmingly Democratic with the coming of the Irish to Massachu-setts before the turn of the 20th century, Republicans still managed to hold on to the sheriff's seat in Essex County. The name Wells became synonymous with sheriff.

An uncle to Roger Wells was the famous movie actor Walter Brennan, noted for playing the old toothless sidekick to cowboy heroes such as Roy Rogers and John Wayne. Periodically he flew in from Hollywood to visit Sheriff Wells, staying in the Federalist 13-room brick house that stood beside the jail. He was always available to help Roger come election time. Brennan provided Roger with the typical frontier sheriff image, conjuring up kid fantasies of courageous cowboys wearing tin stars and six-guns. Roger, however, didn't fit the stereotype. He was tall, but chunky; stoic, but easygoing; stern, but not tough. He neither looked nor acted like the Hollywood version of a wild-west sheriff. I don't really think Roger liked being sheriff. I think he probably ran for the office at the insistence of friends after his father died—it was, after all, a family tradition. Roger was a bachelor and had no immediate family, except for Walter Brennan, and when old Walter died, a little bit of Roger seemed to die too.

Soon after, Roger called a breakfast meeting of all the jail guards and deputies in order to announce that he was retiring from office. He was sick and tired—sick with sugar diabetes and tired of being a Republican sheriff in a political world where Democrats held the purse strings. For ten years he had pleaded with the County Commissioners and the State Legislature for funds to adequately run and maintain his jails, but he received only enough to keep them operating under minimum standards. To the utter surprise and dismay of his deputies and the Republican Party, the last of the Wells dynasty was picking up bag and baggage and moving to a farm in New Hampshire.

The Republican Party was caught off guard. They had no one to replace Roger Wells except possibly Charles Reardon, who was Well's special sheriff. Reardon, like me, lived in Salem, which was center of county administration. I had never met Charlie Reardon, but I went to his home and told him that I was seriously thinking of running for sheriff. Being a state representative from the area and a former Salem city councilor, I was a proven vote getter. Reardon was younger than I was and better looking, but he had no political experience. He loved his position as second in command of the sheriff's department, he told me, so I promised him that he would keep that position if he declined to run and backed me for sheriff. I figured two people running for the same elective office from the same city, even if they were from different parties, would take votes away from each other, and both would probably lose. He wanted a few days to think it over. It was a bold step on my part, making a behind the scenes deal so early in the game, but I had nothing to lose, and as I left, I was convinced that Charlie would become an active worker in my campaign.

Even as I talked to Reardon, I wasn't sure that I wanted to be Sheriff of Essex County. I had little idea of what a sheriff did, or what the job entailed. All I knew is that I didn't want to continue being a representative to the Great and General Court (that's what Massachusetts calls its House of Representatives), as I had been for the past five years. I felt it was time for me to move up or move out of politics. Of course, I wasn't sure that a run for sheriff was a move up. My inspiration came from reading Al Smith's account of his unsuccessful run for President of the United States, in which he stated, "the most wonderful position I ever held was being High Sheriff of New York City." Smith, however, didn't mention why the job was so wonderful. In Essex County, the sheriff's job paid a few thousand dollars more than what I received as a state rep, but that was not incentive enough to leave one position to run for the other. There was also a much shorter commute to work, and a maintenance allowance and free room and board in the old brick house next to the jail for the sheriff and his family, though I didn't think I'd get my wife Sandy to move the kids across the river from our old saltbox. What I did not figure was how much it would cost me to campaign in 34 cities and towns, nor what great horrors would confront me if I won.

After seeing Special Sheriff Reardon, I went to visit FBI Investigator David Lynch, who was attached to the Essex County District Attorney's Office. He had been campaign chairman for the District Attorney; he knew almost every county employee personally; and most importantly, he was my cousin. Lynch, a cock-rooster in appearance and personality, immediately set the county's political wheels in motion. According to Dave, I was running whether I wanted to or not. He wouldn't allow me to have reservations. As soon as I left, he was on the phone lining up campaigners. I then decided to call my old campaign workers to get them stirring. Although most of them were from Salem, they all had friends and relatives in some of the other county communities and were more than willing to extend our old battle lines into neighboring cities and towns.

Essex County is shaped like a banana with the most populous cities, Lawrence and Lynn, at either end, north and south. It's bordered by New Hampshire to the north and the ocean to the south. The old industrial city of Lynn is the most southern and biggest city in the county, and it also shares a border with Salem. About the same time I announced that I was running for sheriff, David Janes of Lynn, a deputy sheriff under Wells, was rumored to be running on the Democratic ticket as well. I tried to head him off at the pass as I had Reardon, but Janes was determined to run. Soon after, Darby McGhee, a Salem Jail Correctional Officer, also from Lynn, decided he would run too. I actually welcomed McGhee's announcement, hoping he would split the Lynn vote, which was almost four times the Salem vote. My spirits were dampened somewhat, however, when Harold Tobin, a retired FBI agent, jumped into the race—also as a Salem Democrat. The 80,000 Democratic voters of the county were split about evenly between the northern and southern ends, and with four wannabe-sheriffs coming out of the south county, it was inevitable that someone would jump into the race from the north. That someone was former High Sheriff William Casey. As a strong Democrat from Lawrence, the second biggest city in the county, he became the instant frontrunner. Casey had been appointed sheriff by the Governor of Massachusetts after Sheriff Earl Wells died, but he was defeated in a special election only a few months later by Roger Wells. Now, ten years later, he was strapping on his six-guns for another shootout. There were no Republican candidates, so the winner of the five-candidate Democratic primary would win it all.

Here I was, a 39-year-old state representative with no experience in law enforcement, facing four opponents, all professional law enforcement specialists. I was completely out-gunned in terms of qualifications, but I knew I was a good campaigner, so if I was going to win, it was strategy and determination that had to carry me. Since Casey was the only candidate from the north, I decided to campaign heavily there. I would start in the heart of Casey country, the mill city of Lawrence, where I didn't know a soul.

Saturday night bean suppers in local churches and clubs were big in Lawrence, I was told, and they were a great way to meet a lot of people at once. The first one I attended was at the parochial school hall located behind the Lawrence Jail and House of Correction, right near the downtown. I drove the 45 minutes from Salem to Lawrence alone on a cold, wet night. When I entered the hall, I was stunned to find well over 500 people sitting at long banquet tables, all occupied in conversation, chomping contentedly on their beans and franks. If you could get fifty people to attend a bean supper in Salem you'd be lucky. I, of course, didn't know a soul there, and although I certainly wasn't bashful, I felt nervous and very alone. I think I was the only one in the place wearing a suit and tie. Standing at the door, I prodded myself to be brave and aggressive—"Com'on, Bob, walk right over to the first plate of beans, stick out your hand, and introduce yourself." But another little voice inside me said, "Get yourself a plate of beans and hot-dogs—even though you've eaten already—and find yourself a seat." I followed the advice of the second voice, stood in the chow line, and with an overflowing paper plate of beans in one hand and a cup of hot coffee in the other, I meandered up and down the aisles between the crowded banquet tables looking for a seat. There was none. I seemed to be the only one in the hall standing up and wandering about; I felt like everyone was looking at me. Oh, that I should be so lucky! In reality, no one was paying any attention to me at all. I finally spotted a little space on a bench in the middle of the hall and squeezed into it, hardly able to move my elbows to eat. Those sitting around me at the table were chatting loudly in animated conversations. No one even said hello to me.

I finished eating. I now had little choice. "There's no such thing as a shy politician," I scolded myself. There was a little balding man sitting across the table from me. Without getting up, I reached my hand across the table to him, smiled and said, "Hi, my name's Bob Cahill and I'm running for Sheriff of Essex County, and I'd like your vote in the upcoming election." The little man stared at me wide-eyed, his mouth ajar. I couldn't understand his surprised reaction. Then he squeezed my hand and shook it like a water pump.

"I can't believe it," he shouted aloud, jumping to his feet. "We've been wondering who the hell you were. Hey fellas," he blurted even louder, "this is the Cahill guy running for sheriff." I was immediately surrounded by five burly men, all talking to me at once. "I'm Frank Murphy," said the little, bald-headed man, still gripping my hand, "and I'm a guard at the Lawrence Jail…all these guys are guards at the Lawrence Jail. Dave Lynch has told us all about you." Murphy was also President of the Elks, the sponsor of the bean supper. Frank and his pals then took me around the hall, introducing me to everyone there. It was a gala evening and a great beginning for my campaign in Lawrence. I considered it a miracle and still do. Of the 500 plus people eating beans in the hall, I had the luck to sit across from one of the six county correctional officers who would lead my campaign in the north against the hometown boy. Casey, surprisingly, wasn't at the bean supper and he kept a low profile throughout the campaign. Frank Murphy said it was because he was getting old and didn't want the people of Lawrence to see how much he had aged since his last run for sheriff ten years past. Whatever the reason, I took advantage of it and dug in at Lawrence, spending almost every day there, meeting as many people as possible, and recruiting campaign workers. Within weeks, Murphy and his pals Joe Carter and Phil Coriveau had influenced every correctional officer at the Lawrence Jail to jump on my bandwagon.

It was only a week after the bean-supper miracle, as I sat in my home office recruiting workers over the phone, that a squat little man with an apple face and Coke-bottle glasses walked in and plopped himself in the imitation leather chair facing my desk. When I hung up the phone, he leaned forward as if he was going to whisper a secret, but a loud gruff voice said, "I will drive you anywhere you want to go, any time, day or night, in my comfortable Cadillac. Just give me a call when you're ready." He stood up and started to leave, dropping his card on my desk.

"Hold it!" I shouted after him. "Who the hell are you?"

He introduced himself as Adam Ricci, a retired firefighter from Beverly, Massachusetts and a part-time deputy sheriff under Wells. It wasn't long before I took him up on his offer, and he was good to his word—he drove me everywhere throughout the county, almost every day and night. He was my sidekick chauffeur for months.

While we drove from meeting to meeting, town to town, Ricci updated me on the workings of the jail and courts, and the running of the "writ business," also called process serving. The sheriff was responsible for the running of the three Superior Courts in Salem, Lawrence, and a quaint historical edifice in Newburyport. Per diem court officers had to be deputy sheriffs, ready and able to serve and protect the judges, juries, and witnesses and to secure all criminals or alleged criminals while they were at court. Court officers received about thirty dollars a day for this work, but were never guaranteed a full week of work. To make up for this possible lack of a week's pay, court officers often served writs. The writ business is the service that lawyers and judges use to deliver complaints, subpoenas, summonses, warrants, and other official documents to people involved in civil law suits and criminal proceedings. The deputy chosen by the sheriff to run the writ business ran it as a private enterprise, being paid by the lawyers or agencies that wanted the writs served. It could be a lucrative business, and I soon discovered that everyone wanted to be a writ-server. Although the sheriff was responsible for this business, he could have nothing to do with it—a real Catch-22. In addition to this, the sheriff was responsible for running the two jails and houses of correction. Ricci informed me that although the Lawrence Jail was newer, having been built just before the Civil War, its interior was as antiquated as the Salem Jail, which was built during the War of 1812.

Adam Ricci often asked why I was running for sheriff, and I never could give him an adequate answer. "Why do you want this job?" he would shout, hands flaying with typical Italian flair to the point where I thought the car would go off the road. "The jails are crumbling to the ground, the inmates shit in buckets 'cause there's no toilets, the guards are dumb-bunnies who couldn't be cops so they work at the jail, the writ deputies are greedy, the court judges are prima donnas, the court officers are ass-kissers, the food in the jails is crap, and the crooked politicians won't give you the money to make anything any better—so why do you want this job?"

"I like the challenge," I'd reply. "Why do you drive me around all day?"

"Cause I'm retired and don't have anything better to do," he replied. "It's not like being a sheriff out West or down South," he reminded me. "They've got hundreds of well-paid and trained deputies and vehicles with all the fixins. You've got crap here—one paddy wagon that's twelve years old, and no training for officers—hell, these guys have to buy their own guns and uniforms and use their own cars to transport criminals. It just ain't right."

"I aim to fix that, pard'ner," I told Adam in my best John Wayne drawl, "and that's why I'm runnin' for sheriff. I'm going to bring the

sheriff's department from the Dark Ages into the twentieth century."
Adam would grunt and give me a suspicious side-glance, but during
these conversations I slowly began selling myself on the idea that I
was the candidate who was going to revamp the old jails and the outmoded way of doing things in the county. I was the Lone Ranger on
the white horse, coming to save the ranchers from doom. I'm not sure
if I convinced myself, but Adam believed I could do it—even though
I was the only candidate without law enforcement experience—and he
was convinced that because of my past political victories that I would
win. He was right.

When the votes were tallied, I received 35,619; Casey got 16,237;
Janes received 14,413; McGhee, 6,520; and Tully, 5,600. I was the new
High Sheriff of Essex County. "The first Democrat ever elected to the
position in the 300 plus year history of the county," was the sub-head-
line of the *Salem Evening News*. "The victory was also remarkable,"
the *News* went on to say, "because Cahill pulled it off without carrying Lynn or Lawrence—the two major population centers in the
county, which most observers say are needed to win a countywide contest. In Lynn, Cahill ran a strong second to Janes, and in Lawrence he
ran second to Casey. However, with the exceptions of Andover, North
Andover, Methuen and Nahant, where he ran second, Cahill was first
in every other city and town in the county...." Who says you can't win
by coming in second?

In the final November election, without Republican opposition, I
received the highest vote that any politician ever tallied in Essex
County, or so Congressman Michael Harrington informed me. I was
flying high—I suddenly had scores of new friends whose names I did-
n't even know and many of them wanted jobs. There weren't enough
jobs in the sheriff's department to fit all the people that wanted
them—and most of these people had worked diligently to get me
elected. I was also some $30,000 in debt, and this was after I had re-
mortgaged my house to pay for brochures and bumper stickers—all
this for a $19,000 a year job; at least I wouldn't have to campaign again
until after a six-year term. Little could I realize at the time that I
wouldn't last the six years.

Before Roger Wells left for the wilds of New Hampshire, he informed me that the beautiful black sedan he drove around was not provided to the sheriff by the county, but was in fact his. The sheriff's department had no vehicle but the old black boxy paddy wagon. On its sides, in gold Olde English lettering, were the words "Essex County Sheriff's Department," making it look even more antique than it was. So on inauguration day, I hired a horse and buggy to drive me to the Salem Superior Court for the swearing-in. When reporters asked the inevitable question about my form of transportation, I told them that Essex was the only county in America that didn't provide at least one vehicle to the sheriff, and that Essex, because of its Republican history, had remained in the Dark Ages in every fashion. The horse and buggy only dramatized the state of the Essex County Sheriff's Department and the need to bring it into the twentieth century.

On that same day, 55 men and 2 women were sworn in as my deputy sheriffs. I had chosen Bob Curran, my campaign chairman, to be chief deputy in charge of the writ service. I had to persuade Bob to leave his well paying job at General Electric in Lynn to be in charge of civil process, though many of my friends' noses were out of joint for doing it, as they all wanted to be in charge of this lucrative business. Very few understood what the job was all about, but everyone wanted to do it because of the rumored high pay. I really didn't care how high the pay was—I just knew that Bob Curran was a good administrator and a tough businessman, and since I was responsible for the process office, I wanted the best man to run it. Charlie Reardon would assist with the writ office, as he had under Wells, and would be my special sheriff, responsible for running the courts, as I had promised him before the election. Warren Bethune of Beverly, Deputy Master of the Salem Jail and House of Correction under Wells, would continue in that position, and I would be the Master of the Jail. Although a lot of old cronies, campaign workers, and a couple of school chums were made deputy sheriffs, I did keep on quite a few of Roger Well's old deputies so at least some of us would understand how the department operated.

The greatest controversy came when I named the Master and

Keeper of the Lawrence Jail. State Representative Bill Ryan from Haverhill, a large northern city, had worked feverishly on my campaign and was the best man for the job, so I made him the offer. Working with him at the state house, I had realized he was a remarkable organizer, improviser, and procurer. He had a great sense of humor, a quality needed to run a grim, outdated jail, and he was a man of action. Bill wanted to run for Mayor of Haverhill, and I had to talk him out of it to become Master of the Jail. The job only paid $16,000, but it supplied a house that was attached to the jail for him and his family, plus free food. Bill finally accepted my offer, but it stirred up some unexpected controversy—he was a Republican. The local press really came down on me, suspicious of the first elected Democratic sheriff hiring a Republican to be his right-hand man in the north; it just didn't sit right with Democratic leaders. I was called before the Haverhill Democratic Committee to explain Ryan's appointment. After an hour of contentious debate, I finally said to them, "If you know of a better man than Bill Ryan to fill this position, give me his name now." There was silence in the room and no mention of it ever again. They knew as I did that Bill Ryan was the best man for the job.

I knew that Ryan, like myself, would beg, borrow, and steal to bring the Lawrence jail up to standard and to begin treating the inmates like human beings. Both Ryan and I were conservatives, but our outlooks now had to be liberal in an effort to better the situation at the jails—neither one of us could just sit back and flow with the status-quo. It seemed like a Herculean task, but we both welcomed the challenge. Bill's wife Maureen opted to live in the house attached to the Lawrence Jail, but my wife Sandy decided to break the old tradition of sheriffs and their families living beside the Salem jail. By law, I had to take two rooms as living quarters in the house or lose control of it to the County Commissioners, but that left eleven rooms in this beautiful old brick Federalist building to do with as I pleased. I decided they could be used as classrooms for deputies and guards, possibly giving them the training they never had, or even as a space to set up a work-release program for inmates. The jail had no room for such programs, nor had there been any inclination in the past to attempt work release.

When I announced my plan, the local newspaper editor, Jim Shea, mocked it as being flamboyant. "Work release will take away jobs from honest citizens who need them," he wrote. Jim Shea and I hadn't gotten along since I was a Salem City Councilor eight years earlier, and it was obvious right from the beginning that I would get no support from the local press in my new position. A further disappointment came when I was handed the keys to the sheriff's house and entered it. There was not a stick of furniture in the house, and many of the rooms were in disrepair. Roger Wells had packed everything up and moved it all off to New Hampshire—he even took the brass door-knocker.

The Sheriff's brick house, thought to be built by famous architect Samuel McIntyre, and the entrance to the Salem Jail, both completed for occupancy in 1813. (Photo by David Matt, courtesy of The Salem Evening News)

CHAPTER I

Keystone Cops

Through every newspaper and radio station north of Boston, I made a plea for furniture, paint, and assistance in fixing up the sheriff's house for training and work release. I also asked for television sets, books and more paint for the jail. It was obvious from the beginning that neither the state nor county was going to spare a penny for my department. Rumor was that Essex County was going to get a new, modern jail, built in the center of the county, in a little town called Middleton. The problem was that this rumor had persisted for at least fifty years. It was just the excuse the county commissioners and my old colleagues in the state house needed not to fund any upgrade. "It would be silly of us to grant you funds to fix up the old jail," was one commissioner's comment, "when we may build a new one in the near future." He, of course, knew that there was no new jail on the horizon; I was already beginning to feel Roger Well's frustration and to understand his reason for quitting the job. Most citizens were apathetic about the jail, but a few pieces of furniture were delivered to our doorstep, and Salem's Hawthorne Hotel—a beautiful old and ritzy hotel located on Salem Common—donated a few old TV sets for the inmates. Bill Reinstein, the mayor of Revere, provided twenty classroom desk-chairs, which we placed in the biggest second-floor room of the sheriff's house, giving us our first classroom. Now all we had to do was find teachers to donate their time.

I immediately wanted to replace the drab black uniforms worn by court officers and deputies serving writs, with snappy forest green uniforms and Smoky-the-Bear wide-brim hats, called Campaign Covers, and worn by the Massachusetts State Troopers. The problem, once again, was that there was no money to do so. "Deputy sheriffs and court officers buy their own uniforms," I was informed by the county clerk. They also had to buy their own badges, which I considered a travesty. How could I appoint someone as deputy sheriff and then tell him to go out and buy his own badge? It was insulting enough that I had to buy my own badge. Bob Curran, my deputy in charge of the writ service, came to the rescue and volunteered to buy the badges, but the deputies would still have to buy their own uniforms. What was really needed was a deputy sheriff's union, but I wasn't about to suggest that. I already had two unions to contend with, one of Salem correctional officers, and the other of Lawrence guards. The latter was affiliated with the Teamsters Union and seemed well advanced in benefits, but the Salem group was independent, and the county didn't even provide them with shoes or coats.

The Lawrence union insisted that I meet with them immediately upon my taking office, which I did. We were embroiled in discussions for almost an entire day, during which they brought in union leaders from the outside who had prepared a long list of demands: seniority, reduced working hours, more uniform allowances, better food—you name it, they wanted it. Their elected steward, a bombastic, outspoken man, began the meeting by screaming out each demand.

"Why are you yelling?" I asked him calmly. "Have I said I was opposed to any of your demands?" The old guard, obviously used to screaming to get attention, looked to his leaders for support. They told him to calm down, which pleased me no end. I nodded my head in agreement to each of their demands as they presented them and watched the mood slowly change from angry and aggressive to excited and hopeful as the day progressed. They were all but patting me on the shoulder when they handed me the document to sign. "Oh, I want you to have all these things," I told them, "but not right now. I certainly can't be under the restrictions of seniority and reduced hours while trying to bring the county in line with existing laws, as I must, at the same time. Let's meet again in six months," and I got up from the meeting and walked out. Hell, there weren't enough guards overseeing the inmates now to meet minimum safety requirements, and the commissioners weren't about to hire more guards, so I certainly wasn't about to reduce their hours. The Lawrence boys weren't too happy. In contrast, with the Salem union, *I* had to call the meeting and convince *them* that they should at least have the county pay for their coats for winter duty, which was often outside the jail walls. I, in fact, had to write up their demands for them to present to the county commissioners and do battle on their behalf at the commissioners' budget meeting.

From the day I took office, the guards of both jails were constantly complaining to me about one thing or another, and even worse, they were always involved in petty gripes and quarrels with each other, often coming to me for redress. Three shifts had to be covered, seven days a week, at both jails. Staffing was so tight that if just one man stayed home sick or feigned sickness with the "blue-flu," the schedules were thrown off and security was in jeopardy, which infuriated many of the guards. Most of the Salem guards thought I should fire Darby McGhee just because he ran against me for sheriff. Darby, an ex-marine, did purposely spark quarrels within the jail, but I soon discovered that he had some remarkable talents as a counselor, and that was in short supply. The internal bickering, which sometimes led to fisticuffs, became so intense that I was forced to call a meeting of all the guards at the jail. I told them that I thought their relations with their fellow workers were awful, and that I would expect better behavior from fifth graders. As if that weren't enough to steam them, I concluded my scolding lecture by saying that I also thought they were doing a lousy job communicating with the inmates. "Yes, you are responsible for security here," I said, "and yes, these people must pay for their crimes, whatever they may be. But you can be cordial to them—hell, you can even be helpful to them. You are called correctional officers, so for Christ's sake, start correcting. I haven't been here long, but I've discovered thus far that most of the problems here are caused by the correctional officers and not by the inmates." Pale, angry faces stared up at me and there was silence. I walked out without saying another word. Now they had something really worthwhile to squawk about—the new sheriff was a son-of-a-bitch.

There was a small room in the jail, not much bigger than a closet, which had been Sheriff Wells' office. I turned that over to Warren Bethune and set up my office in the house next-door. My secretary was Loretta Rainville, a neighbor and friend, who was not only a good typist, but was also very resourceful. With the little bit of furniture we had, she began to make the place look professional. Waters & Brown Hardware Store donated some blue paint, and the sheriff's office soon became "the Blue Room."

One of the first things I realized was that the grounds of the Salem jail didn't seem quite state of the art. Neither the small grassy yard nor the parking lot in front of the jail had a fence around it. Right next door was a playground for the children who attended the Saint John's Parochial Grammar School—not the most ideal spot for a school—and often there were school kids, guards, and inmates all mingling on the front lawn. At the rear end of the jail, where a high wooden wall covered by a few strands of barbed wire separated the inmates from Bridge Street and freedom, there stood a large warehouse with the sign, "Parker Brothers Games", on the roof. The Parker Brothers Games Company is the producer of Monopoly, which always seemed to bring to mind the phrase, "Go Directly to Jail: Do Not Pass Go." I was told that if anyone tried to escape over the wall during working hours, employees from Parker Brothers usually saw him and gave us a call at the jail. I thought that was nice of them.

✻ ✻ ✻

I was looking out the window of my new blue office as three of my new green-clad deputies were stuffing a chain gang of inmates into the paddy wagon. It would only be a three-block ride to the courthouse complex. "They'd probably get there quicker walking," I mused to myself. The old paddy wagon was constantly breaking down, and we needed a new vehicle desperately, but at the moment it was the least of my problems. Only a few minutes after the paddy wagon had left the jail yard, I was discussing some of those problems with Bob

Curran and Loretta when we all heard a loud "pop, pop, pop" sound coming from the downtown area. Bob saw the look of concern crease my face.

"Probably a car backfiring," said Loretta.

"It sure sounded like gunfire to me," I said, "and it came from the direction of the courthouse."

"I hope you're wrong," said Curran, "cause we've got a lot of new green deputies that could really foul things up." Curran was a quiet tough guy, but also an outstanding organizer who was not happy with all my choices for new inexperienced deputies.

One of the deputies on the court detail was my old college buddy Billy Cox of Newburyport. If there was trouble in town, I knew Cox would be right in the middle of it. He was a hell-raiser at Boston University, and although only 5'6" tall, he would take on anyone twice his size. He had been a sprinter on the track team and a crack shot in the rifle club. He had a good job selling pharmaceuticals, but his eyesight began fading, and constantly being on the road was too much for his eyes. Even so, I was surprised when he asked me to be a deputy sheriff. Another on the detail was Travis Smith, a young, chunky ex-bank teller, who had boarded at my house when he went to college not too many years before. He was basically a shy guy, who also surprised me by saying he wanted to be a deputy—possibly just to get a little action into an otherwise humdrum life. I had made it plain to Charlie Reardon that I wanted a least one experienced man on all transportation details and in every courtroom. The experienced deputy on this detail was Tony D'Agnese, a Swampscott policeman who had worked for Wells as a deputy part-time. I thought of calling Warren Bethune on the intercom we had just installed in the jail, but as Curran said, "If things aren't all right, he would have called you." The words were just out of his mouth when the phone rang.

"Sheriff, we've had an escape," an unfamiliar out-of-breath voice shouted into my ear. "An inmate jumped out of the paddy wagon downtown, but don't worry, we'll get him. Gotta go. 'Bye, Sheriff." The phone clicked.

"Who is this?" I demanded. "Who escaped?" There was no answer.

I turned to Curran. "Those were shots we heard...someone has escaped and apparently is running loose around downtown. If that's Billy Cox shooting up the town, we're in big trouble 'cause he's as blind as a bat." I told Curran to run down to the courthouse to find out what was happening and report back to me as soon as he could.

I buzzed Warren Bethune at the jail, but neither he nor anyone else there had heard a thing about an escape. Most of the inmates in the paddy wagon, I was told, were from the Lawrence Jail and were scheduled at the Salem Superior Court for bail review. "Call Lawrence and get me a list of the inmates in the wagon," I told Warren.

He was back to me with the list within two minutes. "Jose Gomez, Jesus Rodriguez, Roberto Carmentine, Santo Romero, Wilson Perez, Percy Roberts and Paul Fitzpatrick—that's it, Sheriff."

"I'll bet you dollars to donuts that Fitzpatrick is the one who escaped," I told Warren. "I don't know why I know that, but I do. He's Irish and probably a rebel. Do you wanna bet, Warren?"

"No thanks, Sheriff," Warren replied, "but you may be right. He's been sitting in the Lawrence Jail for two months, facing extradition to Arkansas, where he's wanted for armed robbery. He's a Lynn boy, just out of his teens, and I'm sure he doesn't want to face those southern rednecks in Arkansas."

Curran was soon back from the courthouse with as much information as he could gather in all the chaos. My hunch had been right. It was Paul Fitzpatrick who'd escaped. The deputies had transported the seven prisoners in the paddy wagon to the courthouse. Parked out front, Deputy D'Agnese unlocked and opened the doors at the rear of the wagon. All the occupants, handcuffed and chained to each other, jumped out of the wagon in single-file. At the end of this tethered, human chain was the tall, lanky Fitzpatrick, but somehow he was no longer connected to the others. With a pin-like tool he designed in jail, he had managed to spring both cuff locks and free himself as he rode in the wagon. When the paddy wagon doors opened, Fitzpatrick bolted, running as fast as he could down Salem's busy Washington Street. D'Agnese pulled out his revolver and fired three warning shots into the air, shouting for Fitzpatrick to stop, but the fugitive kept on running. Billy Cox ran after him, and in front of "The Morning Call" coffee shop, Billy stopped, knelt on the sidewalk, took careful aim and was about to shoot Fitzpatrick in the back at about sixty paces when D'Agnese shouted, "Don't kill him, Billy! For God's sake, don't kill him!" Fitzpatrick dashed into a side alley. Billy gave D'Agnese a dirty look, holstered his pistol, and continued the chase. Hundreds of pedestrians had now gathered to watch the action.

Cox had lost both D'Agnese and Fitzpatrick in the crowded street, so he continued the search alone. A concerned citizen informed Cox that the escapee had ducked into the Masonic Building. Drawing his pistol once more, Cox rushed into the building. He came to a long corridor and saw a door slam shut at the other end. He ran to the door and cautiously opened it. Inside the dark and dingy room, a cloth drapery hung from ceiling to floor. Billy tiptoed up to it, aimed his gun and threw the drapery back. There sat a fat, gray-haired woman, her mouth stuffed with cotton, staring wide-eyed into the barrel of Billy's gun. She moaned and tried to say something as Billy backed out of the room, apologizing to her and to the frightened dentist who had peeked in from a side room. Fitzpatrick had ditched his pursuers and was now on the loose, and nobody knew where.

Meanwhile, the other six inmates, all cuffed together, standing in the street outside the courthouse, had been forgotten by D'Agnese and Cox, both in hot pursuit of Fitzgerald, and by Deputy Trav Smith, who was inside the courthouse. It had been Trav who had called me on the telephone announcing the escape. The leader of this chain gang, realizing their unique situation, started edging the others towards busy Washington Street. At first the others resisted being pulled down the street by their lead man, but then they realized what he was attempting to do. They tried to look inconspicuous, but that was near impossible. When they got to the street corner they gathered close together, hiding the handcuffs as best they could, and pretending that they were waiting for a bus. Trav came back out of the courthouse in time to see them sidestepping up the street and managed to drag them back to the courthouse.

I had explained to all the deputies when I swore them in that, whether they worked full-time or part-time, they were expected to volunteer their services during any emergency—I considered Fitzpatrick's escape an emergency. I had Bob Curran begin calling them all to show up at my office in uniform, with their weapons. Fitzpatrick wasn't a convicted felon, so we couldn't shoot him—which was the message D'Agnese was trying to get across to Cox—but I still wanted my men armed as they went out searching for him. Convicted or not, a man on the run and desperate is a dangerous man. Charlie Reardon informed me that Sheriff Wells never tried to chase down his escapees, leaving that task to the local or state police. "If we lose them, we've got to find them," I told Reardon, which pleased him, for he loved police work. He immediately took over control of the search, and as deputies showed up at my office, he would assign them to various details of the search.

Charlie Hardy, Assistant Deputy Master of the Salem Jail, provided us with a jail photo and description of Paul Fitzpatrick: "Six-foot two inches, thin, clean-shaven, long brown hair that was usually worn in a ponytail, wearing a white T-shirt and jeans." Each deputy had a peek at our only photo and then joined in the search. I told them all that either Bob Curran or I would be in the office, so if anyone got a lead or spotted Fitzpatrick they were to call me immediately.

From the moment of the escape, I was inundated with calls, not only from the overzealous deputies and over-bearing newspaper reporters, but also from seemingly helpful and sometimes frightened citizens, who had heard of the escape from a local radio report. There were sightings of Fitzpatrick in every far-reaching corner of Salem and beyond. He seemed to be everywhere. I would have needed over 100 deputies just to follow up all the phone leads, many of which were obvious pranks. There were two calls from people who said they saw a tall man with a ponytail walking the railroad tracks towards

Lynn, which sounded plausible to me, so I had Reardon and a flock of deputies check it out. We also staked out Fitzpatrick's girlfriend's house on the Lynn-Salem border and searched a few downtown Salem buildings from basement to attic. One of the biggest problems I had was obtaining a clear phone line to alert all 34 police chiefs in Essex County of the escape and to describe the escapee. We had an extremely poor communication link between law enforcement agencies, creating a definite need for the sheriff's department to have more than one telephone. I added that to my growing list of improvements for which I had no money.

In the midst of my calling the police chiefs, an incoming call sneaked through from Carl Harris, an old friend who owned a downtown furniture store. "There's a young man who keeps walking in and out of my store," said Carl, whispering, "and he's acting very suspicious. I think it's your man."

"Follow him wherever he goes," I told Carl. "I'll send someone right over." I hung up and realized that Bob Curran and I were the only ones left in the office. Leaving Loretta at the phone, we jumped into Bob's car and sped downtown. By the time we rushed into Carl's store, he was gone. His wife told us that he followed some man up the street. Bob and I trotted up Washington Street and bumped into Carl. "He's in the drugstore," he said, pointing, and walked back towards his store, not wanting to be caught in any potential crossfire.

"Do you have a gun?" I asked Bob. He didn't, and neither did I.

"You go in the back door," I told Bob, "and I'll go in the front. If he's facing me, you grab him from behind, and if he's facing you, I'll grab him." We gingerly entered the drugstore at both ends. I was in my forties and Curran was in his early fifties. Could we handle the wily Fitzpatrick, I wondered. I steeled myself for a fight, assured that we could take him. I entered the long, narrow store with the checkerboard, black and white marble floor. There were only a few people at the counter, and another one at the magazine rack. None of them looked young, but I couldn't clearly see the man at the magazine rack. I spied Curran at the other end, staring intently at those around him, and when Curran spotted me, I pointed at the man reading a magazine. Curran rushed to the man's side and grabbed his arm, causing him to drop the magazine to the floor. Then Curran turned red in the face. Apparently he thought that I was signaling for him to capture the man with the magazine. The poor fellow, a middle-aged man who was graying at the temples, was in shock, and Bob was embarrassed. As I ran up to them, Bob was quietly apologizing. The man was wide-eyed and sputtering.

"I'm the sheriff," I said, "and we're looking for an escapee…sorry, we thought you might be him."

The man gave us both an angry stare and walked off in a huff. Everyone in the store was staring at us. My face turned red to match Bob's. We quickly left by the front door. There was no young man with long hair. It was just another false alarm. We would have many more before the day was over.

Shortly after Bob and I returned to the office, the phone rang with another supposed encounter with the escapee. It was Deputy George Dobson, a zealous volunteer, who sounded out of breath.

"I'm in a phone booth, only a block away from Fitzpatrick's girlfriend's house," he said, "and I've got Fitzpatrick here in the booth with me."

I wasn't sure I had heard Dobson correctly, so I had him repeat himself

"Yes sir, Sheriff, I'm holding him by the ponytail. It's him all right—it's Fitzpatrick." Dobson looked and acted like a marine drill-sergeant. He was such a gung-ho guy that I was immediately afraid that he had grabbed the first young man who walked near the girlfriend's house and now held him captive.

"What do you want me to do with him, Sheriff? Can you get a car down here quick?"

"Just hold on for a minute, Dobson," I said. "Describe him to me."

"He's tall, thin, wearing a soiled T-shirt and jeans, long brown hair, scruffy beard and mustache—."

"Let him go!" I shouted over the phone.

"Let him…? But, Sheriff, it's him—it's Fitzpatrick!"

"Fitzpatrick is clean shaven—no beard, no mustache. It's not him. Let that guy go before we have a lawsuit on our hands."

"But, Sheriff, I'm sure it's him," Dobson pleaded.

"It can't be him, unless he was able to grow a mustache and beard within three hours. Tweak his beard. Make sure it's real." I heard a yowl.

"It's real all right," said Dobson.

"Then let him go, damn it," I shouted. "That guy can't be Fitzpatrick."

"Okay, whatever you say, Sheriff—screw off, punk!" I heard Dobson say.

"You've got to be careful," I shouted at Dobson. "We've got enough problems here without arresting innocent people."

"He thrives on this police stuff," said Curran. "You're going to have to keep him in line."

No more than five minutes passed from Dobson's phone call when Deputy Charlie Hardy walked into my office from the jail and stood before my desk.

"Something's been bothering me, Sheriff," big Charlie said. "It's about this photograph of Fitzpatrick." He held up the mug shot that was lying on my desk. "I don't think it's right."

"What's wrong with it?" I asked, somewhat perturbed that Charlie would bring up some trivial imperfection in a photograph when so many important things were going on around us.

"Well, I'm pretty sure when I saw Fitzpatrick in the wagon this morning, he was sportin' a beard and mustache. I asked some of the other inmates inside, and they agreed with me—Fitzy's been growin' a beard for the last few weeks."

I was stunned, frozen in my seat, unable to move. "Holy shit!" I finally yelled up at Hardy.

"Dobson was pulling on that beard five minutes ago. Quick! Get me the address of Fitzpatrick's girl's house in Lynn. Come on, Curran, we've got to get to Lynn, fast! Call every County police station again, starting with Lynn," I shouted at Loretta, "and tell them that Fitzpatrick has a beard and mustache."

Curran is a cautious driver and we had no siren, so by the time we pulled up to the curb near the girlfriend's house, I was jumping out of my skin. Six deputies, including Dobson, immediately crowded around Curran's car. Dobson opened the car door for me, and as he did, said, "Gee, Sheriff, I'm sure that was—."

"I know, I know. Dobson, can I speak to you in private for a moment?" I asked, pushing him away from the other deputies. Out of earshot of the others, I wrapped my arm around his shoulder. "You were right, George. It was Fitzpatrick. Now, tell me, which way did he go?"

Dobson pointed to the end of the street, to a heavily wooded section. "He went into the woods," said Dobson.

"Curran," I shouted over my shoulder, "call Reardon and the Salem Police and tell them that we have good reason to believe that Fitzpatrick is in the woods off Highland Avenue."

Leaving one deputy to watch over the girlfriend's house, I gathered together the deputies on the scene. "If anyone spots Fitzpatrick, fire a shot into the air," I told them. With Dobson in the lead, we spread out to comb the woods. As we pushed through the underbrush, I lost sight of the deputies and soon realized that since I had no weapon, even if I did bump into Fitzpatrick, all I could do was shout. I began sweating under the collar and loosened my tie. Fitzpatrick would certainly think it strange to see a dressed up man walking in the middle of the woods. My pants legs were scratched and torn by thorns and briar patches, and my shoes were caked with mud from what was becoming a swampy area. I decided not to proceed any further, fearful that I'd get lost, bringing further ridicule to my department of greenhorns and myself. I found a large boulder and sat for twenty minutes, absorbing the silence and solitude. I hadn't visited a wooded area for years—probably not since my Cub Scout days—and it felt good to be alone and at peace with myself. I wondered if maybe Fitzpatrick was sitting on a rock nearby, also enjoying the quiet solitude of the woods.

I meandered my way out of the woods to the street and found two Salem police cruisers waiting, along with "Ace," a black German shepherd police dog. Ace was famous in Salem for sniffing out hidden marijuana patches. The police had walkie-talkies, so I sent them out individually. My deputies, who were arriving one at a time, on the other hand, had no way of keeping in communications with each other, so I sent them into the woods in pairs, hoping that one pair wouldn't stumble into another and start shooting at each other. As darkness set in, most of them walked out of the woods to inform me that they had to go home for supper. If their wives allowed, they would be back after supper. "If you come back, bring flashlights," Charlie Reardon told them. I too decided to go home and change clothes before returning to search. Reardon and a handful of deputies remained on the scene, searching the edges of the woods along Highland Avenue.

The evening newspaper was wedged inside my storm door with the headline: "Fleet-Footed Prisoner Flees Van, Eludes Deputies." With a palpitating heart and twitching fingers, I sat down at the kitchen table to read the lead article:

SALEM—A fleet-footed, nimble-wristed jail prisoner amused pedestrians and embarrassed the sheriff's department today when he wiggled out of his handcuffs and leaped out of a parked paddy wagon and escaped down Washington Street in broad daylight. The guards, three deputy sheriffs, provided the comic relief as they shouted, fired guns into the air, and ambled hopelessly behind... The escape, which occurred shortly after 10:30am, unfolded before some 100 on-lookers, whose initial shock from the crack of gunfire quickly turned to delight as a confused contingent of police and correctional officers gathered for a futile search of the courthouse area.

One witness, chuckling at the spectacle of the bullet-punctuated chase, told on-lookers, 'Better keep low around here; it's dangerous.'

And while some witnesses were laughing over the road race, others joined the official search party in speculating on the wily prisoner's whereabouts. One of Fitzpatrick's pursuers, Deputy

Sheriff William Cox, is a former high school track star. But according to witness accounts, Fitzpatrick left Cox in the dust....

I could read no more. My wife said that our home phone had been ringing off the hook since the newspaper hit the streets. Most were from so-called friends asking if they could "join my track team," or "provide physical training for my out of shape deputies." I wasn't in the mood for such jokes, but was thankful that news reporters hadn't ferreted out George Dobson's story of Fitzpatrick's "capture."

I was eating supper and hadn't yet had time to change my clothes when I heard sirens coming from the direction of Highland Avenue. I ran from the house and climbed into my 1972 Mustang, and even though it hadn't been running well lately, drove it as fast as I could. When I arrived where I had left them only a half hour before, the place was abandoned. I began cruising the four miles of Highland Avenue to the Lynn border and back, but saw nothing unusual—no deputies, no cops. The siren I heard had probably been a fire engine on the way to a fire somewhere else. My radiator cap started leaking steam like a hot kettle, so I decided to head home, somewhat surprised that everyone had given up the search so early.

Coming into the downtown area, two police cruisers sped past me, lights flashing, sirens blaring, heading in the opposite direction, toward Highland Avenue. I spun the old Mustang around and headed after them. My radiator was now boiling over, and the car sputtered and coughed, but I pushed on. I just knew in my bones that their emergency had something to do with Fitzpatrick. Trying to pass other vehicles in order to catch up with the cruisers, I leaned on my horn, waving other drivers out of the way. Both cruisers crossed the highway and came to a screeching halt near a junkyard, close to a rocky gully that led into the woods we had been searching earlier. I followed, my car screaming in pain and spitting steam. I pulled in, leaped out of the car, which kept on rumbling long after I'd taken the keys out of the ignition, and followed four policemen and Ace the dog as they headed into the deep, dark gully. It was pitch black and I had forgotten to take a flashlight.

"What's up?" I asked one of the cops.

"Got a call," he replied. "The escapee was seen climbing around the cars in the junkyard. Then he was seen running into this gully just minutes ago." The police kept walking, flashing their lights on and behind the many tall boulders that peppered the gully. One of them flashed a signal to Bob Tarnowski, the dog officer, who was behind me, and Bob let go of the leash. Now, I love dogs, but I have always had a powerful fear of German shepherds—and there was Ace, heading right towards me. My legs began to wobble and I braced myself for a pounce, but Ace sped right by me and headed for a nearby boulder. Less than thirty feet from me, Ace stopped and started barking. A tall figure leaped to his feet from behind the rock, hands cupped behind his head.

"I give up!" he shouted. "Call off your dogs. Hi, Sheriff," he said matter-of-factly, noticing me standing close by. "You sure do have a lousy communications setup, don't you?" he said with a wry smile, while the police cuffed him.

"Yes," I replied, "it's the worst in America."

They escorted Fitzpatrick up the hill to one of the cruisers. I waited until I was sure the police were all on their way, with Fitzpatrick securely cuffed and in the back of a cruiser, before heading back to my car. My car wouldn't start. I sat there a long time before I started my three-mile walk home. It gave me time to consider my first crisis as sheriff. Would there be other days like this, I wondered, or would this be my worst day as High Sheriff of Witch County?

In the morning, I signed a court order against Fitzpatrick for his escape, which added six months to his jail term in Salem, further delaying his extradition to Arkansas. It was just what he wanted—probably the reason he escaped in the first place. This was turning out to be a strange job, recapturing inmates who escaped from prison in order to stay in prison longer.

*Bob Curran, Chief Deputy Sheriff in charge of Writ Service,
High Sheriff Bob Cahill, and Bill Ryan, Master & Keeper
of the Lawrence Jail.*

*Warren Bethune, Deputy
Master of the Salem Jail and
House of Correction.
(Photo by Jim Wilson)*

*Funnel for dumping
human waste from
inmate buckets, located
outside the dining-hall
at the Salem Jail.*

*Called "the flats" by some inmates, this is the only recreation area
inside the Salem Jail and House of Correction. (Photo by Peter Main)*

CHAPTER II

Storming The Bastille

There was only one working toilet in the Salem Jail and anyone who used it could be seen from the cellblock catwalk. It sat in a little wooden cubicle, without a door, near the shower area in the basement. It often clogged and overflowed, flooding the shower area with a soupy mess that smelled terrible; nobody ever wanted to clean it up. The crumbling cement shower stall contained three dripping showerheads, although usually only one worked, and it often supplied no hot water. The constant smell of strong disinfectant, attempting to hide the scent of feces, permeated the whole bathroom area. It was where, in the summer months, flies and mosquitoes thrived, and in the winter, an occasional rat could be seen lapping at the water. Inmates were allowed one shower and one dump in the real toilet each week, if they so desired. Otherwise, all one hundred-plus inmates did not bathe, and were forced to relieve themselves in six-gallon plastic buckets kept in their cells. There were no toilets or sinks in the cells, just an iron cot covered with a soiled mattress, one itchy woolen blanket, and a "shitbucket," as it was fondly called. The only other item provided in each cell was a naked light bulb that had to be twisted on and off. The five-foot by eight-foot cells often held two inmates, which meant an extra bunk and bucket, leaving little room to move and no room to escape the smells. Many inmates were not provided sheets or pillows. When I arrived on the job, the county clerk told me that the county could not afford them. "We're not running a country club here, you know," he told me.

"You certainly aren't," I retorted. Although there were some issues that couldn't be corrected without big money and major reconstruction—like laying plumbing pipes through six-foot granite walls—I was bound and determined to solve the little problems—like the shortage of sheets, pillows, toilet paper, and towels. After being locked in the cells from 8:30pm to 7:30am each night, the first chore in the morning for every inmate was to empty his bucket. It was poured into a funnel-shaped receptacle attached to a sewer pipe, located just outside the dining hall. Although an open water spigot was attached to the top of this funnel and a barrel of disinfectant was standing close by, the foul fumes from the funnel kept many inmates from the breakfast table.

There were four groups of inmates within the jail and each had to eat separately from the others. First to the dining hall in the morning were those residing on the "jail side," those awaiting trial for some crime they may or may not have committed. These were the "innocent until proven guilty" set, all of whom professed innocence. Within this ever-changing group could be found petty thieves, income tax evaders, bank robbers, drunk and disorderly persons, rapists, and murderers—a real mixed bag. These folks ate first to give them time to prepare themselves in their Sunday best to appear before the sitting judge. It was a bad idea and against the law to mix the jail side residents with the "house side" residents. The house side was also known as the "work side," and housed the men who had already been convicted of a crime and were serving sentences, usually not more than three years. Most, however, were repeaters, men who were constantly getting themselves into trouble when they weren't behind bars, thereby spending most of their lives as residents of the Salem House of Correction. Some had spent so much time in jail that they considered it home. Hardly any arrived on the house side without a warm and usually loud welcome, with handshakes and hugs all around, like a homecoming for an old friend or family member returning from vacation, or just back from war.

The house and jail sides literally split the ancient building into two fort-like wings, each three stories high, extending from a central tower. Within the wings were tiers of cells running the length of the building, facing narrow corridors with waist-high railings. Below the railings was the "flat," a wide basement corridor extending beyond the first tier where the inmates played cards, chess and ping-pong. It was the only place in the entire building where they could gather to have recreation, or any physical activity during the winter months. The fenced in recreation yard behind the jail was hardly bigger in total area than the flat—about the size of two tennis courts. It had a basketball hoop, but didn't allow enough elbowroom for house-side residents to sun themselves and play basketball at the same time. It was usually closed off from November through April, as most inmates didn't have coats or warm clothes to protect them from the cold. The jail itself provided enough chill and cold draft during the winter months without stepping outside. The heating pipes that snaked up the walls beside the long, barred windows, hissed and banged day and night, all winter long, adding more puddles of water to the flats, but providing little warmth. Those living on the lower tiers froze as the heat rose in great waves, scalding the third tier and beyond to the central tower, where the other two types of inmates lived—"the outcasts."

In a large room at the top of the jail, containing ten cells and a sitting area for sewing, was where the female inmates lived, usually between five and ten of them. It was called "the penthouse." Most of the women who spent time up there were awaiting trial, and after trial would be moved off to a woman's prison. Also in the tower was a small four-cell area called "lockup," "solitary" or "protective custody". The men kept here couldn't be kept with the inmate population for one reason or another. They were the dangerous men, or the squealers who were in danger of being beaten to a pulp if allowed in with the others. Often, those awaiting trial who had allegedly raped children were kept in lockup for fear that other inmates might attempt to kill them. The boys behind the bars had their own unique justice, and child molesters, without fail, would suffer cruel torture from fellow inmates. We had to keep them separate and alone. The women and those in lockup hardly saw the light of day from the moment they arrived at the Salem Jail, for they had but one window in their section. In order to allow them into the recreation yard, all house-side inmates had to be locked in to let them pass through. When either the women or the lockup men were allowed to walk by the tiers of the house, there would be a hullabaloo that could be heard in downtown Salem, and it usually didn't subside until the girls or the "hated ones" were returned to their cells. They also weren't allowed to enter the dining hall, so they ate all their meals alone in their cells.

The sounds inside the jail on a daily basis were enough to cause ear damage, or at least drive any normal person slowly insane. The stale air was constantly filled with obscenities, growls, and shrieks from morning to night. There were frequent quarrels and petty arguments, compounded by radios and loud music competing with the TV set and the card players. There was a constant din, rising and falling through the day, without letting up, until the electricity was shut off at midnight. Then, only the occasional car on Bridge Street could be heard passing by, and the echo of the guard's footsteps as he made his rounds.

In the mornings, bells rang to wake everyone up, rang again to open the cell doors, and rang once more to herald breakfast. Another bell sounded at lunch and again at dinner. At night, a bell rang pronouncing a two minute warning that cells were about to be locked and that everyone should be inside their iron and brick enclosure. The final bell rang at 8pm and all doors slammed shut. If you didn't know you were in a jail, you'd have thought you were in school; people shuffling in single file from here to there, to the sound of bells. On weekends there was no wake-up bell, leaving inmates to rouse themselves for breakfast, or to make it to the little chapel above the guardroom for Protestant services and Catholic mass.

Few inmates took advantage of the religious services, leaving the chapel largely unused. It struck me as a perfect setting, with a few modifications, for a library. One of the chapel walls was covered by a mural of the Last Supper, painted by inmates, under which were the words, "In Memory of (the late) Sheriff Earl Wells." It was painted directly onto the brick wall and was chipping in spots. It certainly was not a masterpiece, and took up wall space that could have been used for bookshelves. At the time, our library consisted of some comic books and a total of 66 dog-eared paperbacks, donated by the Salem Women's Republican Club. The minister and visiting priest, of course, didn't want the mural covered, and it did seem a bit sacrilegious to do so. Further complicating my plan for a library was the fact that a guard would have to be on duty at all times if we were to open the chapel for daily activities. Also, under security requirements, the chapel windows would have to be double-barred, which would cost $1,100. Our resources were already stretched to the limit, and there were not enough guards to cover other jail duties, so the library idea would have to wait.

There was just nothing for these inmates to do all day. There wasn't even any place they could sit. The few who played cards sat on orange crates at a card table made of another orange crate. After my newspaper appeal for furniture, a Gloucester restaurant donated some well-worn tables and chairs, a blessing for the card-playing inmates. Warren Bethune, who had been deputy master of the jail for some fifteen years, warned me that the donated tables and chairs wouldn't last long. I didn't believe him. I thought the inmates would surely welcome sturdy tables and chairs for their marathon card games. Within two weeks, all the tables and chairs had been torn apart, the arms and legs converted into clubs and hidden under mattresses as potential weapons. I also thought suggestion boxes in the cellblocks would be an ideal way to find out what ideas the inmates might have to improve their lot. One of the suggestion boxes was ripped off the wall and left on the floor in splinters after the first night, and the other, two nights later, was filled with the contents of a shit-bucket. It was not exactly the kind of suggestion I was thinking of.

"That would never have happened in the old days, Sheriff," said Assistant Deputy Master Charlie Hardy. "We used to get mostly drunks in here that we'd take in out of the cold in the beginning of winter and let them go free in the spring. We've gone from manageable drunks to pill-popping punks. We just don't get the good class of guys we used to get."

Since the inmates were not allowed to have money, cigarettes and candy bars were used as currency and trade items within the jail. "I'll give you ten cigarettes for your pork chop," or "a pack of Marlboros for that meatloaf," were typical phrases that could be heard at dinner, and since there were no seconds on food, bartering for eats was often times furious and sometimes violent. "They'd kill for a sugar donut in here," said Hardy.

I was determined to improve the food situation and to allow second helpings to anyone who wanted them. The reason for scrimping on food was, yet again, the budget. There wasn't money in the budget to buy enough food to adequately feed the ever-growing population. Sheriff Wells, I was told, was forced to feed the inmates Jello and coffee for dinner on two occasions at the end of the fiscal year when the food money ran out. When it came to food, I refused to adhere to the budget. If the county commissioners were shouting, "Let them eat cake," then we would do just that. When I started spending over budget, George Hollum, the correctional officer in charge of finances, came to me in a panic. The Wells sheriffs had never spent a penny over budget. They would be called before the commissioners and the county treasurer and scolded if they did. The commissioners might even impeach the sheriff for over-spending, Hollum warned me; he was near tears. Hollum was a big man, weighing nearly 300 pounds. "Could you live on just one helping of food if you were an inmate here? Could you tolerate the bland meals they serve here?" I asked him. He shook his head. "They feed the same amount of food to the guy who weighs *120* pounds as they do to a guy who weighs *250* pounds. Not only is it not right, but it's a wonder it hasn't caused a riot. Don't you worry about the budget," I told George. "When it comes to food and fuel, we're not going to scrimp, and when I overspend in these areas, I feel fully justified in going to my old pals in the legislature to get the dough in a supplementary, or even an emergency budget. And speaking of dough," I added, "start buying sugar and jelly doughnuts—and honey dipped while you're at it—instead of those day-old plain donuts you feed them every morning. You don't eat those plain doughnuts, do you George?" He shook his head. "Then from now on, don't feed the inmates anything that you wouldn't eat, George." The inmates were pleased and so was George.

One food item we had to stop supplying the inmates with was fruit, in all its forms. No fresh fruit or canned fruit, and no cereal with fruit in it. They'd pick out the raisins from Raisin Bran cereal, stuff them in a pocket, and bring them back to the cell to ferment in a clean shit-bucket to make home-brew. Some booze-buckets were discovered, usually hidden under another bucket filled with excrement, making it a distasteful place for guards to search for contraband. We knew that other homemade alcohol stills must exist in the jail, but were well hidden, probably where guards feared to tread.

There was no doubt that the inmates were getting marijuana and other forms of dope. Sometimes you could smell it wafting out from the cellblocks into the guardroom late at night. Flashlight inspections of the tiers accomplished little more than assuring us that we weren't imagining the smell. The source was almost impossible to track down. One way of getting such contraband into the jail was through a furloughed inmate. He could be bribed or even forced to bring narcotics back when he returned to the jail. Although men returning from furlough were thoroughly searched before re-entering the population, there were many ingenious ways devised to fool the guards. One was to swallow a deflated balloon filled with the pot or pills before entering the jail, and then releasing it into a bucket once they returned to the cell. If only a short time had elapsed since swallowing it, one could vomit it up by inducement, but if delayed too long by the guards, the customers would have to wait until the furloughed inmate deposited the dope into the bucket in nature's due course.

One constantly harassed inmate named Peaches, an admitted homosexual, was threatened by three others with physical abuse if he didn't return from his furlough with a supply of pills and marijuana. The threatening inmates even managed to pay him before he left so that he could purchase the narcotics. When Peaches returned to the jail two days later, he passed the guards' skin-search inspection and was greeted eagerly by his three financiers. Peaches reported that he had stuffed a balloon full of dope far up his rectum where the guards couldn't find it. He retired to his cell to remove the contraband while his three partners waited eagerly outside, but he soon announced that he needed help. Peaches couldn't reach the balloon himself. So, one by one the others entered his cell and stuck their fingers as far as they could into Peaches' rectum, attempting to find the balloon and pull it out. As long and as hard as they tried, none of them could reach the balloon. It finally dawned on one of them that Peaches was enjoying all this attention a little too much, and that he just might not have a balloon stuck up his ass after all. Peaches at first denied the allegations, but when pressure was brought to bear, he admitted that he had spent their money on his own pleasure while on the street, and had returned to the jail with nothing more than a fairytale. He then, literally, got the shit beat out of him.

Narcotics were also brought into the jail by outside visitors. Often a wife or sweetheart successfully passed pills from mouth to mouth as they kissed through the small openings in the screen that separated all inmates from their visitors in the lobby. Guards had found marijuana stuck in between pages of books being brought to inmates as gifts, or within cookies or cakes.

One day, a not very wise guard found a bag of cocaine powder hidden in the wastebasket of the visitors' waiting room. It had obviously been left by a visitor who meant it to be picked up later by the inmate who emptied the wastebaskets. The guard, without saying a word to anyone, emptied the cocaine from the plastic bag, refilled the bag with sugar, and returned it to the wastebasket. The guard then witnessed an inmate bring the wastebasket into the cellblock, remove the bag and pocket it. The guard immediately reported the incident to me, quite pleased with his own detective work.

"I would like to be the one to arrest him," said the guard.

"What shall we arrest him for?" I asked.

"Why, for bringing narcotics into the jail, of course," he replied indignantly.

"But he didn't bring narcotics into the jail," I shouted menacingly. "He brought SUGAR into the jail, and you can't arrest him for that!"

Drugs weren't the only threat to the safety of the prison; if so much as a spoon was missing from the dining hall after breakfast, lunch or dinner, there was a general shutdown and lock-up until every inmate and cell was searched. A spoon could easily be made into a stabbing weapon, as could the handle of a fork, or a piece of a steam pipe. Almost anything, given a little time and ingenuity, was a potential weapon. Many inmates kept makeshift weapons in their cells, but word of an impending search or shakedown always seemed to trickle through the cellblock, and all the makeshift weapons would be found on the flats in the morning, thrown out of the cells the night before. The flats, in fact, became the receptacle for all trash, day and night, as there was no other place to deposit trash, garbage, or contraband. Anything unwanted in the cells or on the tiers was thrown over the railing and onto the flats. Those playing cards or ping-pong in the flats below had to be constantly on the lookout for flying objects, the most prevalent being lighted cigarette butts. The trash would pile up on the flats and sit for hours until it was swept clean before breakfast, only to have a new pile of trash begin to develop. If contraband or weapons were found in the morning trash, there was no way of telling which cell it came from. A full bucket was once dropped from an upper tier onto the flats, hitting a guard in the head and disabling him for life. The culprit was never identified.

I decided to wipe the slate clean and rid the Salem Jail and House of Correction of all contraband, home-brew, dope, and makeshift weapons, in one fell swoop. I realized that more would eventually trickle back in again, but I didn't want to take command with leftover contraband from the previous administration. This was my war on all illegal garbage, and I would beat the system by staging a secret, surprise raid. I wouldn't even tell the guards about the search, thereby guaranteeing the absence of leaks to the prisoners. I would tell no one—I would storm my own Bastille.

It was a chilly, frosty morning at 4:30am at the Hawthorne Hotel parking lot, across from Salem Common, where I met with 31 deputies and guards. I had taken Special Sheriff Charlie Reardon and Deputy Master Warren Bethune into my confidence the night before. Only they knew the reason for this clandestine meeting. Reardon said that the men were not pleased at having to assemble at this forsaken hour, but there they were, stomping their feet, blowing into their hands, cursing under their breath, and eyeing me suspiciously.

"Is everyone here?" I asked.

They all looked at each other with blank expressions.

"How the hell do we know?" said Jim Walsh, an old out-spoken friend of mine, who I had asked to become a deputy sheriff. Now I wondered if that had been a mistake. "Not only don't we know who's supposed to be here, but none of us knows why we're here!" His ruddy round face was aglow, but his eyes were droopy from lack of sleep. He wore a yellow plaid woolen coat over his new green uniform and Smokey-the-Bear hat. The others, most of who didn't know me as well as Walsh did, were surprised and openly snickered at his bold-ness.

"Is that the coat your grandfather wore pickin' potatoes in Ire-land?" I asked.

"We were told to wear old clothes, Sheriff," Walsh retorted, "but please note that I have my new green uniform on underneath. For you, Cahill, I come prepared for anything." The others laughed at him, but the old Sheriff Wells' deputies were more hesitant than the new deputies, as they weren't used to somebody wisecracking with the sheriff.

"This is my first assignment," Walsh shouted to the others, "and I'm already beginning to think I need this new shinny badge like I need a hole in the head."

"You may also receive one of those before the morning is over," I assured him. That got a good laugh, and it jolted everyone awake at the same time. "We are going to attack the Bastille this morning," I informed them all. "We are going to raid our own jail and shake it down like it's never been shook before. And this time, it will be as complete a surprise to the inmates, as it is to you. That's why I asked you to bring old clothes, because much of what they possess in weapons, dope, and home-brew, is hidden in their shit-buckets where they don't think we'll look too diligently. But this morning, we shall leave no shit-bucket unturned. We are going to search every nook and cranny of the jail." I turned to Warren Bethune, whose red nose and pursed lips protruded from his upturned coat collar.

"There are six correctional officers here," Bethune's voice bel-lowed, echoing across the Common and causing pigeons to scatter.

"They will each lead a team of four deputies, each team covering one tier of cells. We'll all go in at once and hit all the tiers at the same time. Those who haven't been involved in a shakedown before will do what the guards tell them... Any questions?"

"How long will this take?" Walsh asked.

"About two hours," replied Bethune, which even surprised me. I thought we'd be in and out within half an hour.

"Hell, I got to be to work in Boston by seven-thirty," cried Walsh.

"And many of us have to be in court by eight," another deputy piped up, "and we have to go home and change first."

"Can't help that," replied Bethune, squinting at me. "The Sheriff wants this shakedown."

"We'll do it as fast as we can," I assured them. Charlie Reardon arrived with coffee for all, and his arrival stopped the questioning. As they all gathered around his car, I whispered to Bethune, "Get some-one down to the jail, so we'll know when to go in."

"It's too early to go in," said Bethune. "The inmates don't get up 'til six-thirty."

"It's a hell of a time to tell me that!"

"I thought you knew," said Bethune. "We want them all in the dining hall before we go in, otherwise they'll just throw any contra-band over the rails onto the flat, and we'll never know who was hid-ing stuff"

"Well, we can't wait here 'til seven. These guys will hang me. Imagine having to listen to Walsh for another two hours? We've got to go in soon. Have the boys on duty wake them early and get them into the mess hall."

"They won't like that," said Bethune.

"Tough," I replied. "I don't like getting up this early either."

Bethune walked the few blocks to the jail to tell the on-duty guards to get the inmates up and out of their cells. He didn't return to the hotel parking lot for a half-hour. The sun was coming up and the deputies were getting restless. They were huddled in little groups, blowing steam breath into each other's faces as they mumbled and grumbled among themselves.

I expected a question on why they had to be there at four-thirty if we didn't intend to hit the jail 'til after five-thirty but "Where's the doughnuts?" was the only comment from Walsh. No one caught on to the fact that we were an hour and a half early and stalling. When I saw Bethune rounding the corner of the Common, I walked over to greet him, not wanting the others to hear what he had to say.

"We'll have to wait until six. They won't be able to get all the inmates into the dining hall until then."

"Don't tell the others that," I said to Warren, "or they'll tear me apart before they have a go at the cells. Hell, we all could have easily slept another hour." The deputies walked over and slowly circled Warren and me.

"All right," I shouted into Warren's face, acting as if he were to blame, "if we have to wait a little longer we will," and I threw up my hands and walked away from the crowd. If the deputies were going to vent their anger and frustration, I figured it should be on Warren instead of me. I saw lips tighten and heard a few groans.

"Why don't we move closer to the jail," Reardon suggested. "That will at least get circulation going." A good idea.

"Okay, men," I shouted, "let's line up in the designated teams and head for the jail."

A few commuters slowed their cars as our group of mostly overweight, middle-aged men crossed the main street and headed for the jail. Walsh marched off at a fast clip as others lagged behind, laughing and jostling each other. I halted the group and asked them all to stick together. When we reached the church beside the jail, I halted them again and let Bethune enter to make sure all the inmates were at breakfast.

Getting the all clear from Bethune, I sounded the charge, cautioning them all to walk and not run, and not to make a sound; it was like taking fifth graders on a field trip. The on-duty guard opened the front doors, and we entered into the lobby facing the visitors' screen, where there was hardly enough room for all of us to struggle out of our coats. The gates to the cellblocks were opened, and gingerly the teams entered the tiers to begin the hunt. I grabbed a chair and sat facing the tiers to watch and listen. The inmates were all locked into the dining room, both jail and house-side together, so by this time they had to be aware that something out of the ordinary was going on. I heard the clinking of keys in the locks and the squeaking of cell doors opening. There were whispers and mumbling as cells were literally torn apart. The heat was up and the steam pipes were clanging, drowning some of the grunts and curses of the deputies as they lifted mattresses and opened the lids of shit-buckets. Many of the buckets were full because the inmates were moved into the dining room so quickly that they weren't given time to empty them.

I heard a cough, a familiar cough, from one of the upper tiers. It was Jimmy Walsh's constant hacking from smoking too many cigarettes. His cough soon turned to groans of pure agony — deep-throated eruptions and gasping. I looked up just in time to see Jimmy Walsh rush to the railing, dip his head, and vomit onto the flats—a shower of brown liquid spraying deputies below. There was deep gurgling, then more coughing, and another spray. Two deputies rushed to his side. Tears dribbled down his round cheeks.

"What's wrong with Walsh?" I shouted, my voice echoing throughout the cellblock.

"Walsh just heaved his guts out," came a reply from within.

"What's wrong?" I asked.

"He opened up one of the full shit-buckets," came a reply, with a few giggles and guffaws behind it.

In the shakedown, the deputies uncovered: eight makeshift knives, eight handmade clubs of wood and iron, one gun made of soap, a few pills, and over one pound of marijuana. Those who occupied the cells where contraband and weapons were found had charges filed against them, which added time to their sentences. In one shit-bucket was found fermenting fruit, pieces of apples, oranges and raisons used to make the home-brew, "kickaboo juice," as they called it. It smelled almost as bad as what was normally found in the buckets. I asked Jim Walsh if he would like to taste the brew to see if it had fermented, but he refused. Walsh was escorted out of the jail into the open, crisp air where, as soon as he caught his breath, he feebly said to me, "I will never go on another secret assignment of yours again, Cahill, so there is no need for you to call."

"You sure you won't have a little waker-upper of home-brew before you go to work?" I asked. But he walked off without a reply—not at all like my talkative old pal who always seemed to have a witty remark on the tip of his tongue. On the next emergency call, however, Jim Walsh was right there, bright eyed and bushy-tailed, ready for another misadventure with the Essex County Sheriff's Department.

CHAPTER III

A Night Of Terror

It's a disgrace—a joke of justice," I heard Deputy Charlie Geary tell Charlie Reardon in the next office, purposely loud enough for me to hear. Charlie Geary was an old Salem friend and a former school committee member. I had gone through the Salem schools with his brothers, and all the Gearys had helped me in my campaign. Charlie Geary was a fiery redhead with a hot temper, although his flaming hair had begun to recede as he approached middle-age.

"What's a disgrace and a joke?" I asked from the next room, knowingly playing into their hands. The two Charlies walked into my office, grim-faced, as if the weight of the world was on their shoulders.

"The court system. It's ridiculous!" said Geary, taking a seat next to my desk. Reardon followed and stood behind him. Special Sheriff Reardon was in charge of the courts, and except for checking the lists of court officers on duty in the three superior courts each day, I left the running of the courts to him, so I could concentrate on the jails. Reardon was still shy about revealing his concerns regarding department problems and the conflicts involved in mixing my new deputies with old members of the Wells' regime. He didn't know my capacity to take criticism, so he played it close to the vest. He did, however, take Charlie Geary into his confidence, and Geary, like my pal Jim Walsh, had no qualms about confronting me on any issue. "How the hell can we run a half-decent court when most of the people we subpoena never show up?" he demanded, noting the look of surprise on my face. "It's a joke—the judge shows up, the lawyers and plaintiffs show up," continued Geary, now waving his hands for effect, "but the guilty party doesn't show up—it happens all the time."

"The judges are getting mad," piped up Reardon.

"I didn't know that," I managed to say.

"Some have been subpoenaed five or six times," Geary continued, "and they never show up in the court room."

"That doesn't sound right to me," I said.

"It isn't right," they nodded in agreement.

"So what do we do about it?"

"Sheriff Wells never allowed us to go after people who don't show up in court," said Reardon.

"Why not?" I asked.

"I don't really know," he replied. "Wells was often cautious about arresting people."

"I just came from the courthouse," Geary boomed, "where five of us, including the judge, waited an hour for this guy who refuses to pay his bills, and he never showed up. This is the third time I served him with a summons to be in court at a specific time, and he just never shows. It makes us look like fools."

"Why don't we just go out and arrest these people who don't show up in court when they're supposed to?" I asked, looking up at Reardon.

"We can if you allow us to," said Reardon, a look of pleasure crossing his face.

"I think we should go after them and lock them up," Geary said.

"Then do it," I said. "If a person skips a court session more than once, he'll have to spend a night in jail. Then we can be sure he'll be in court the next morning, right?"

"Right!" echoed my two deputies, Geary smiling up at Reardon like a kid who just heard there was ice cream for dessert. "We'll go after all the shirkers next Friday night," Reardon assured me as the two Charlies left my office elated. Certainly, it only seemed proper that those accused of something, no matter how minor, should make their appearance in court when they were supposed to, and if not, they should be arrested and made to appear. The plan seemed sound, and I was relieved that we had found an easy solution.

A week later I was relaxing on my den couch at home, watching the football game, when a tap-tap came at my back door. It was such a soft knock that I thought it was one of my kids' little friends.

"Come in!" I called. "The door's open."

Silence. Then, tap-tap-tap. Not wanting to leave my comfortable couch, I shouted, "Come in!!" I heard the doorknob slowly turn, and the back door opened a crack. A woman's face filled the crack. "Sandy has gone shopping and she won't be back for awhile," I said, recognizing the intruder as one of the neighborhood housewives.

"I'm not looking for Sandy," chirped a timid voice. "I'd like to talk to you, if I may?"

I sat up. "Certainly," I said, somewhat surprised, "come in, have a seat." She tiptoed into the room like she was treading on glass and took a seat on the edge of a chair near the door. I tried in vain to remember what her name was and at the same time wondered why she'd want to see me. Had my dog torn up her garden, or one of my kids offended her in some way?

"This won't take long," she said, glancing momentarily at the TV set. She may have thought me rude for not turning off the TV as she talked, but I wasn't about to miss part of the Patriot's game to hear some petty complaint.

"What can I do for you?" I asked.

"Phil has left me, you know," she began in a hardly audible voice.

"No, I didn't know that," I said. I didn't even know who Phil was. Her lips tightened and she squirmed in the chair. "I'm sorry to hear that," I added, afraid she was about to burst into tears. Who the hell was this woman? I racked my brain for a name, a clue, anything that would help me recall who she was.

"Well, I just wanted to come over and thank you," she said, staring at me, tears welling up in her eyes. The crowd at Foxboro cheered. Sam Cunningham, the star halfback, made a forty-yard run right up the middle.

"He threw a big bowl of spaghetti at me, sauce and all," she proceeded. "Maybe Sandy told you about it?"

"No, I don't think so," I said, "but I'm sorry to hear that." The Patriot's were on the Jets' 8-yard line.

"He was drunk—he's always drunk."

"Well, maybe he's got a lot on his mind," I said on Phil's behalf.

Why, I asked myself, does everyone come to see Sandy with their domestic problems, and why doesn't this woman at least wait until Sandy comes home to tell her tale of woe.

"It's all over," she sobbed, bowing her head. "I can't take it anymore." They didn't make it—three downs and they couldn't make eight yards. Now they'd have to kick a field goal, and they're losing by seven points. I felt like screaming. "There, there," I said soothingly, "I'm sure everything will be all right." I glanced at the TV. The field goal was good, but what the hell were they cheering about? They should have scored seven points, not just three.

"Well, I just wanted to come over and thank you," she said, staring at me, the tears now streaming down her face.

"Thank me? For what?" I asked, genuinely curious for the first time in the conversation.

"Why, for taking Phil in, of course." Stunned, I missed the Jets runback.

"Taking him in? Taking him in where?" I knew my wife was kindhearted and sympathetic, but I was sure she hadn't taken in some guy to live with us.

"Why, taking him in to your jail...didn't you know? Two of your men came to take him away about an hour ago. Phil was drunk, so I don't think he knew where they were taking him. I just couldn't do anything with him, and the local police got sick and tired of me calling them all the time..."

The more she talked, the further my jaw dropped. "You mean, two of my deputies walked into your house and took your husband away to jail?"

"Why yes," she smiled. "I've taken him to court three or four times for wrecking things in the house, breaking windows, threatening me, being drunk and abusive, but he never shows up in court. But he'll be there tomorrow morning, thanks to you...your men said it was your idea to arrest Phil...and I thank you, very much." She reached down and squeezed my shoulder. "Holy shit," I whispered to myself as she headed out the back door. "I can't thank you enough."

She waved and left.

I walked into the kitchen and poured myself a stiff shot of Irish whiskey. Never in my wildest dreams did I imagine that the two Charlies would be arresting neighbors of mine in their sweep of court shirkers. Should I stop them, I wondered? But no, they're right, these people should be arrested. In shock, I went back to my couch and the game.

About twenty minutes later there was a loud thumping on the back door. "Come in," I said, a little gun-shy from my last visitor. In walked Joe Ingemi, a city councilor and a good friend, but I didn't remember him ever visiting me at my home.

"What are you trying to do to me?" he shouted before he even entered the den. He was rubbing his big hands together, and I hoped it was to ward off the cold and not in preparation of strangling me. "I thought you were my friend," he said, glaring at me from the doorway.

"What did I do?" I laughed, thinking that Joe was possibly spoofing me as he often did, but my light-hearted attitude only seemed to anger him more.

"What did you DO?!?" he shouted to the ceiling. "You know what you did. You arrested the cook right out of my father's restaurant—that's what you did. There's people in there waiting to eat, and the cook is in the hoozgow."

"Well, we needed a good cook at the jail, so I sent my deputies out to find one." Joe didn't appreciate my sarcasm, but I just couldn't resist.

"Come on," he shouted, "this ain't no joke. Two of your guys just came in to our kitchen and grabbed him as he was turning an omelet—really. I got people waiting to eat…I can't cook…what the hell did you grab him for?"

I made Joe sit down and I explained to him why the deputies were going around town arresting people. Joe nodded his head up and down. "Yeah, he's been sued a few times for owing people money."

"And obviously he's not showing up for his court trials. So tomorrow morning, he'll show up in court." The Patriots had gotten the ball back and were ready to score again.

Joe waved his hands over his head. "I'll make sure he shows up. I'll come to court with him. I'll tie a leash around his neck, but please, Bob," he folded his big hands together as if in prayer, "forget this football game and get my cook out of jail so's he can finish the dinner meals."

"Just watch this one play, Joe. You're a football fan, aren't you?"

"BOB!" he shouted, despair in his voice. "I've got people sitting there. The waitresses are feeding them free drinks while I raced down here to see you. I mean, why no notice?" he asked. "It's like the Gestapo. Two guys just walk in, flash their badges, cuff him—spatula in his hand—and drag him out of the restaurant. What happens now? Can't I bail him out? Can't I get him out?" Joe reached for his wallet. The Patriots scored and I jumped off the couch with a holler. Joe stood, sloop-shouldered.

"It's ten to seven, Joe. Aren't you excited?" He gave me a hangdog look. "Put your wallet away," I said patting his shoulder. "You won't have to bail him out. Come on in the kitchen and I'll call the jail to get him out." I turned to stare him in the eyes. "But you better damn well promise to have him in court by morning, or I'll have the Gestapo arrest you!"

"What time?" said Joe, following me to the telephone. "If he has to be there by nine, I'll have him there by seven. I promise."

Correctional Officer George Hollum, my hefty doughnut eater, answered the jail phone. I gave George all the details. "Yup," said George matter-of-factly, "he's getting into his jail clothes right now. He doesn't look very happy. Those deputies really purged the town tonight."

"How many have they arrested so far?" I asked.

"Six," said George, "all from the Salem-Peabody area. I think they're going to Beverly next. There's a lot of bullshit people here."

"Well, when Reardon returns, have him call me here before he arrests anyone else. In the meantime, please let the cook go, so's he can finish his work at the restaurant. People are still waiting for their dinners there." Joe, his ear close to the phone, nodded and wiped imaginary sweat from his forehead. But his relief was premature.

"Can't do it, Sheriff," Hollum said.

"What do you mean, you can't? I want that cook out as soon as possible. I'll see to it he's at court in the morning."

"You can put them in jail, Sheriff," said George in a sing-song voice, "but you can't get them out. Only a judge can do that."

"You've got to be kidding. You mean I can't get the cook out, now that I've put him in?" Joe was shaking his fist at me.

"Only a judge can get him out. That's the law," said George. "All you gotta do is have one of the judges call me, and I can let him go—any judge will do." I hung up and stared at Joe with a dumbfounded look on my face.

"What now?" said Joe through clenched teeth. "What now, you bastard? What am I going to do?" He started dancing around my kitchen like a lunatic, tearing at his hair.

"Don't panic, Joe," I said. "What judges do we know who might be willing to help? How about Sam Zoll, or Dave Doyle?"

"Yeah, try Doyle," said Joe, color returning to his face. "Dave's a good guy, he eats at the restaurant…he might help us."

I called Dave Doyle. "You watchin' the game, Judge?" I asked. "What do you think?" Joe danced around me, his hands waving, his eyes bulging.

"The Patriots don't look that good," said the judge. I agreed. Judge Doyle continued to analyze the game, and I thought Joe Ingemi would burst. I then asked the judge if he had ever made a big mistake during his early years on the bench. Then I told him about Joe's dilemma. "No problem," said the judge. "I'll call the jail right away." Joe Ingemi was ecstatic. I thought he was going to kiss me.

"See Joe, nothing to it," I laughed.

"C'mon down the restaurant, I'll buy you a meal," said Joe.

"Are you kidding me?" I laughed. "Your cook would poison me after what he went through tonight. I don't want a meal—I don't want anything. I just want to watch the rest of this game. You just make sure you personally bring the cook to district court in the ing."

"Done," agreed Joe. "Can I go up to the jail and get him now?"

"Sure, but let me call Hollum to tell him you're coming."

"Geez, everyone at the restaurant will be drunk by the time we get back."

"Hi George. Did the judge call? Good! Can you get the cook out of there as soon as possible? Joe Ingemi is coming down to drive him back to the restaurant... Gone? Like a flash? Thanks, George." I hung up and turned to Joe, "He's already out of the jail yard."

Joe's face paled. I thought the information would please him, but instead panic flooded his face. He headed for my back door.

"What's wrong, Joe?"

"Tell George to stop him," he shouted back to me. "He won't go back to the restaurant. He's so bullshit that he'll hit every barroom in town. It'll take me another hour to find him." Joe ran down my driveway to his car and sped off. I went back to the phone.

"Too late for me to catch him," said George, "He's gone. Oh, by the way, Sheriff, we've got one of your neighbors in here too," said George with a touch of glee in his voice. "He says he's gonna kill you."

"I know that George. Next thing they'll be arresting the mayor."

"They've just brought in a guy who says he's the mayor's cousin. It sure has been an interesting night. By the way, Sheriff, the Jets just scored and are leading fourteen to ten with only two minutes left to play." Sometimes I wondered whose side George Hollum was on.

CHAPTER IV

Taking The Heat

Art Farley, the county's court reporter for the *Salem Evening News* and an old high school pal of mine, was at the *News* office on election night. He informed me later that the paper's publisher, Cy Newbegin, and his editor, Jim Shea, were both angry that I had won the sheriff's job. "You were the only one of the five candidates without law enforcement or correctional experience, and that bothers them no end." They felt I had spent too much time and money campaigning. "Over-campaigning," they called it, and Shea had a reporter write a story on my being "over-organized," which I considered quite humorous. How could a candidate for office over-organize, or not shake the hand of that last potential voter? "What if I lost by one vote?" I asked Arthur. "Would they then have felt that I 'under-campaigned'?"

Al Marrs, both Arthur Farley's and my pal, became a major influence in the early years of my administration. All three of us were Boston University grads, and Al and Art had been roommates there. Al, who had spent years in marketing and had directed various federal programs for the state and for the city of Salem, drew up and submitted a federal government grant request for the sheriff's department. It was a request for $70,000 to start several new initiatives, including a work release program at the jail. Only a week after I took office as sheriff, the State Committee on Criminal Justice announced to local newspapers and radio stations that the grant request had been approved and that in addition, "another $5,000 would probably be granted for renovation of the third floor of the sheriff's house. That part of the 1813 structure was never used at all in the memory and knowledge of Sheriff Roger E. Wells", wrote the Lawrence Tribune. "Most of the 13-room federal construction house is barren. Only two rooms have lighting fixtures. Sheriff Cahill hopes to use these upper rooms for a work release program.... This is the first federal grant to go directly to a penal institution in Essex County...."

After only a week in office, I announced to the newspapers that I intended to ask for an additional $400,000 increase in the sheriff department's budget for fiscal year 1975 in order to meet daily expenses such as food and heating oil. "I don't intend to run a country club here," I told news reporters, "but I don't intend to have some two-hundred plus inmates starve or freeze to death either. We have a long way to go in this county, mainly because nothing has been done for years in the areas of maintenance, rehabilitation and security."

"Jim Shea is really pissed at you now," Art Farley told Al Marrs and me on the day I announced that my old pal Al Marrs would become the department's new Program Director at a salary of $16,000. I put Al to work immediately trying to drum up more federal funds for renovations of the ancient bastille. *News* Editor Shea responded with a scathing editorial:

> There is a continuing campaign of new Essex County Sheriff Robert E. Cahill to get more money spent on jails and other structures within his jurisdiction. In a year of austerity when taxpayers are rebelling against such meritorious projects as a regional vocational school, Cahill is whistling in the dark. Cahill wasn't even in the sheriff's office five minutes before he initiated a drive to spend, spend and spend. He should get his feet on the ground, stop issuing self-serving press releases and remember that the long-suffering taxpayer deserves some consideration. This past week was the week, apparently for hip shooting actions. I am not easily stunned but some of the goings-on seemed outrageous.

There was a rise in Jim Shea's blood pressure a week later when the Lawrence Tribune announced that:

> The Essex County Commissioners have voted unanimously to seek legislative approval to spend up to $5-million to modernize the Lawrence and Salem County Jails. The vote followed a plea

by new County Sheriff Robert E. Cahill that the commissioners begin to upgrade the long neglected penal institutions.' We are the second or third largest complex in the state,' said Sheriff Cahill, 'yet the lowest in personnel and facilities..." Suddenly Commissioner Burke called for a ten-year bond order, 'to provide money now for capital improvements and equipment.'...Then the commissioners voted a $5 million bond order. 'At least that amount of money could bring us out of the dark ages,' said Sheriff Cahill, 'but I don't know if it will bring us into the 20th century.'

I was prepared to meet heavy resistance from the county commissioners in calling for an expensive bond order, so my plan was to make it plain to them that the two jails were far from meeting minimum state and federal standards, and that if nothing was done, I would petition the courts to close them down. If closed down, the state would be forced to come in and take them over. I knew that the county commissioners were constantly losing power to the state legislators, and there was a strong movement to have the state government take over all county functions. In essence, I made the commissioners an offer they couldn't refuse—vote me the money to repair the jails, or I'll help the state take the jails away from the county. The commissioners, however, were only one hurdle. I still had to convince the legislators, the state Committee on Counties, and the 34 members of the County Advisory Board, made up of local city mayors and town selectmen.

I also had local editor Jim Shea to contend with. He went so far as to write in a front-page article that "Cahill's bond order is so full of holes, it's a piece of Swiss cheese." The bond order had to go through many committees and subcommittees, and I didn't really give it much hope of passing into law—Jim Shea's caustic comments weren't helping. The other Essex County newspaper reporters and editors had been fair in their coverage during my first few weeks in office, but Shea and his staff of reporters were unrelenting in what I felt was unfounded criticism:

New Essex County Sheriff Cahill seems to be out of touch with
the political and economic realities when he proposes spending
$5 million-plus to fix up the ancient Salem and Lawrence Jails.
And for the county commissioners to go along with the asinine
and extravagant request compounds the problem. The money
just isn't there this year in the public bucket. Bob Cahill is an energetic, personable, public-relation wise sheriff, with good Democratic political connections among the county commissioners
and in the state legislature where he served a couple of terms.
Because of these obvious assets in a state and county run by Democrats just about exclusively, Cahill brings a heavy bat into play
when he asks for additional money to run the county jail system.
But it should be made perfectly clear that Cahill did not discover
bad penal conditions in the county. They have been with us for a
century or more, but for two basic reasons, there has been no action... Its hard to get steamed up about making life comfortable
for an armed hoodlum: secondly, the ideas proposed for solving
the Essex County jail situation have had no broad-based community support....

Yet, Jim Shea, in the very same editorial, went on to say:

Cahill would like to settle for a measly $5 million to patch up the
Salem and Lawrence jails, both of which are not only unfit for
human habitation but would not be adequate for the storage of
cattle....

Making life comfortable for armed hoodlums? I really believed
Shea was talking out of both sides of his mouth. I just couldn't sit still
and let him pummel me and my department without responding so I
called him and I let him know how I felt—he wasn't pleased.
He continued to write editorials critical of my efforts to upgrade
the jails. Among other things, he wrote, "Cahill has given a new di-
mension to the office and has completely politicized it.... It is the
worst of Boston politics brought to Salem." I never minded being crit-

icized, but I considered Shea's comments undeserved.

It was a near-disaster at the Salem Jail that forced Shea to bite his tongue, or at least temporarily holster his stinging editorial pen. Seven women housed in the attic "penthouse" of the jail inadvertently came to my aide in the fight for increased spending.

To say that the few women inmates housed at the Salem Jail were trouble would be an under-statement. Most were hard-core armed robbers or accused murderers awaiting trial, mixed in with a few petty criminals and dope addicts. There was not room to separate the convicted women from those awaiting trial. Unlike 90% of the male inmates, they did not have to use buckets to defecate in, but had portable chemical toilets in their pink painted cells. We had one matron per eight-hour shift to watch over them. I inherited these matrons from Sheriff Wells, and although aging, they seemed sufficient to handle these tough female inmates. However, the constant squawking and quarreling from what we called "the penthouse" was unnerving to all within earshot. Their foul language exceeded the male prisoners polluted vocabulary, and from time to time there was scratching and hair-pulling bouts. Male guards on occasion had to rush up the three flights of stairs, open the locked gate to the women's tier and break up fights. The matron had her own little closed off room in the attic if she wanted to get away from her sometimes boisterous brood, but often her room and the entire attic compound was so terribly hot that doors were left open for circulation. As the old boiler and pipes hissed and banged trying to heat the lower tier cells, the upper tier was sweltering. The women were hardly ever let out into the fresh air of the prison yard because to do so meant all the men had to be locked up in their cells, and all the women had to agree to go outside together. If one female inmate wanted to stay inside, none of them could go out; our manpower situation at the jail wouldn't allow it. There had to be unanimity among the women, or they would not see the light of day, and since the few women would hardly ever agree with each other on anything, they usually didn't leave their enclave.

Matron Marjorie Rankin was in her tiny third floor room on the early morning of February 10, 1975 with her door closed when she smelled smoke. She opened her door and spotted two raging fires with black smoke billowing from cells at the other end of the attic. The seven inmates started screaming and yelling. Two hefty ones slammed the door back into Marjorie Rankin's face and then pressed their bodies against the door so Marjorie couldn't get out. Marjorie pressed a shoulder to the door and pushed with all her might, opening it enough to stick her foot in the crack and shout for the guards on the lower tiers. The women inmates tried to drown out her shouts with loud laughter. The putrid smoke now filled the attic; all the women began coughing, and some joined Marjorie in calling the guards. Two guards came to the rescue, opened the tier, pulled the two women from pressing against Marjorie's door and cuffed them. "Sound the alarm!" shouted one guard down to the Deputy Keeper "and call the fire department." The guards tried to put out the fires but couldn't. Two of the women had torched their cells and the storage cell at the end of the tier where mattresses, bedding, blankets and personal clothing of inmates were stored. Flames were now whipping out the high, open, barred window and were quickly spreading across the old, polished wooden floor. It was out of control. The guards led the matron and the women in a single file to the first floor. The male inmates whistled and howled as the women passed their cells. The women giggled and shouted obscenities in response.

The Salem firefighters were quick to arrive on the scene, discovering first that there was no water in the jail hydrant, and then that the jail-house hose was so old and decrepit that it all but crumbled in their hands. By the time the firefighters were ready to attack the flames, the deputy chief announced that the fire was "too hot to handle" and that the entire jail had to be evacuated.

"Impossible!" I told the deputy chief. "We can't just let 120 inmates walk out the front door. We don't even have enough hand-cuffs to cuff them all together,"

"If that roof comes down we won't have any time to get all those men out, and I'm not sending my men back into a burning building to fiddle with locks and keys," the deputy shot back. We argued back and

forth as the fire raged on. Reluctantly, he agreed to my proposal of letting all the inmates stand and wait in the first floor corridor, and if the
fire couldn't be contained, we would trek them out the front door into
the yard. Warren Bethune got on the phone and called in more
deputies and guards to be prepared for all possibilities.

With hardly space enough for them all to stand shoulder-to-
shoulder, the inmates were corralled onto the first floor. They were, of
course, anxious to leave. Surprisingly, they remained in good order, but
the women, who we tucked into Bethune's small office, were shouting,
screaming and laughing loudly at me.

"How do you like them apples, Sheriff? Maybe you'll get us an
air-conditioner now." The catcalling and harassment went on for an
hour and a half while the firemen fought to quell the fire from an aer-
ial ladder outside the one window of their penthouse. Once the wood
floor and all the bedding and clothes were burned up, the flames had
no place to spread, and the fire fighters could bring it under control.
The damage was substantial. Certainly, no one could live in the attic
any longer.

"Girls," I announced, squeezing into Bethune's office with them.
"You are all going to be shipped to separate jails within the state,
mainly to Plymouth, Springfield and Framingham. You will find
things a lot tougher in these jails, and the two who tried to lock the
matron into her room will have charges pressed against them by the
District Attorney. If we discover who lit the fires, they will go away for
a long time. But I do want to thank you girls for destroying the only
place I could keep you so I won't ever have to see any of you again,
which pleases me no end. We will not repair the attic, but will use it
for other purposes. I will never accept another female prisoner in this
jail as long as I am sheriff of this county. So, goodbye girls, and thank
you again. Your little surprise, I think, may be a blessing in disguise."
And indeed it was.

The smiles and sheepish grins on the women's faces quickly disappeared. Most of them realized that their scheme for mischievous
adventure or attempted escape backfired on them. Two women who
were alleged first-degree murderers awaiting trial and a third inmate

serving time for armed robbery were transferred to Framingham State Prison, which most inmates detested. Deputy Dugie Russell was handcuffed to one of them in the rear of the old paddy wagon for the one-hour ride to Framingham. Dugie later informed me that though angry and upset at having to leave her cozy attic conclave in Salem, she still had enough spirit to attempt to seduce him during the transfer. "She's the one that they think murdered her husband," said Dugie.

The damage to the jail by the fire was estimated at $10,000. "I do not have budget funds to repair it," I told the press the next day. Then, Dave Goggin, the Salem Fire Marshal, gave the county commissioners and me an ultimatum to provide additional items and procedures needed immediately at the jail:

1. Establish fire drills. (Which meant we'd need money for proper fencing outside the jail to prevent inmates from pouring into the neighborhood.)
2. Install an automatic fire alarm in the jail office, not directly accessible by inmates.
3. Replace the fire hose (relic from the last century), which, even if it had worked, was not long enough to reach the third floor of the jail and didn't have fittings that matched the connections the fire department was now using.
4. Any storage areas should be enclosed with a self- closing door that can be locked.
5. Water pressure must be increased and the jail needs new piping.

The Fire Marshall then set up a meeting with county treasurer Tom Duffey and the three county commissioners to provide emergency funds to update fire safety and fire prevention at the jail. While I had the attention of the press, I called for all judges and members of the state legislature to come and tour the Salem Jail to force a decision as to whether I should get the $5 million for repairs of both jails, or spend some $30-million of tax payers money for a new jail. I was sure Jim Shea was choking on my words, but those were the only two choices we had. A few members of the legislature trickled in, and I gave them the grand tour. All were appalled at what they saw, but most were non-committal about voting for the bond order. Then, Louis Glaser, a district court judge with seventeen years on the bench, decided to take up my offer of a jail tour. Neither Editor Jim Shea, nor any of his *Salem Evening News* reporters were around when Judge Glaser finished his tour, but reporters from Beverly, Lawrence, Gloucester, and Lynn papers were there, as well as a reporter from the *Boston Herald*, and staff writer Gary Thatcher from the world renowned *Christian Science Monitor*.

"That building went up in 1813," said the judge to the press, after his inspection, "and has absolutely outlived its usefulness. It should be destroyed. It could not pass minimum fire, sanitation, or safety standards...It is the most archaic, outmoded public institution I've ever been in and it should be closed. It reeks with old age. If the county commissioners were in the same position as property owners, they'd be summoned into court...I will never sentence anyone from my court to the Salem Jail again..." Then the reporters turned to me. "I think the judge is right," I said. "There is no question that the Salem Jail is the worst in the state—probably the country. A judge has already closed down the Charles Street Jail in Boston, and that was a palace compared to what we have here in Salem." It was great to have a judge singing the same tune that I had been singing for some two months.

"*Salem Jail Is Not For Viewing,*" headlined the *Christian-Science Monitor* on February 27th. Gary Thatcher wrote:

> SALEM, MASS. – This city has one historic building that will not be open to the throngs of U.S. bicentennial visitors expected here in the next two summers. The Salem Jail and House of Corrections, built during the War of 1812, is a classic example of everything the prison-reform movement loathes—Gothic architecture, antiquated radiators hissing steam, small cells with chamber pots instead of toilets, and massive granite walls. The reason visitors will not be allowed to see the jail is that it is still in use.

Thatcher described the Judge's visit and reaction, my feelings about the jail, and the commissioners and legislators twenty-five years of fruitless talk about building a new jail. He concluded:

> Sheriff Cahill has opted for renovation of the two jails and is asking for $5-million for new flooring, wiring, plumbing and construction to showers, toilets, and a recreation area. The sheriff says that until these improvements are made he has a 'real fear' that the facility may be closed down by a court order for failing to meet minimum standards. Until the Legislature acts...122 men will get recreation by using one Ping-Pong table placed in a corridor, or study in a small room that doubles as an attorney's conference room and library. And youthful offenders will be mixed in with hardened criminals awaiting trial.... Meanwhile, the sheriff attempts to convince the legislature that something must be done to change the 'inhuman' situation in Salem.

If I had seen my seven female inmates, now residing elsewhere throughout Massachusetts, I would have kissed each one on the cheek. They were instrumental in getting that county judge to visit the jail, and his outspokenness had opened Pandora's Box. Though Jim Shea tried to ignore the jail's blearing defects, *The Boston Herald's* and the *Monitor's* attention to our woes, complete with photos, prompted more feature articles from such newspapers as the *Gloucester Times*, the *Beverly Times*, the *Lynn Item*, and the *Haverhill Gazette*, which in turn prompted more mayors, selectmen, and legislators to tour the jail. "I was dead against any expenditures for the Salem Jail, but after going through the place, I came out singing a different tune," commented one legislator. "The conditions are worse than I expected," said a local councilman. At least the politicians who would vote on my budget were now coming to visit instead of putting their heads in the sand, or trying to wish away the conditions at the jail, as they had done in the past.

Warren Bethune wasn't too please with all the reporters and legislators tramping through the jail; it upset his routine. But I convinced him that it was important for others to see how these inmates had to live. That made me wonder how the inmates were feeling about all the politicians visiting their squalid, cramped quarters, and all the publicity they were getting from the press. My answer came in the form of the new jail newspaper, called *Decision*, which the inmates asked to publish. In the first issue, delivered soon after the fire in the women's' section, the editorial read:

> Welcome Sheriff Cahill—'The Decision' would like to go on record as saying that your recent arrival is second only to that of the Messiah 1975 years ago in terms of importance to the inmate population…. Your arrival is an indication that we are about to depart the 18th Century and the most backward correctional system in the State of Massachusetts, if not the country. Anything but naive, we realize that the brick walls aren't going to miraculously transform into gingerbread, nor the bars to candy canes. Neither do we expect society's image of its incarcerated members to change from its current 'hide 'em or hang'em' mentality. But we at least have the luxury of hope. I mean the phrase 'work release' is bouncing off the walls, on everybody's mind…. You see, the problem lies not so much in our physical existence here but rather in the fact that, until now, there appeared to be no hope of improvement. At last there is reason to hope that we will be able to serve our sentences with dignity as members of society, detained temporarily, rather than as stagnating zombies.

I showed the first issue of the jail newspaper to Art Farley, the court reporter. He read the editorial, looked up from the desk and smiled wryly at me.

"Do I dare show it to Jim Shea?" he asked.

"Christ yes!" I replied.

Jim Cahill, the Sheriff's brother, holding up a copy of the competing newspaper Beverly Times, *behind Jim Shea, editor of the* Salem Evening News. *Shea was Sheriff Cahill's nemesis throughout his term of office.*
(Photo courtesy Beverly Times*)*

Sheriff Cahill with fifty of his deputy sheriffs before the Lawrence Jail to march in the Lawrence Saint Patrick's Day Parade, 1975.
(Photo by A. Reynolds)

CHAPTER V

Buddy And The Beast

If an inmate caused disruption or serious problems within a county jail, he would be sent to a state prison, usually Walpole—better known as Cedar-Junction—or Concord State Prison. If the sheriff thought an inmate had mental problems, he might ship him off to Bridgewater for incarceration and observation. If, however, the sheriff had an inmate that was causing problems within his jail but not serious enough to justify sending him to state prison, he might be carted off from one county jail to another. The eleven High Sheriffs of Massachusetts were constantly in trade negotiations, trying to pawn off troublesome inmates. An inmate who was a real problem at one jail could be as docile as a lamb at another. Nobody really knew why that was, but it was assumed that the bad company the inmate kept acted as a catalyst for mischief, and if he was removed from that prison and those particular fellow prisoners, the behavior would change. Sometimes, feuding inmates or rival gangs had to be separated before or, too often, just after physical violence erupted. Every once in a while an inmate requested to be moved to another part of the state, and if both sheriffs agreed to the move, we'd often accommodate him. There were also occasions when sheriffs made trades for other than safety concerns. If the one toilet at the Salem Jail was clogged beyond the abilities of my guards or inmate mechanics to repair it, I might call on Sheriff Bowes of Barnstable or Sheriff Marshall of Norfolk to transfer an experienced plumber from their population, so I could get my toilet running again. There were many such good-will gestures between sheriffs.

It was with that spirit of good will and cooperation that I received a call one morning from Sheriff Jerry Bowes, who ran the prisons on Cape Cod.

"You'll really like this guy, Bob," I recall Sheriff Bowes telling me over the phone. "His name is Buddy and he is causing me some minor problems, but only because of the company he's keeping down here. He won't know anyone at your place, so he should be fine."

"What's he in for?" I asked, somewhat suspicious that Bowes would want to send me a guy I'd "really like."

"Just for breakin' a window and raisin' a little hell," said Bowes.

"You know I'm real crowded, Jerry. If he's just causing little problems, why transfer him to me?"

"My guards and the other inmates can't take him anymore, Bob. He's driving us crazy. He's not a troublemaker—believe me. He's just a pain in the ass. I've had him for a year and he only has a few months to go. It would be awhile before he'd become acclimated to your place, and by that time, you could either ship him to someone else or let him out. He's really a good guy…he just talks too much. Please, Bob—remember the plumber?"

"Okay, Jerry, I'll take him. But if he's really trouble, you'll get him right back. What's his name again?"

"Buddy. Buddy Jerome…I'll have him to your place within two hours."

"You must really want to get rid of this guy bad," I said. "You've never lied to me before, Jerry. I hope you're not sending me a problem, 'cause I've got enough to contend with here."

"Bob," said Jerry with a chuckle, "you're going to love this guy."

Buddy Jerome arrived, all 300 pounds of him, and Warren Bethune was in my office some twenty minutes later. "He can hardly fit in the cell," said Warren. "He had to squeeze in sideways…and he's already driving people nuts—inmates and officers."

"If he's causing trouble, I'll send him right back," I told Warren.

"He's not causing trouble," said Warren, "he just won't stop talking. His mouth has been going from the minute he arrived."

"Do you think he's crazy?" I asked Warren, thinking that maybe he belonged in Danvers State Hospital or Bridgewater State Hospital.

"Not quite," Warren replied with a pencil smile, "but almost. I know what you're thinking, but Bridgewater wouldn't take him. He's not spaced out or anything. In fact, he's a funny, likable guy. He just won't stop talking."

I went to the cellblock to see Buddy for myself; I could hear him before I entered the block. "Hi, Sheriff," he shouted when he saw me, "very pleased to be here. I did like Cape Cod, don't get me wrong, but I needed a change. Nice place you have here. Best food in the state, I hear. I love to eat," he said, patting his big stomach. The inmates, now gathered around, were all smiling, as were the duty guards. "I was a short-order cook once," he continued. "Can I work in the kitchen here, Sheriff, please can I?" I opened my mouth to answer him, but couldn't get a word in. The inmates were now roaring with laughter, but Buddy didn't even crack a smile. "I've been in every institution in the state, you know. I'm a good friend of the attorney general, and I know every sheriff—except you, of course— but now I know you." He stuck out his hand to shake mine. "Glad to know you, Sheriff. All I did was break a window, you know, and I got three years. I'm a victim of circumstances. Even though it was Sheriff Courtney's windows, that's big time for a little crime. And Courtney never would have known it was me...except I told him. Jeez was he mad, but he's my friend. I was mad at him too, for a while. That's why I broke his window. Maybe the devil made me do it..."

Buddy kept talking non-stop. He wasn't loud and he wasn't vulgar. Actually, he was funny, but he just wouldn't stop. I felt guilty leaving the others with him. They were laughing now, but I knew that Buddy would soon wear on peoples' nerves. I wondered if he talked in his sleep. I was mad at Jerry Bowes. He had been honest about Buddy; he did say that he talked too much and that his only crime was breaking a window. He just didn't tell me that it was Sheriff Courtney's window. I called Courtney, and when I told him I had Buddy Jerome, he laughed so hard and long that I had to take the phone from my ear. Between laughs, Courtney managed to tell me that Buddy had thrown a brick through his office window, dented his desk, and broke a lamp. Then, he walked to the front of the jail and demanded that he be incarcerated for the deed. Courtney had gladly passed him on to Bowes. "Wait 'til he starts singing in the middle of the night," said Courtney. "You're going to love this guy," he laughed.

"That's what Bowes said," and I hung up.

Here were my own fellow sheriffs passing a hot potato to me; it wasn't fair. I began racking my brain trying to figure out how I might pawn Buddy off onto my good friend and colleague, Sheriff Cliff Marshall of Norfolk County.

Meanwhile, Buddy started sending me lengthy notes on a variety of subjects. None of them were about the typical concerns and complaints of the average inmate. Buddy's letters were on car racing, baseball, court procedures, cooking, and politics. One of his letters announced that he was running for governor of Massachusetts, and he wanted to know if I'd be his campaign manager. Every time I entered the jail, he would have his pudgy face pressed to the black iron bars facing the visitors' screen and guards' room, talking to anyone and everyone who passed by.

"He's really getting on everyone's nerves," Warren complained, "but no other jail will take him. His reputation precedes him, and every jail-master has heard of Buddy the Non-Stop Yakker...last night in the dining hall, some of the boys threw their mashed potatoes at him 'cause he wouldn't stop talkin', and he yaks at everyone when they're trying to watch TV. Even after they're all locked in at night, he tells them bedtime stories. Some still laugh at him, but most are fed up. He's been the center of attention since he got here, and he's starting to make everyone a little edgy, including the guards."

Almost everybody in the prison seemed fed up and frustrated with Buddy Jerome, and I knew people were looking to me to find some solution to the problem, but I was really at a loss on what to do with him. I could put him in solitary confinement, but that wouldn't be right, as he hadn't done anything wrong, nor was he a hazard to himself or anyone else—although a few inmates were complaining of belly aches from laughing so long and hard. It was Warren who finally suggested that maybe we could solve the problem by just letting Buddy out of jail. It was a dangerous precedent to set, for if other inmates realized what we were up to, they might try to imitate his antics as a way to get out themselves. At Warren's request, I approached the parole board for an "Early Out on Good Behavior" for one Randolph "Buddy" Jerome. According to my report, backed up by Warren, Jerome was the most delightful, easy, and model prisoner at the House of Correction since Paul Revere spent a night here in 1813 for disturbing the peace. In order to accomplish this without a hitch, I had to call Buddy into my office and have him swear to secrecy that he wouldn't blab a word of his early release to anyone. If he said one word to anyone, guard or inmate, I promised him that he would finish out his entire three-year term in state prison. I also made him promise that he would never come into Essex County again. He was confused but happy, and he was convinced I was letting him out early because I liked him better than anyone else in the jail.

"Jeez, how can I thank you, Sheriff," he said as he left my office.

"You can thank me by never coming into Essex County again."

"Jeez, that's what Sheriff Courtney said when he sent me to Sheriff Bowes in Cape Cod."

I reached into my pocket and handed Buddy twenty dollars. "Two deputy sheriffs are waiting outside to drive you to the bus station in Boston," I told him, "and I want you to take a bus to Hyannis, Cape Cod. It's not too far from Sheriff Bowes' jail, which you loved so much. Dinty Moore's Restaurant on Main Street needs a short order cook. See Mr. Welch tomorrow...and behave yourself." I stuck out my hand and said good-bye to Buddy.

"Jeez, Sheriff, I'm overwhelmed," he said, seemingly stumped for words for the first time in his life.

"So am I," I replied. He kept on waving to me out the back window of the car as the deputies drove him away. I had learned a hard lesson from my fellow sheriffs, especially my mentor Jerry Bowes. I hoped in my heart that Buddy Jerome would succeed at his cooking job in Hyannis, but I had my doubts. If he did get himself in trouble, however, he would again become Jerry Bowes' responsibility and be impossible to transfer. I wasn't mad at Jerry any more; I was just getting even.

✳ ✳ ✳

Not two weeks had passed since the release of Buddy when Sheriff Cliff Marshall called me. "Bob, I've got a guy here I'd like you to take off my hands. He's from your county originally, and I don't know how I got him, but I did."

"Is he dangerous? Does he cause problems? Is he emotionally unstable? Does he talk a lot?" These were the questions I now asked of any sheriff who wished to transfer an inmate to Salem Jail, and most important, "Why are you getting rid of him?"

"He's sort of a loner," said Cliff, after answering no to all my previous questions. "Two other guys at my jail are out to beat him up, and I don't know why. They've already managed to blacken his eye."

"Is he queer?"

"I don't think so," said Cliff. "He's just a nice, quiet guy, who doesn't seem to bother anyone, but I have to transfer him for his own good."

I wondered if I was swallowing the bait again. "Cliff, I'll take this fellow from you, but you're sure there's nothing else about him that you're not telling me? What's he in for?"

"He's in for petty theft, Bob, and there's really nothing more to tell. I'll have him down to you within an hour." Cliff seemed awfully anxious to get rid of this inmate. Like Jerry Bowes, I had served with Cliff Marshall in the state legislature, and we had won our sheriff's positions in much the same way and at the very same time. The House of Representatives was an old-boy network then, and Cliff, Jerry, and I used to kid around with each other a lot while we were there. It was fun then, but now I considered the responsibility of running the sheriff's department and my antiquated jail a serious business. I hoped that Cliff was not pulling a fast one on me as Jerry had; I couldn't help thinking that there was something about his black-eyed inmate that Cliff wasn't telling me. Of course, maybe I was just getting paranoid after the Buddy Jerome fiasco.

I peeked out of my office window when the car from Norfolk County arrived, and two of Cliff's deputies escorted this stoop-shouldered, pimply-faced, bespectacled, little character into the jail and into what I hoped was oblivion. I thought surely that this sad looking, seemingly benign creature, named Vincent Fuller, could not possibly be a troublemaker.

"Any problems with Vincent Fuller?" I asked Warren after Fuller's first full week.

"Wouldn't even know he was here," said Warren. I was relieved to hear it, and the issue slipped easily from my mind.

The first inkling of trouble came two weeks later, however, when a correctional officer on the third shift—a.k.a. the Dog Watch—mentioned in his report that Vinnie was "asleep in his cell with a pair of worn woman's panties draped over his face." When questioned about the panties, an embarrassed Vinnie Fuller stated that his girl-friend, who had visited the day before, had left the panties with him as a reminder of her. That didn't seem especially bad to me. A bit bizarre perhaps, if not a little uncouth, but it certainly didn't warrant disciplinary action.

"At least now we know he isn't queer," Warren assured me. But two days later, Vinnie was discovered lying prone, face up, on the floor near the shower stalls.

"If he's trying to watch other guys take showers then he's got to have a problem," I concluded. But Warren had a different theory. He believed that Vinnie wasn't trying to view men taking showers, but was attempting to spy on anyone using the toilet.

"What on earth for?" I asked Warren.

The deputy master shrugged. "I have no idea," he said, "but I still don't think he's queer."

"What then?" I demanded, perplexed and a bit uncomfortable with the whole idea of it.

Warren shrugged his shoulders again. There was something ab-normal about Vinnie Fuller, and I was sure Sheriff Marshall knew exactly what it was, but asking him was futile because he'd never admit it to me. "Have the boys keep an eagle eye on him," I told Warren.

"The toilet is the one place an inmate can go to get a little privacy; he sure as hell doesn't want someone staring up at him from the floor."

It was another few days before the next clue fell into place and we could begin to figure out Vinnie's problem. Although the inmates were usually pretty tight-mouthed when it came to squealing or revealing the character flaws of fellow inmates, his cellmates had nicknamed him "The Beast" and avoided contact with him, always giving him a wide berth in the corridors.

Warren finally got the story from an inmate source of his and eased into my office to educate me. "As crude and nasty as it sounds," Warren reported delicately, "it seems that Vinnie's main hang-up is the toilet-bowl, or more specifically, what's *in* the toilet when someone fails to flush, or the bowl is stopped up."

My stomach did a flip-flop. "I don't want to hear any more," I told Warren. "We've got to send this guy to Bridgewater immediately."

As with Buddy Jerome, we found it impossible to get rid of The Beast. After explaining our discovery to the authorities at Bridgewater, they refused to take him, even temporarily for observation.

"We're full up—no room," said the director, "and we've got guys here with much bigger problems than a fetish for shit."

When I told Warren, it was the only time I ever saw panic creep into his eyes. "We can't keep him here," he said. "Next thing you know he'll be into the buckets." I hadn't thought of that.

My last and only hope was Danvers State Asylum, a mental institution located only a few miles away, but they hardly ever accepted anyone coming directly out of a jail. I assumed they feared ex-cons could be dangerous to their entire population. I made the call and was pleased to discover that the head nurse in charge of admissions was Carol Brown, an old high school classmate of mine. I hoped she would be sympathetic.

"You can bring him up for observation, Bob," said Carol, sounding not too optimistic, "but we can't keep him unless we find that he's really got a problem."

"Really check him over good," I said in a pleading tone. "The guy has a problem, Carol, and unless I get your help, I have no where to turn."

"We'll see," concluded my old classmate. "Send him up." I immediately shipped Vinnie off, hoping I'd never see him again. But early the next morning, I got a call from Carol.

"Send your deputies to come pick Vinnie up," she said. "We can't find anything wrong with him, and therefore we can't keep him. He seems normal in every way... quiet and retiring, but normal."

"But I told you what he was doing, Carol. That's not normal. I can't have him mixing in with the regular population here. Please take him!"

"I'd like to help, Bob," said Carol, sounding truly apologetic, "but I have to follow orders." I was devastated and angry at the inept system that couldn't find the problem in an obviously troubled man. I had no choice but to send the deputies to pick up Vinnie and return him to the jail. I decided to call Sheriff Marshall and demand he take Vinnie Fuller back. That, of course, would not solve Vinnie's problem, but I could not allow The Beast to disrupt my jail.

I was about to make that call when my phone rang. It was Carol Brown. "Bob, I sent your deputies back without Vinnie Fuller...we've decided to keep him." I was surprised but I felt a great weight lift off my shoulders. How could I be so thrilled at the fate of a shit-eater?

"What made you change your mind?"

"When your deputies got here, Bob, they couldn't find Vinnie. I had left him in the waiting room unattended, and he slipped away. We had an all-out search here, and when we found him, he was in the visitors bathroom...with his head in the bowl."

"That's wonderful," I said, "so you caught him in the act. What happens to him now?"

"We just have to give Vinnie some personal attention," said Carol, "like right now I'm sitting with Vinnie beside me, cleaning his teeth with a toothpick and floss. All you have to do, Bob, is send up his papers for the transfer."

"I'll forever be indebted to you, Carol," I said. "And just to show my gratitude, when I send my deputy up with the transfer papers, I'll have him stop off at the pharmacy to buy you a bottle of Listerine."

My fellow sheriffs, I now concluded, had thoroughly initiated me into the brotherhood of law enforcers with their two nightmarish transfers to the Salem Jail. I would be quite leery of okaying any more transfers in the future. It was all, I supposed, part of the learning process, but if you can't trust your friends, whom can you trust? In a jail, be you sheriff or inmate, the answer was obvious—you can trust no one.

CHAPTER VI

Going To The Dogs

For courage, discipline, devotion to duty, and investigative powers, there was no law enforcement person in Essex County as capable as Ace, the Salem Police dog. I was so impressed watching Ace capture Fitzpatrick in the pitch blackness of the field off Highland Avenue that I decided the sheriff's department should have a dog of its own. We could then hunt down our own escapees without having to rely on the dogs of local police departments. The dog could live inside the perimeter of the jail fence, acting as a deterrent to any inmate escape plans and to outsiders climbing the fence to hand dope, cutting tools, or weapons to inmates through the barred windows. The dog could be trained to sniff out narcotics, and when inmates returned from furloughs, instead of a guard demanding they spread their cheeks to search for contraband, the dog could just stick its nose where it usually does anyway. If there were narcotics hidden within, the dog could be trained to take a hefty bite. Instead of guards having to get their hands dirty searching cells for narcotics, the dog could be trained to conduct spot inspections. A dog seemed to be the answer to many of our problems. Maybe we could even get two or three dogs, I thought, since there seemed to be no real expense to the county except food, and we could save on that by feeding them jail food, which I was convinced was better suited to dogs anyway.

I asked some of the guards and deputies what they thought about getting a dog and training it, but didn't receive much enthusiasm in response, until one day, a quiet, unassuming correctional officer named Ernie Comeau approached me. "The boys are saying you'd like to have an attack dog," Ernie inquired in a stuttering French accent. Ernie was born in Canada and had worked as a guard for a few years under Roger Wells.

"Not so much an attack dog, but one we could use to track down escapees, sniff out narcotics—that type of thing," I said.

"If there's a riot, there's nothing better than a dog to quiet things down," said Ernie. I agreed. "I can get a dog, Sheriff," said Ernie, a touch of enthusiasm in his voice.

"We not only need a dog—we need a qualified trainer," I said.

"A friend of mine has a German Shepherd that he'll give me to train. I can keep it at my house. I've always wanted to train dogs…I have dogs…I love dogs." Ernie kept rattling on, his accent getting thicker the more enthused he got. He was one of the most conscientious and capable guards in the jail, and he was obviously sincere.

I finally heard myself saying, "All right, Ernie, let's do it." Not knowing Ernie's skills nor the dog's capabilities, I was somewhat reluctant, but the Boston Police Department provided an eight-week course in training dogs and their owners in investigative work, so I signed Ernie and his dog up. The county commissioners, of course, would not pay for such a frivolous expense. If they wouldn't pay to train correctional officers or deputies, they certainly wouldn't pay to train a dog. It was also going to be difficult to spare Ernie for eight weeks. I asked the deputies to chip in to send Ernie and his year-old shepherd to school, and I convinced Warren Bethune that someway, somehow, he had to spare Ernie in the jail and have other guards cover his assignments. No one seemed happy about this four-legged addition to the sheriff's department, except Ernie and me. When I told Ernie about going to Boston with his dog, he shook with excitement.

Ernie had been gone five days when I received a phone call from Sergeant Buchanan of the Boston Police Canine Corps. When I signed Ernie up for the training, Buchanan agreed to provide me with a progress report every week.

"I just wanted to report that your dog trainer is doing fine," said the sergeant, "although he's a bit nervous. But I'm sure he'll get over that before the next seven weeks are up. He's very attentive and conscientious. The dog is the best we've got here, he's the most aggressive canine we've seen, he's even managed to bite a tire off my captain's new Volkswagen." The sergeant chuckled softly to himself "So, I really think you've got a great team." I thanked him and asked him to give his captain my apologies. I was really pleased with Buchanan's report, although Ernie's timidity and the dog's aggressiveness bothered me a little, but then again, he had called them, "a great team."

Seven days later I received another call from Sergeant Buchanan. "Sheriff...I have some bad news for you. Your shepherd? Well...you see, it was trying to jump over this wooden wall on the obstacle course—It wasn't a very high wall, maybe four feet or so...Uh, the dog got caught, sir...it caught its balls halfway over the wall...and...well sir...the dog went berserk..."

"Will he die?" I asked.

"No sir, but it'll be no good for training anymore. It really hurt itself... maybe in a few months you can try again, but I don't think this dog will follow commands any more."

I was very disappointed. "Thanks, sergeant," I said. "At least we tried. Maybe we'll find a new dog and start all over again."

"Well, you see, that's not all, Sheriff," the sergeant continued. "The dog was attached to a leash when it happened, and your training officer—Ernie I think he is—well, he was holding onto the leash and when the dog went berserk, it pulled Ernie over the wall with it. Ernie broke his leg. Sheriff, he's all right, but he'll be laid up for a few weeks."

Seven weeks later Ernie reported back to work at the jail. It was another week before he came to my office, almost in tears, to apologize and try to explain. "The dog was too frisky," he concluded, and so he gave the dog back to its original owner. "My wife is sick of cleaning up the dog mess anyway," said Ernie, and he had no desire to attempt to train another dog. Before he limped out of my office, he presented me with a piece of paper. "My wife told me to give you this", he explained. It was a $71.00 bill for dog food.

This was a major set back in my quest for a canine deputy, but I didn't give up hope. Word of my desire to have a department search dog apparently spread throughout the county, for hardly two weeks passed from Ernie's return when a handsome, energetic, young man from Newburyport with wavy gray hair sat before me in my office, stating that he was an experienced dog trainer and wanted to work for me. His name was Paul Ferguson, and his deal was that if I made him a deputy and commissioned him the department's canine officer—non-paying of course—he would train two of his shepherds in police work at a farm he recently purchased. Ferguson had worked part-time as a police officer, and he had trained dogs in the past, so I agreed. What could I lose with a deal like that?

Ferguson went to work immediately, and periodically he would bring one of the German Shepherds to the jail to demonstrate its progress. I had met enough shepherds during my door-to-door campaign days to give them and Dobermans a wide berth. Although he was training the dogs to search, they were more tempered and talented as attack dogs, and Paul could see that I was nervous having them around. I delicately explained to him that I was more interested in their search and rescue capabilities than their ability to maul inmates. So, with my approval, he contacted a Georgia sheriff who bred bloodhounds and convinced him to give our department a one-year-old hound, already trained in search and rescue, as an added specialist to our pack. The only problem was that when the bloodhound arrived at Ferguson's farm, it didn't get along with the two shepherds. "This is normal," Paul explained to me. "All dogs living in the same area have to fight at least once to decide who is leader of the pack...the bloodhound beat both shepherds," which surprised me.

"Bloodhounds are cruel fighters," said Paul, "and the shepherds now keep their distance from Charlie."

"Charlie?? I hope you didn't name the dog after my special sheriff, Charlie Reardon?" Ferguson blushed at my question and never answered me. I suppose having the toughest dog in the pack named after you could be considered a compliment, but I wondered about it, for I knew Reardon was opposed to the idea of using dogs, "except for a major riot." Whenever Ferguson and Reardon met, they would argue the pros and cons of a canine corps within the department. This, I assumed, was the reason the bloodhound was named Charlie.

Ferguson seemed to spend almost every waking hour dragging the shepherds and Charlie from one special training session to another. Charlie was especially popular with the kids, and many schoolteachers called on Ferguson and his canine team to put on demonstrations for their classes. After being with us a few weeks, Charlie, in fact, pulled off a minor miracle. The deputies had chipped in and bought Paul a canine car, an old 1970 Ford sedan, rigged with a rear seat screen for the dogs. Paul agreed to pay for gas, but no one could afford to register and insure our K-9 vehicle, so we brought it in as a special budget item to the county commissioners. I didn't give it much of a chance of passing, even though we weren't asking for much money. As the item came before the commissioners in their meeting room, Paul Ferguson, with Charlie on a leash, entered the room. Charlie became an immediate hit. Kay Donavan, the female commissioner, wilted before our eyes and fell in love with Charlie. Ferguson pleaded that the vehicle was needed to offer assistance to all 34 police departments within the county. He explained that Charlie was the only bloodhound available within the county to track lost persons—"this breed being the best trackers in the world." And as the local newspaper reported the next day, to the great surprise of all, "Without another word or bark, the commissioners approved the request."

I informed all the police chiefs that Charlie and the two shepherds were available to them at any place or time. But we never got a nibble from them, and the dogs were never used on their behalf. Ferguson, however, kept busy with the dogs, giving lecture-demonstrations and marching in local parades.

On the Fourth of July, Paul marched with the shepherds on leashes in the Salisbury Parade. As they turned the corner onto Beach Street, a little beagle came sniffing around the shepherds. In front of hundreds of children and their parents, the shepherds attacked the beagle and one of them bit off its left ear, forcing Paul to leave the line of march. Charlie also appeared in the Newburyport Parade, sitting in the back seat of the K-9 car, driven by Paul. Charlie just stuck his nose and ears out of the window and the children cheered, but when the Ancient and Honorable Battalion, dressed in bright red uniforms, galloped by on horseback, Charlie went wild. He began howling and pawing madly at the screen that separated him from Paul. The horses flinched and reared up on their hind legs. The crowd cheered as the horses bumped into each other and the riders almost fell off. The Ancient and Honorables, an artillery outfit dating back to pre-Revolution days, were extremely upset with Charlie and Paul. Needless to say, Paul and the dogs were not invited back to any local parades, and it seemed that all our potential goodwill dog-gestures were creating ill will.

The last straw came when Ferguson entered one of the shepherds into the United States Annual K-9 Association competition on the grounds of the Plymouth County House of Correction. "The large black German shepherd was over-zealous," local newspapers reported, and when the wife of the assistant jail keeper walked out her front door she "was bitten very hard" by Ferguson's dog, which he was trying to restrain with a tight leash.

As Fergy later explained, "she was just at the wrong place at the wrong time, and the dog took a nip." Paul said that he told the woman to "remain still and don't move" when she suddenly appeared on what was being used as the K-9 training and exhibition field. "I just can't understand her reaction," Paul told me. "She began screaming and flaying her arms in panic." I could understand that reaction. It was the same as mine on many occasions when I'd knock on a door with my political brochure, and a dog would growl or leap forward—my legs would turn to jelly. "Anyway," Paul continued, "our good shepherd caught hold of one of her flaying arms and wouldn't let go." I cringed. The victim of the bite, Mrs. Miriam Barron, sued Essex County for $25,000. Certainly, my determination to have a search dog like Ace led to this terrible incident. Mrs. Barron eventually won her case. It was the end of the Sheriff's Department K-9 Corps.

It was, admittedly, a costly and embarrassing failure, and it wasn't the only one I would make as the sheriff. But I wasn't going to stop trying new ideas, and the dire circumstances of the county jails insured that we had to be creative and bold. I only wondered if the county commissioners would ever allow me another special budget item again. Needless to say, there was never again the talk of dogs within the sheriff's department.

CHAPTER VII

Messiah On A Motorbike

They came in droves: thin ones, fat ones, young ones, old ones, males and females, all with one purpose, to break *into* the Salem Jail & House Of Correction. It was as if they had been waiting for centuries to get in, hungry to right every wrong those old walls had stood for. One would think that since they all represented organizations that wanted to assist the inmates in some way, they would be a peaceful, non-aggressive lot, but they weren't. Most of them barked at me, insisting on entry so that they could work their collective wonders. Deputy Master Bethune and his assistant, Charlie Hardy, former U.S. Army heavyweight boxing champion of Europe, wanted nothing to do with these do-gooders. Bethune felt that outsiders involved in jail life could cause serious disruptions to security, and Hardy just didn't like the way most of these liberal volunteers talked or dressed.

"I'm tellin' ya', Sheriff, they're gonna cause trouble if ya' let 'em in," said Hardy.

"I agree," echoed Bethune, " and there is little or no room in the jail for them to do anything."

I informed Bethune and Hardy that we had to allow the more legit groups to enter the jail, but only in limited numbers, and for a limited time, to counsel the inmates on a volunteer basis. The problem was that when I allowed a couple of agency representatives inside the jail, others clambered even louder to get inside, accusing me of playing favorites. It was a notion I found funny because at that point in time, none of them were my favorites. They were like gnats, constantly tapping at my office door and windows, wanting to see me "only for a minute" about this solution and that idea for turning criminals into stalwart citizens. The especially shaggy characters, seemingly leftovers from the Swinging Sixties, just wouldn't take "no" for

an answer, and their persistence prompted me to call for a general
meeting of all concerned. On a Wednesday morning, in the small
conference room we had recently constructed on the first floor of the
sheriff's house, we all met. It was packed with counselors and agency
representatives, a few wearing suits and ties, but most of them looking like they had just come down from a lifetime in the mountains.
They all tried to speak at once, some banging the table with their
fists—it was chaos—but out of the verbal melee came one strong
voice of logic. Others were starting to quiet down and listen to him,
and he was making sense. A leader had emerged from the masses,
and I knew right then and there that I would make him my "King of
the Ultra-liberals and Chief Coordinator of the Jail's Human Services." I announced that we would begin a coalition, and that this
man would head up the group. Then I left the room.

Jack Jerdan had a thick black beard and moustache. He wore san-
dals, a tan robe with a knotted tie around his slim waist, and a large
leather pocketbook strapped over his shoulder. If he had worn a
wooden cross around his neck, he would have passed for a holy man.
He drove a vintage motorbike with a large mesh basket behind the
seat, where a big, amiable, drooling dog of questionable heritage, rode
with him. It lay quietly at his feet wherever he plunked himself to
discuss human services. Jack Jerdan approached projects and problems like gangbusters, head on, no holds barred. He was project director of Project Rap Intervention Hotline in Beverly, a crisis
intervention and rehabilitation agency. After his first full meeting
with the new coalition, Jack came to see me. His first major complaint was not being able to get in the jail door.

"Usually the guard at the door tells me I can't come in."

"Unless there's a countdown or some inmate problems affecting
the security of the jail, I'll see that you can get in any time you want.
Come to see me first, and I'll call the Deputy Master to let you in."

"I don't think they like me in there," he said. " I mean the
guards—the inmates like me just fine."

Jack was right, but I wasn't going to tell him that. "They like you,
but wearing pants and a nice shirt might help your image. Plus, they

don't want the dog in there slobbering over everything." Jack protested. "Leave him here in the house with me or Loretta when you go inside. It will help ease any tension."

"What about new programs?" asked Jack. "The coalition has all kinds of ideas and projects for the residents." Jack called the inmates, "residents", and he wanted me to do so as well, but I never could get use to the idea of it, so they remained inmates to me.

"You can try any new program you like," I told Jack, "but if it doesn't work well, or my Deputy Master or correctional officers have legitimate problems with it, whatever it is, it will be stopped. But otherwise, the sky is the limit."

" Are you pulling my leg?"

"Nope," I replied

"I can try anything I want in there?" he smiled deviously behind the beard.

"Yep."

My feeling was that we really didn't know what would work, but we knew there needed to be improvements, so we might as well try as many different programs as possible. Some services, such as drug and alcohol abuse counseling, were obviously needed. Jack started what he called "rap sessions" twice a week, in the jail's only available room, the chapel/library. Warren informed me that a guard must be present whenever inmates were in our decrepit chapel/library because the barred windows were old and crumbling.

"Anyone with a hacksaw could cut through these bars in two minutes, lift the window, climb down the water spout to the sidewalk leading to the front door, and just stroll down Saint Peter's Street." The solution, Warren explained, was to double bar the windows. I told him to find out how much it would cost.

"Eleven hundred dollars."

"Do it," I told Warren. "We'll find the money someplace." When I said it, I didn't know where the money would come from, but it was necessary for Jack Jerdan to work his magic, and that's all that mattered. I had already overworked the county coffers, and the legislature was still grumbling over my 5-million dollar bond order. And even if the Feds would come to my aid again, it would take a long time. So, I decided to contact old friends and wealthy constituents who had contributed money to my past campaigns and ask them to fund the project. Soon after, we had our bars, and Jack had his meetings.

The Salem Public Library, Salem State College, and North Shore Community College donated books for our jail library/chapel, which soon became a reading room, a therapy room, a lecture hall, and a class room for inmates striving to learn how to read and write. The average inmate read at an eighth grade level and, surprisingly, twenty prisoners in the Salem jail alone could not read or write. We also had a few who were studying to take the high school equivalency exam. If they wanted to study further, North Shore Community College offered college courses at the jail. The inmates took to these new programs slowly, but once they saw the successes of their cellmates who did participate, most of the new programs began overflowing with interested inmates. Some, of course, were taking them just as a way to relieve the boredom, but even then, in many cases, they became interested and excelled in their studies. That old chapel that had remained idle six days of the week and had provided comfort for only a few on Sunday mornings had become the most exciting and active part of the prison.

Reverend Webster, a tall and stately looking man with a deep resonant voice, was the jail chaplain; he had a meager following. His old, brick Unitarian Church was just down Bridge Street from the jail, and he was always ready to assist us in any way, on a moment's notice. He didn't want us to paint over the Last Supper wall mural in the library/chapel, which hindered us from erecting bookshelves for the volumes we were receiving from Salem State College, the Salem Public Library, the Beverly Public Library, and North Shore Community College. Reverend Webster was definitely into the new swing of things at the jail, but he stood his ground on our wish to dispose of the Last Supper. It was Jack Jerdan who matter-of-factly found an agreeable solution to the impasse; his agency provided funds for a velvet curtain that could be opened or closed at will, and four-tier portable bookracks that could be wheeled to the rear of the room on

Sunday when the curtain was opened to reveal the crude painting of the Last Supper. Reverend Webster reluctantly accepted the compromise. Jack Jerdan also convinced Warren Bethune that he would not have to spare a correctional officer to be present at meetings, lectures, or classes when Jack was there, if we made him a correctional officer. So, when the department received funds for two new correctional officers from one of Al Marrs' federal grants, Jack Jerdan was hired as a counselor/correctional officer and relieved Bethune of some of the worry that these new "liberal programs" had placed upon him. But that wasn't the end of the conflict between Jack and Warren—not by a long shot. Warren came down hard on Jack when he introduced an art class and hired a beautiful young woman to do the teaching. Warren visited the class in the library one afternoon, only to find the art teacher and an inmate art student in a compromising position. He canceled the art program immediately and sent the art teacher packing. Jack was furious, and he came storming into my office.

"It was just a flirtation," he stammered, "nothing serious, and certainly not enough to cancel the art classes."

"They are canceled for now," I told him, " and maybe we'll start them up again later, with a male teacher."

"This woman was the best," shouted Jack.

"I'm sure she was," I snickered.

"I quit!" Jack said, "I'm giving my resignation right now."

"Why?" I asked. "Just because one of your ten new programs is temporarily closed down, for the sake of security in the jail?"

"Security???" What security? It was just a guy and a girl hugging or something like that."

"Not in the jail, Jack. If the other inmates, or guards, or, God save us, the press gets wind of this little peccadillo, there will be hell to pay all around. It could cause the cancellation of all other programs for the inmates—for good. So, don't let this one setback spoil everything."

"I quit!" He insisted, sitting down before me to pout.

"When you started this job as our inmate-advocate and coordinator of all human services programs, I told you that you could try anything, but if something didn't work, we'd cancel it and try something else."

"But this was working."

"Sure, for one creative, over-zealous, love sick inmate. No way, Jack. And I'm sorry you're quitting after so many successes and just one failure—I thought you were tougher than that."

"I'm not tough," replied Jack. "I don't want to be tough. I just want to do my job."

"Then, go do it," I said, pointing to the door, "and stop blubbering over just one setback."

"It's not just one setback," said Jack with a dejected look on his face. "I've had hundreds of setbacks in there," he said, pointing to the jail. "They don't like me in there and were just waiting to close down one of my programs."

"Jack," I said, leaning in to stare into his bearded face. "I am surrounded by old-school conservatives here. You are my only liberal, so you must stay to carry on with all the needed programs here. Don't let one setback bowl you over. Go in there," I said, standing and pointing towards the jail again, "and give them ten more programs. I promised you that you could try anything unless it caused great problems—this one did. Go try another, and don't give up."

Stoop shouldered, he headed for the door, giving me a meek wave goodbye. I think this was the same "get in there and fight" speech I had given the weekend before to my Pop Warner football team.

Things didn't get any easier for Jack, and he continued to be browbeaten by the crew. He wasn't use to being surrounded by men who thought exactly the opposite as he did. He wanted to be liked and was constantly bringing gifts to Bethune, Hardy, and the jail guards—usually large rubber tree plants that he carried to work in his motorbike basket. Most of the correctional officers didn't know what to do with a rubber plant, and why Jack considered these little trees as a suitable gift, was anyone's guess. His dress started changing for the better; he now wore faded jeans, a tee shirt, clogs, and a red bandana, either tied around his head like a wreath, or worn as a neckerchief. The beard and moustache even seemed to me to be getting a little trimmer. He still had a crudeness about him, however, and when he ate lunch, some of it was always stuck to his beard for a time afterwards. Although he was thin-skinned, he came on like gangbusters, and many guards took this as an affront. But Jack pushed on and accomplished much in bettering the inmates' lot.

Jack approached various groups in the county's many cities, like Rotary, Kiwanis and the Chamber of Commerce, to assist the jails with money and services. He continuously spoke at these club meetings, emphasizing to them that "crime is a community problem" and that "every segment of the community should get involved." He invited them all to lunch at the jail and to take a tour, where he continued to hammer home the need for their involvement.

Jack's tours, plus the ones I was giving simultaneously to mayors and legislators, drove Warren Bethune to near insanity. Though Warren was beginning to appreciate Jack and his ideas, most of the guards just wouldn't accept him, no matter how hard he tried to please them. It wasn't long after the art class fiasco that he was back in my office quitting again. Our most notorious, bull-headed guard would not let him in the jail one morning, and through the thick steel door, had called Jack, "Mary."

Jack was furious and hurt. "I can't work this way," he told me. "That guard is a horse's ass, and he shouldn't even be in corrections." I agreed.

"I inherited him from Wells. He's a former frustrated football player who once was kind of famous, and now he's forgotten. He's angry at the world. He has troubles at home, and he lives behind bars all day. Besides, I told you to call me if you ever had trouble getting in."

"Well, I won't call on you again, 'cause I quit."

"No you don't," I told him. "You can't quit now. You've started all these programs, and I'm sure you have many more in mind, so go back to the door, and I'll call the jail." Jack walked out of my office, dejected. I had never met a man, only 26 years old, who had such developed counseling, organizing, and leadership skills, yet was so thin-skinned. I called the jail, and the bull-headed guard, who shouldn't have been a guard, answered. "Open the door for Jack Jerdan," I told him.

"Can't do it, Sheriff. We're having a countdown."

"Open that door now, or you can count yourself out of here," I roared over the phone. He got the message, but my outburst didn't help Jack's cause. The constantly sulking guard continued to call him "Mary" whenever he was on duty.

There were some guards, I felt, that acted like criminals, and some inmates that would have made excellent correctional officers. To their credit, being a guard is not an easy job; there is a lot of stress and it's easy to become cynical and jaded. In fact most of the guards spent more of their lives behind bars than any of our inmates did. The average age of our guards was about 40 years old, and the average age of inmates was 22 years old. About 65% of the inmates had emotional, drug, or alcohol problems—sometimes all three—and my guess is that serious emotional and substance abuse problems were almost as prevalent among the guards. As Jack Jerdan struggled to bring proper counseling and assistance to the inmates, I tried to improve the attitudes, understanding, and skills of my employees.

In 1973, the federal government created the Comprehensive Employment and Training Act (CETA), a work/training program to help the unemployed find new careers, and the cities provided us with workers to train at federal government expense. We put the CETA trainees to work as guards in the jails. This, to Warren Bethune's horror, allowed me to ship two guards off to the University of Massachusetts in Amherst for eight weeks to study at a new Correctional Institution for Jail Guards, sponsored and financed by the state. None of my guards had ever trained in corrections, and some weren't even high school graduates. I also invited various lecturers in psychology and the science of counseling to begin a re-learning process for some of our "old school" officers, who believed in the "lock 'em up and throw away the key" philosophy. The fact is that the inmates' sentences would eventually end, and they would be set free, and I felt a responsibility to let them out in better shape than they came in. The first step in improving the inmates' behavior was to first improve our own.

* * *

There were a lot of groups who wanted to change the way we did things in Essex County. I was informed by the Human Services Coalition that I wasn't even close to meeting minimum standards in providing African-American and Spanish speaking correctional officers. Lawrence Jail had a fairly heavy Spanish speaking or Latino population, representing just about every South and Central American country and the West Indies. Salem had about an 18 percent Spanish speaking population and only one CETA guard who spoke Spanish. So North Shore Community College provided a Spanish teacher and we began teaching Spanish to the guards and any inmate who wanted to learn the language.

I only had a few African-American inmates at any one time, but I only had one African-American on my payroll, and that was Charlie Manuel of Beverly, who considered himself a mulatto (half black and half white). Charlie and his father were famous for an orchestra called "Manuel's Black And Whites" that had been around the North Shore for years. Charlie had also been a well-known football star for Beverly High School. On the wall of his living room, he displayed a large photo of himself, scoring one of his many touchdowns, with a chunky Salem lineman barreling down the field after him, too slow and too late to make the tackle. Unfortunately, I was that chunky lineman. Salem and Beverly have been Thanksgiving rivals for over 100 years, and Charlie Manual is a legend of this ancient rivalry. I begged him to take the photo down— he refused, of course—but I hired him as a deputy anyway. But that wasn't good enough for the Coalition, the Commonwealth of Massachusetts, or the Federal Government. It wasn't good enough for me either, but there hadn't been any African-American applicants for the correctional officer positions. It was only by chance that a tall, well-built African-American man walked into my office one day, looking for a job. He had been a CETA employee and had had a short stint on a local police force. I questioned him for about five minutes, and then asked him to follow me. I marched Leon Breckenridge out my front door and three blocks down the street, without telling him where we were going. I walked into Superior Court with Leon close beside me, and asked for Jim Leary, recently elected Clerk of Courts. Jim appeared from out of the back office and asked how he could help.

"Can you swear this man in, Jim?"

"Sure," he replied. "Raise your right hand," he said to Leon, and he swore the bewildered man in as a deputy sheriff. That over, Leon and I walked leisurely back to the jail.

"I can squeeze you in for a couple of days as a guard in the jail, mainly because I have two men at school and a couple more on vacation, and then I can give you two to three days a week in the court. All that may vary a bit from week to week, and you may have to keep changing uniforms from day to day, but you're hired. Welcome aboard." I stopped half way down the street and shook his hand. Leon still looked bewildered—pleased, but bewildered. He opened his mouth to ask why the rush, but stopped himself. It was as if he had been shanghaied off the street, and I realized that I was going to have to come clean with him.

"Leon," I told him before I sent him in to Warren, "you are an old CETA employee, which is good, 'cause it saves us money. You have police experience, which is good, for few of us in the sheriff's department do. So you are more than qualified. But the truth is, I have a form sitting on my desk that I have to turn in tomorrow to the state Corrections Administration listing my Equal-Opportunity employees. You, Leon Breckenridge, have just allowed me to come into compliance and keep my badge." Leon understood and smiled. "And in addition, you've just doubled the diversity of the department." He thanked me for my honesty and the opportunity, and I thanked him for his good timing.

Jack Jerdan was pleased as punch with Leon, and he immediately received a rubber tree plant. The next time Jack saw me, he smiled, which he didn't do very often and said, "I can see that you're making progress too, Sheriff."

⁂ ⁂ ⁂

Al Marrs had miraculously gotten us a grant to begin the work release project, and surprisingly, the County Commissioners and the Advisory Board chipped in $8,000 in matching funds. With the help of John Kuczun and Don Richards, two correctional officers who also happened to be talented carpenters and plumbers that I would constantly steal away from Warren Bethune for construction detail, we got to work on the transformation of the sheriff's house into lodging for work release inmates. The third floor of the sheriff's house was converted into bedrooms, a kitchen, and a living room. They also installed one bathroom, complete with a working toilet, to be shared by six men—a blessing to those who had been using buckets in the main prison.

Our first job, once the facility was ready, was to set up a screening board, made up of our best correctional officers from Lawrence and Salem and four local businessmen. It was their job to decide which inmates would be first into the program. They would select ten men, and then I would boil it down to the final six. In talking to these ten inmates, some for well over an hour, I was surprised to discover that their greatest fear during their time in jail was that they had lost their work habits. This new program, we hoped, would build these habits up again, and in turn, build their self-esteem and motivation to stay clean. It really wasn't difficult finding jobs in the community for the six chosen men. One was an experienced fisherman, another got a job pumping gas, another worked in a plastics factory, the fourth got work at the nearby Sylvania Electric Plant, packing light bulbs, the fifth became a short-order cook at a restaurant, and the sixth work release "resident" got a job selling used cars. We even acquired an old vehicle in order to get them to and from work each day. Correctional officers turned counselors, like Harry Healy and Phil Corriveau, kept tabs on the inmates, on and off the job. The work-release men returned every evening to their little enclave, two stories above my office, where they were guarded at night and on weekends.

At first, we allowed weekend visitations by family and friends to the third story home, until Harry Healy caught one of the six being jerked-off by his girlfriend in a bedroom. We then set up tables and chairs outside the house and only allowed friends and family to visit out in the open. Except for a few minor problems, like the over anxious girlfriend, the program worked exceedingly well, with more and more local businessmen eager to employ inmates. The first batch of men served four months in work release before leaving for good. Not only did they start savings accounts for themselves, leaving with a total of some $4,000 in the bank, but two of them got their families off of welfare, plus paid County Treasurer Tom Duffy, $694 for room and board. All six men, who started their jobs while still in prison, remained on the job after they were released. How much better was this system at keeping men out of prison, than handing a released inmate fifty cents for bus fare, sending him back to the streets without savings or a job, where he had nothing to keep him from reverting to his old ways? As Jack Jerdan said in his speech to persuade local businessmen to help us:

> The challenge is to find some way to make these men and boys change while they are incarcerated, otherwise they are unmotivated men who will spend most of their time in jail simply waiting to get out...and they will get out. Isn't it better to integrate them slowly, as we improve their educational and vocational skills? Except for eating and sleeping, these men waste their time and your money in jail.... Remember, you as taxpayers are paying $10,000 to $12,000 per year to incarcerate these men. Under work release, they pay for room and board and become earning, taxpaying citizens themselves. Recidivism rate at our jails, like jails all over America, is 70 percent, so three-quarters of those who are released from jail, return within the year to become a burden on the taxpayers once again. In work release, however, recidivism is only seven percent, meaning that 93% of

those who participate in work release at the Salem and Lawrence Houses of Correction become contributors to society.

My first sad experience with the seven-percent that don't make it and return to jail from work release was with an inmate named Joe Rowe. Joe was a conscientious worker and a fellow well met. He was quiet and witty, and his employer liked him, but after spending four months in the program without a single problem, he disappeared. The counselors couldn't find him, and we had to put out an escape warrant on him. We didn't have to search for very long though, because the next day he turned himself in.

"Why did you run away, and why did you return?" were my first questions to him, for neither action made much sense to me. Finally, after hemming and hawing, Joe Rowe admitted that he left work release because he would be let out for good in a few days, and even though he had a good job and money in the bank, freedom frightened him.

"I came back, Sheriff," he said, his head bowed, "'cause I got no where to go." Joe Rowe was what we called "institutionalized." His home was the jail, and he'd do anything to stay in jail, so he escaped just days before he was scheduled to be let out for good. Jack Jerdan didn't want me to charge Joe with escaping, but I did.

"Right now he needs the jail," I told Jack, "as bad as it is, he likes it here. It's his home."

"He needs a break. Let him go," insisted Jack.

"He got his break and he messed it up. You know what we tell them before they're placed in the house. 'You screw up once and you're back inside', and that's where Joe Rowe is going."

"I quit," shouted Jack, a phrase I was getting use to from him.

"You can't save them all, Jack, and this one I'm sure will fall to pieces on the outside."

"If you won't let him graduate from this place, then I quit," Jack repeated.

"Then quit," I replied, watching his eyes light up with surprise. "You've started a lot of good programs here, so I guess we can carry

Iright without you. See you later," I said, standing up from my desk and offering my hand.

"You'd really let me go?" he said with a touch of sadness in his voice.

"Only if you want to, Jack. It's your choice, but I'm sure a couple of those fat grumpy guards would be as pleased as punch to see you out of here. Got any names of who might replace you?"

Once again, Jack didn't quit. In fact he went on to provide even more wonders for the Essex County Sheriff's Department. One new idea, called the Victim-Restitution Program, asked a work release inmate to sign a contract to pay back the victim of the crime that sent him to jail in the first place. Before the inmate entered work release, he would meet face to face with his victim, and they would work out a manageable payment schedule on a weekly or monthly basis. The only eligible men were those who committed crimes against property or non-violent crimes against people. After signing the agreement to pay for his sins, his money was automatically taken from his paycheck and delivered to the victim. The incentive to the inmate is not only work release, but also early parole. Jack, with the help of Al Marrs, got a federal "Law Enforcement Assistance Administration" (LEAA) grant, to launch the Victim-Restitution Program at Salem and Lawrence, and Jack was made project director at an increased salary. I gave him an office of his own on the second floor of the sheriff's house, and to make him feel really at home, I had a large leafy rubber tree plant delivered to his door. With that promotion, Jack started wearing a shirt, tie, and sport coat, and miracle of miracles, one morning he shaved his beard. When he came to work, nobody recognized him, not even the grumpy guard.

The Lawrence Jail and House of Correction.

Independent news reporter Bill Pike inside the Lawrence Jail with Master Bill Ryan. (A Dierdorff Photo, courtesy of Bill Pike)

CHAPTER VIII

The One Two Punch

Bill Ryan, my Republican keeper of the Lawrence Jail, was always coming up with surprises and new ingenious ways to better the lot of the inmates. When he came and asked me to come up to the Lawrence Jail to see a new innovation he and his deputy master Joe Carter had concocted, I didn't know what to expect.

"You know the large wooden floor surrounded by the cell blocks, the one in the center of the jail?"

"Of course," I replied. It was as big as a dance hall, with a mirror-like oak floor, where inmates currently held their visits with family and friends. In the late 1800s and early 1900s, it had been merely a showpiece that inmates were forced to scrub and wax every day, but couldn't be walked on, per order of the Jail Master.

"I've found a new, good use for it," said Ryan over the phone. "Come on up!"

I had often commented to Ryan and Carter that I wanted to use the floor for something constructive, but I couldn't think of anything to do with it. The Norfolk County Jail at Dedham was a twin to the Lawrence Jail, only built later, and Sheriff Cliff Marshall had inmates build bookcases along the oak floor and made it into a library. This created a problem, however, for the library was too close to the front door of the jail. Two supposed bookworms who had confiscated a gun, made a dash for the door one day, and shot a guard who tried to stop them. They escaped, but were later caught and sent to maximum-security prison. Sheriff Marshall then had to restrict inmates' access to the library, thereby defeating its initial purpose of providing them greater freedom and productive opportunities. After Cliff's experience, Ryan and I made sure that our new libraries were well within the confines of the jail, with no easy way out but through the pages of a good book.

Ryan's use of the wide expanse of floor was a pleasant surprise. He and Carter had built a professional boxing ring in the center of the floor.

"The inmates built it," Ryan informed me, "and I managed to scrounge the canvass, pads, rope, and bunting, with the help of Joe Carter."

"When are we going to have a fight?" I asked.

"I've already had a few matches—some real good ones—and the inmates love it. A couple were grudge fights—I thought the boys were going to kill each other, but they wear protective headgear. It's been great for morale, plus it cuts down on the wild fighting and feuds in the cellblocks. We've got some real good fighters here in Lawrence."

"I'm sure we have a few good ones in Salem, too," I said.

"Prove it!" said Ryan, turning to stare me in the eye. Without even a clue, I had fallen into his trap. "I'll give you four weeks to find your best men in each of six fighting categories: featherweight, lightweight, welterweight, middleweight, light-heavyweight and heavyweight. Train them and bring them up here to fight on the first of next month."

"You've got a deal," I said, shaking his hand.

Bill and I then walked on into the block area to talk to some of the inmates. "I'm going to be let out for good next week," one inmate told me, "but would it be possible, Sheriff, for me to come back on the first of next month, just to watch the big fight between Salem and Lawrence?"

"Sure!" I replied, turning to Ryan who wore a sheepish grin. "You bastard," I shouted at him. "You had this match all planned before I even got here! I suppose the invitations are all mailed out, and the tickets are on sale?"

"Well," laughed Bill, "the boys are anxious to fight, and I knew you wouldn't refuse a challenge. And just to make it interesting, I'll bet you a dinner at Dini's in Boston that we beat you four out of six matches."

I shook his hand again. "You're on, you cocky bastard. But just remember, I'm sheriff of both jails—I don't have favorites—but just to bring you down a peg, I'll take and win that bet." I was thrilled at the challenge and couldn't wait to get back to Salem to inform Warren Bethune and Charlie Hardy that we were to prepare for battle. Hardy had been European heavyweight champion in the service and would be a natural challenger to the pugnacious Joe Carter, at organizing and managing our team.

To my surprise, neither was enthusiastic about starting a boxing team. Warren worried about security during training. "We just don't have the room in the Salem Jail that they have in Lawrence, plus the Lawrence boys have obviously been training for awhile." Said Bethune. Charlie Hardy informed me that he didn't think we had one fighter presently in our jail—at any weight level— nor did he have the time or the desire to train an entire team of loafers. This was a great disappointment to me and I got worried about my bet.

"I don't think we even have a qualifying heavyweight in the jail," said Warren.

"Except for Bucky Brown," said Hardy.

"But he won't fight," added Warren.

"Who's Bucky Brown, and why won't he fight?" I asked in desperation.

"He's a big black guy," replied Hardy, "and I know he can box, but he won't fight. He beat up a guy real bad once, I heard, and hasn't been in a fight since then."

"Bullshit!" I cried. "Talk him into it!" I wondered if maybe we could call around the state to see if the other county jails had any incarcerated boxers that we could borrow temporarily, but I was sure Ryan and Carter had already done that—probably the reason they were so confident their team would win. "Do we have anyone who can train some of our guys into fighters in four weeks?"

"Leon Breckenridge, our new correctional officer, says he's done some boxing, and he's willing to train them, but the only place to train is the jail yard," said Warren. "These guys can't go out jogging. The ones that volunteered to box aren't the most reliable we have in here, and I'm afraid some of them will just keep on running."

"Hell, they'll have to run around the jail yard 100 times to make a mile," sighed Hardy.

"I know," said Warren, "and I was just forced to take a wager with Joe Carter, who called to bet me a dinner that his team would beat ours, five out of six fights."

"That bastard!" I exclaimed. "How did you get better odds than me? He got me with four out of six. I think we're in big trouble, fellas," I told the others, "but we have to do the best we can. Obviously those Lawrence fellas have something up their sleeves. They've got ringers up there that they think will crush our guys to a pulp. Talk it up in the jail," I insisted. "If nothing else, let's send up a spirited team."

There were few volunteers for the Salem boxing team, and those inmates who did step forward were out of shape. Breckinridge had them exercise vigorously and run in place in the jail yard, weeding out the shirkers and the misfits. He had them box each other, which further weeded out the weak and the weary, and dwindled our numbers. There were no real incentives for joining the boxing team except for extra time outside in the yard, and one, free, all expenses paid, round trip to Lawrence on Boxing day.

Breckenridge complained constantly to Warren and me about space to train and running room, but we always answered that he had to make do with what he had; there was no equipment and no chance of being let out in the street to run. It was frustrating, but Breckenridge did seem to be making progress. His boxers seemed a little less sluggish in the morning, and their sparing sessions were a little less flailing.

On the morning of the fights, I was in great need of moral support, so I asked a good friend, former navy boxer Bob O'Meara of Salem, to join me in what I assured him would be a memorable day of fisticuffs in Lawrence. On the ride up Route 114, Bob confided that he felt somewhat uneasy about going into a jail for the first time in his life, but was willing because he loved to watch a good boxing match. I was surprised that my tough, devil-may-care friend was nervous about going into a jail, so I assured him that he'd be in safe, secure surroundings.

We climbed the granite stairs and entered the old stone bastille. Joe Carter, mouth firm and eyes squinting, greeted us at the door. "You're late," he told us. "We're holding up the fights for you, Sheriff." Carter's baldpate was dotted with perspiration. He was noticeably nervous, which was out of character for him. He opened the locked door to the arena and the noise was deafening; we could feel the excitement in the air. Inmates, correctional officers, and outside guests mingled around the ring, which was decorated with red, white, and blue streamers and bunting. Other inmates sat outside their cells along each of the two tiers above the ring, their legs and feet dangling down. They were yelling, laughing, talking, smoking, and staring down at the colorful scene below. Folding chairs were set up around the ring to seat almost 100 people, and Carter led us through the throng to the front row. A hazy blue smoke settled over the entire scene, and I felt a pride at the fitting atmosphere that Bill and Joe had provided. It was, however, an atmosphere that seemed to make Bob O'Meara extremely fidgety.

"Are we locked in here?" he asked, as we entered ringside.

"Yes," I replied, "but a guard stands behind the locked door to let us in and out when we desire"

"But all the inmates are out of their cells, right?"

"Right, but don't worry about it. They're harmless. Most of the guys in here are in for petty crimes...nothing really serious." I could tell that Bob still wasn't convinced of his safety, but I figured that once the boxing began, he would calm down. Sitting with us in the front row was a rugged-looking man in his mid-forties, whom Carter introduced as Paul Pender, former middleweight champion of the world. O'Meara was impressed. Pender and I were to be judges for the fights, along with Joe Carter's father, Nick, who was also known in Lawrence as "Mister Sports." Nick Carter was a walking sports encyclopedia, and he had his own local radio program, where people would call in and reminisce about memorable sports events and characters. Callers would attempt to stump Nick on local sports facts, but Joe Carter said that they never did.

"There's a hell of a lot of inmates here, and I see only a few guards," I whispered to Joe Carter as I took a front row seat next to his father. All of O'Meara's questions had made me a little uneasy as well.

Joe's neck twitched—a nervous habit. "That's because the inmates are all out, Sheriff," he said loudly, waving his hands, "but don't worry," he confided in a lower tone, "I've got ten extra guards on duty here, dressed in civilian clothes, who volunteered to come in to work for free. We'll be all right." I believed Joe, but I could tell that Bob was still nervous, and truth be told, I didn't feel comfortable with so many inmates shouting down at us from above. Bob kept eyeing the second tier, where longhaired men in sloppy prison garb were hoopin' and hollerin'. I didn't mind the noise, for I knew this was a good outlet for their pent-up frustrations. They had been waiting for this day for weeks. This was their Christmas, New Year's, and Fourth of July, all wrapped up into one event. I only wished that more Salem inmates could have attended. Only Breckenridge, his six fighters, two substitutes, and two inmates chosen as his assistants were there at ringside from Salem. Charlie Hardy was in the crowd too, but Warren Bethune reluctantly remained behind; somebody had to watch the store, and way down deep, Warren was convinced it was going to be a slaughter.

Leon Breckenridge looked nervous as I walked over to his corner to talk to him and the Salem boxers.

"How do you think we'll do?" I asked.

"We'll take them all," said Leon.

"Well, I'm rooting for Salem today, even though I can't show it openly."

The boxers smiled and a couple of them banged their gloved fists together. I needed to let them know that I was with them, for they certainly had to feel outnumbered and somewhat overwhelmed with the Lawrence supporters booing and hissing at them from above. "Just remember it's all in good fun," I told them, knowing that the razzing couldn't be helping their self-confidence, "and one more thing—just beat the shit out of them."

I returned to my seat as Joe Carter stepped into the ring with a megaphone. Joe didn't need the megaphone; his voice carried up to the rafters without it. It was a familiar voice to the Lawrence inmates, and a respected one. It was like someone had pulled a switch. One word from Joe Carter and the place went silent; when Joe Carter spoke, the inmates listened. Joe circled around the ring like a pent-up lion, his face looking up to the boys on the second and third tiers. He introduced Pender, his father, and me as judges, and correctional officer Joe Deshanes as the referee. Then he pointed to Bill Ryan, Master of the Jail, to a round of applause. I hadn't noticed Bill come in. He was acting aloof, leaning against the exit door, and sipping a cup of coffee, just looking on, smiling like the Cheshire cat. He nodded to me when I looked back at him, but he obviously wasn't going to sit with us. He was letting Carter run the whole show.

The first two contestants entered the ring. The crowd cheered for the Lawrence inmate and booed the Salem boy. O'Meara and I clapped as loudly as we could for Salem. Sitting next to O'Meara were two nuns from the church located behind the Lawrence Jail, wearing their black habits. They came in just as the fight began. They were volunteer social workers at the jail whom Ryan had coaxed into daily charitable service, and they were apparently big fight fans as well.

"See," I said, nudging O'Meara. "They're not nervous about being here."

"True," he replied, "but God protects them."

"The Punching Puerto Rican, Ramos Romeros," Carter shouted through the bullhorn, and the inmates cheered. "And in this corner, wearing…wearing cut-off jeans," stuttered Carter, "from Salem, Jumpin' Johnny Sullivan." Boos and hisses rained down from the balcony. Two skinny kids, neither looking a day over 17 years old, touched gloves, adjusted their head gear, and at the sound of the bell, began dancing, and continued dancing around each other for three minutes.

"Somebody throw a punch, please," shouted Carter. There were three 3-minute rounds for each fight, and if all were like this first round, we'd be bored to death. Apparently at the first break, the trainers gave their boxers the word, because at the bell for the second round, my man Sullivan came out swinging. Unfortunately he swung like he was sickling grass, pulling his arms so far back in preparation for a long wild swing that he gave Romeros all the time and warning that he needed to duck every punch. As Sullivan wound up for one of these wide arching punches, Romeros hit him so hard in the forehead that he knocked Sullivan's headgear off. Then a right uppercut knocked out Sullivan's mouthpiece. Every telegraphed punch from the great John S. was blocked, and Romeros kept darting inside with quick, hard jabs. Sullivan's white freckled skin was covered with red blotches. In the third round, Romeros staggered Sullivan against the ropes, which held him up while he used his fists like jackhammers. The referee finally had mercy and stopped the fight, and Romeros won by a TKO—Lawrence, one, Salem, zero.

In the second fight, the contenders were a bit meatier than the first fighters, but not much taller. The match wasn't very exciting, as neither boxer had much speed or power. The Salem guy was out of shape, and the Lawrence boxer easily wore him down, so that by the third round, the Salem boy couldn't lift his gloves any higher than his stomach to protect himself—Lawrence, two, Salem, zero.

The third fight was an obvious mismatch. The Lawrence inmate was a mass of muscles, and the Salem fighter was a scarecrow. It was over early in the second round—Lawrence, three, Salem, nothing.

I decided to talk to Breckenridge in the Salem corner, not only in an attempt to lift his obviously sagging spirits, but to get away from Bob O'Meara, who was beginning to barb me with wisecracks to the delight of everyone around. As I left my seat, O'Meara whispered loud enough for Nick Carter and Paul Pender to hear, "Tell Brecken-ridge we've got a nun over here who wants to take on his next guy."

Leon was sweating profusely, and his eyes danced angrily in his head. He was so furious that he stuttered. "We'll get the next one, Sheriff," he said. "I've got Rocco Bussone. He's done some fighting on the outside…and I know we'll take the heavyweight class, 'cause Bucky Brown's our man, and he's real good."

"I'm glad Bucky has decided to box today, Leon," I said, "but our guys don't seem to be in very good shape."

"How the hell can they be," shouted Leon, "tryin' to run around that little pigpen at Salem? We've got to get them running in the street!"

"You're doin' a good job, Leon, but we've just got to win the next one. Hell, they're embarrassing us." I didn't lift Leon's spirits; I only aggravated him further.

Salem's Rocco Bussone had obviously done some fighting all right, but not in a ring; he was a street fighter. Luckily, however, his Lawrence opponent fell into Rocco's style of flaying arms, butting heads, and swinging wildly at anything that moved. I had never seen two men throw so many furious, meaningless punches within three minutes, in my life. They took turns tripping over each other and pushing each other to the canvass. They were constantly tangling themselves in the ropes, and at one point, the Lawrence boxer almost fell into O'Meara's lap. When O'Meara jumped out of his chair, it at least gave me something to laugh about.

My scoring at the end of the second round put Rocco ahead, but the Lawrence boy seemed to get a second wind in the third round, and Rocco looked worn out. It was a split decision. I had it scored 2 to 1 in favor of Rocco. Pender had it scored 2 to 1 in favor of Lawrence. We waited in frenzied anticipation of Nick Carter's decision, which based on the third round performance, came in favor of the Lawrence boy. I loved ol' Nick, but I wasn't pleased with his judgment. Granted, Lawrence won the last round, but Rocco had clearly won the first two. I was fuming inside—Lawrence, four, Salem, zippo.

"I think he's right," said O'Meara. "Of course, when it comes down to a close decision, Nick Carter will pick the Lawrence boy every time."

Joe Carter came over to pat me on the shoulder. "Pretty good show, huh, Sheriff?"

"Very good, Joe," I said, smiling, though I'm sure Joe knew I was steaming inside.

"After all, Sheriff," said Joe, "Lawrence is your jail too, and you don't want to show favorites."

"Where'd you get all the ringers?" I asked, still smiling.

"All local boys, Sheriff, cross my heart," and he did. "Wait 'til you see our heavyweight…Big Black Mama, we call him. He'll tear the Salem guy apart."

"We—I mean Salem has Bucky Brown," I said with pride.

"I don't care if Salem has Mohammed Ali for this one. He'll have no chance against Big Mama," Joe boomed triumphantly, still smiling down at me. "It's gonna be a shutout—you just wait and see."

The light heavyweight match, which came before Big Mama and Bucky Brown, was also a mismatch. Either the Lawrence fighter had eaten a lot since the weigh in, or somebody had tampered with the Lawrence scale, because he must have weighed 250 pounds and was at least six foot two inches tall. A light heavyweight, he was not. Salem's boy, named "Killer Coogan," was five foot nine and he couldn't have weighed over 160 pounds. The big man pulverized him in the first round; Coogan couldn't even reach far enough to touch the big Lawrence boxer. Huffing and puffing heavily between rounds, Coogan looked like he might throw in the towel early, but Leon Breckenridge whispered something in his ear, and Coogan seemed to perk up. When the bell rang, his fighting style changed. Suddenly, from the starting bell of the second round, the mismatch dramatically turned in Salem's favor. Coogan was ducking inside the big fellow's defense and pounding his fat belly in close. He began wearing the big man down with his body punches. Halfway through the third round, the Lawrence fighter surprisingly threw his hands up into the air and gave up. Breckenridge was beside himself with glee, jumping into the ring and hugging Killer Coogan. It was the best fight of the day— Lawrence, four, Salem, one.

There was electricity in the air, mixed in with the heat, humidity, and cigarette smoke, when Big Black Mama and Bucky Brown entered the ring—two very big men with glistening purple-black skin. Mama looked heavier and was definitely taller, but Bucky had arms that would make Popeye wince. Even the little referee was bug-eyed as he brought these massive men to center ring for instructions. There, they grunted at him and at each other, then returned to their corners, ready to fight. The boys in the balcony were shouting hoarsely until the bell rang, then all you could hear was snorting and the thud of gloves smacking flesh.

"This is going to be a good one," mumbled O'Meara, leaning forward.

Mama danced a bit at first, imitating Mohammed Ali, but seeing that Bucky wasn't going to chase him, he settled down, and the real hitting began.

WHAM!!! WHAP!!! The sounds echoed. Mama took a stab to the ribs and a clout to the cheek. Bucky wore a constant furrowed brow as he stalked his prey. The anger of the world seemed to spit from his eye sockets, and those big arms moved fast as lightening. Bucky Brown wasn't just fighting this big guy from Lawrence, he was out to whip every no good bastard that ever crossed him in his long, hard life. Bucky was a tough boy who wasn't stepping into the ring for the first time, and Big Mama knew it. WHAP!!! THUD!!! Big Mama took a hard left to the stomach and a right to the nose. Blood trickled into his mouth. Big Mama punched back hard, but Bucky Brown didn't seem to feel a thing. He was pressing Mama hard, and Mama had a touch of panic in his eyes. WHACK!!! Bucky smashed Big Mama's ribcage again, and Big Mama flinched. Mama caught Bucky one on the jaw as he attempted to escape the ropes, but Bucky kept coming, slowly, deliberately, without a change of expression. He wasn't out to box Mama; he was out to kill him, and even the boys in the balcony felt it and were sucking in their breath.

The crouching referee, his eyes glued to the sweating tangle of flesh, failed to see a fourth man enter the ring. It was the big Lawrence inmate whom Killer Coogan had defeated. He still had his trunks on, but his gloves were off. He quickly sneaked up behind Bucky Brown, took a fast step forward, and with his teeth clenched and fists tight, he hit Bucky as hard as he could on the side of the head. Bucky didn't see the punch coming, and he reeled off balance. Stunned but not hurt, he quickly caught himself, and without a change of expression on his face, he went after his new opponent. Big Mama was spread-eagle against the ropes, a look of shock on his face. I'm sure he was relieved that someone had come to his aid. Bucky got off two good hits to the intruder's face before the little referee grabbed the bare-knuckled man around his throat, and tried to hold Bucky off with the other hand.

The room exploded with shouting and stomping. Joe Carter jumped into the ring, waving his finger at the intruder. Another man, wearing a sports shirt and jeans, slipped between the ropes to enter the ring, and Leon Breckenridge, like a football linebacker, dove across the canvas and tackled him. The two began wrestling. I recognized the man Leon attacked as a Lawrence correctional officer, but apparently Breckenridge thought he was another Lawrence inmate looking to do battle with Bucky Brown. Bucky, at this point, was desperately trying to slip off his boxing gloves, so that he could take a good poke at the intruder. The referee now had the intruder pinned to one of the ring posts. A fellow Lawrence inmate crawled through the ropes, onto the canvas, to free his friend from the referee's grasp. Luckily, Joe Carter saw him in time, kicked him in the head, and then used his foot to push him out of the ring.

I stood up, as did the others around me. It looked to me like a real riot was about to commence. I felt pretty secure with former world-champion Paul Pender on one side of me, and former Navy boxer Bob O'Meara on the other, but I noticed the nuns were making their way to the only exit, and O'Meara was close on their heels. Now there were skirmishes erupting in and out of the ring. The ten plain-clothed guards that had volunteered for duty could not be distinguished from the inmates, who began rushing down the stairway from the second and third tiers, and charging across the polished oak floor toward the ring. Old Nick Carter was watching his son who, with the mere holding up of his hand, had managed to stop many of the inmates in their tracks. Joe had dropped the bullhorn on the canvas, and without thinking, I jumped into the ring and grabbed hold of it.

"All right! That's enough!" I heard my voice echoing throughout the hall, but it didn't seem to me that anyone was listening. The inmates were yelping like wild dogs. "Back to the upper tiers," I shouted louder. "If you're not back to your cells in two minutes, we'll lock you in, and you'll miss the rest of the fights."

Someone pushed me from behind, and I hit the ropes, almost knocking my teeth out with the bullhorn. "Sorry, Sheriff!" It was Joe Carter, his head glistening with sweat. He was trying to shove everyone out of the ring. "Are you all right?" he asked, squeezing my shoulder, which he always did as a form of greeting.

"Yes," I said, gritting my teeth, "but let's get these guys back to their cells, or we'll have a riot on our hands."

"I think we have one now," he said, jumping out of the ring to break up another fight between a defeated Salem boxer and a harassing Lawrence inmate.

I got on the bullhorn again. "If you don't stop now, that will be the end of our boxing program—and I mean it." Correctional officers were rushing from one side of the room to the other, and I spied another wave of inmates heading down the stairs to join in the fun. "Stay where you are!" I shouted at them at the top of my lungs, pointing my finger at them, and surprisingly, they stopped, turned around, and went back up the stairs. In the form of an old football-type wedge-formation, Joe Carter and his uniformed and volunteer guards managed to herd all the whooping inmates back into their cells.

"The inmate who started all this will be punished," I announced at ringside, "but I'm not going to stop this program just because one guy wants to start trouble." We waited a few minutes until everyone had calmed down.

"What now?" asked Carter.

"We continue on," I replied. "Keep the troublemakers in their cells, and let the others out to watch the rest of the fight."

"Think we should?" said Carter.

"Damned right we should," I replied. "We can't let one or two idiots mess up your program. Besides, the Salem guy was beating the piss out of your Big Mama." I smiled at the frowning deputy master. "Let the games continue," I shouted through the bullhorn. I noticed

Ryan, still leaning on the exit door, sipping coffee, as if nothing had happened, and O'Meara standing beside him, ready to leave the hall at a moment's notice. The inmates were laughing and joking as they returned to their balcony seats, their feet dangling from the tiers above.

The scene settled. Black Mama and Bucky faced each other once more, and Bucky proceeded to pulverize the bigger man. The inmates started to get restless again. They didn't like to see their biggest and toughest contender get slaughtered. Again, an inmate jumped into the ring and tried to sucker punch Bucky. Bucky saw it coming this time and whacked him so hard that the intruder fell backwards out of the ring. The jail exploded again with rebel yells, and inmates flooded down the stairs to get to ringside. This time, Joe Carter and his men met them head-on and physically drove them back up the stairs and into their cells—locked up for good, this time. The fights were over. It was obvious, even to Joe Carter, that Bucky was beating Big Mama pretty badly and would have certainly won the fight. During the melee, Bucky Brown had also managed to lay out two other bare-fisted contenders on the canvas, but he never did get his gloves off.

Paul Pender, Nick Carter, Bill Ryan, and Bob O'Meara were waiting for me in the jail's outer lobby, and we all went to lunch at Bishops Restaurant. Nick Carter couldn't get over what a great boxer Bucky Brown was, and Paul Pender kept repeating that although he had been in boxing all his life, he had never been to a match quite like this one. Ryan felt it was a good morning, allowing the inmates to vent their frustrations, and he intended to keep the program going. O'Meara was uncharacteristically quiet at lunch until I gave him hell for running off with the nuns.

"Never again, Cahill," he said, his jaw clenched. "Never again will I set foot inside a jail."

CHAPTER IX

Kidnapped

It was another one of those phone calls that numbs the body and dries the throat. "Sheriff, we've had an escape at the Lawrence Jail."

I tried to regain my composure as I asked for details: Marvin Grayson, in for four years on a forgery conviction, was on kitchen detail and had bolted through the open rear gate as a meat delivery truck pulled up to the jail kitchen. Grayson had been one of four inmates selected to unload the meat from the truck into the jail freezer.

"When the gate opened, he ran," said Lawrence Correctional Officer Ed Talbert with a wavering voice.

"Wasn't there a guard around?" I asked.

"Yes sir, but the guard couldn't catch him. Jacobs was on duty and you know about his bad knees." Jacobs was sixty years old and could hardly walk. "According to Jacobs, Grayson just shouted, 'I can't stand this place any more,' then he ran across the yard and jumped down off the high granite wall to the sidewalk. That's about a twenty-foot drop, Sheriff, and although Jacobs almost had him at the wall, he thought better of jumping after him. He was afraid he'd break his legs."

"Tell Jacobs I'll break his neck for not going after him."

"But don't worry, Sheriff, Jimmy Carter's after him now," said Talbert. "He was just coming to work when the escape happened and Jimmy chased Grayson down the street until he jumped into a passing car."

"You mean that Grayson just flagged down a passing car and jumped into it?"

"Yes sir. Some old lady was driving, Jimmy said. But Jimmy ran back here and jumped into his car to go after them."

I'm sure Eddie Talbert heard me swallow hard. "Are you telling me that we have an escape and a kidnapping on our hands?"

"I'm afraid so, sir, but maybe Jimmy caught up with them. He hasn't come back yet."

"Where's Ryan?" I asked, trying to remain calm.

"He's in Boston at the Committee on Counties meeting."

"Where's Joe Carter?"

"He's on vacation this week."

"Who the hell is in charge up there?" I shouted over the phone.

"I am, sir," replied Talbert. "I regret to say, I am."

"Look, Eddie," I said, "don't talk to anyone else. If the press gets wind of this, tell them nothing. I'm on my way. It'll take me about 45 minutes to get there. Try to contact Ryan in Boston. Do you think Grayson is desperate enough to hurt that old woman?"

"I don't think so, Sheriff. He's an artistic type. He's the one who did that neat sign for you in front of the Salem Jail—."

"Okay, Eddie," I interrupted, "get all the info on him: his friends, relatives, description, etc., and get it to the Lawrence Police. I'll be right there." I slammed down the phone. "Get me a driver, quick," I shouted to Loretta.

"A driver?" Loretta stared at me quizzically. I had never asked for a driver before. "We don't have drivers," she said. I only recently received a vehicle from the county commissioners–the first ever for the Sheriff of Essex County. It was a year old Nash-Rambler, "an embarrassment" said Bill Ryan, "to all in law enforcement."

"Get me one of those new CETA employees that the city lets us use. I need to get to Lawrence, and I'm too nervous to drive myself— we've got a kidnapping on our hands."

✳ ✳ ✳

"I sure do like being a correctional officer," said Angelo Coppio, my driver and a newly acquired CETA employee. We now had four of them in our employ. Most merely took up space, but some, like Angelo, seemed to have potential, and we hoped to hire him full-time at county expense some day.

"I'm glad you like the work, Angelo, but step on the gas, will you? I have to be in Lawrence, subito."

I knew Angelo was an Italian immigrant, but what I didn't know was that Angelo had been a professional racecar driver in Italy. He pushed the pedal to the floor. He had a Pinocchio look to him, and his black beady eyes danced with glee as he hunched over the wheel. He occasionally stole a sidelong glance at me to make sure I was paying attention as he babbled on about his childhood in Verona.

"Watch the road, Angelo," I had to say more than once, and as we hit heavy traffic on the long straight road to Lawrence, I told him to turn on the siren. His face beamed.

"Siren? Where is it?"

"The switch is under the dashboard, near your left knee," I pointed, "and turn on the blue bubble on the roof, too." He was in his glory. Ignoring all signs and lights, dodging traffic, and humming an Italian opera under his breath, he flew up Route 114. I was scared to death, and Angelo sensed my fear.

"Don't you worry, Sheriff," he said. "I was champion in my country—they call me 'The Angel,' because I drive smooth, like on a cloud."

I closed my eyes as vehicles whizzed around us and thought of the poor old woman that our escapee had kidnapped. Maybe he'll throw her out of the car, I thought, or maybe she'll be so frightened that she'll suffer a heart attack. Was Grayson so desperate that he might kill her? I had a sick feeling in my stomach. I knew that I wasn't going to hear the last of this escape for a long time. The bumpy, swerving ride was also making my stomach queasy, and the blaring siren was giving me a headache. Angelo, a broad grin across his puppet-like face, was at the Verona racetrack again.

When we skidded into the Lawrence Jail driveway, I quickly jumped out of the car. I felt like a sailor who had been out to sea for weeks and had just landed on solid ground. With wobbly legs, I ran up the granite stairs to Ryan's office.

"I haven't been able to contact Ryan," said lanky Eddie Talbert, standing at attention as I entered.

"What have you found out about Grayson and the old woman?" I asked, as he followed me into Ryan's office. Ryan had hanging plants all over the place, and photographs of prominent Republicans lined the walls—I made a mental note to speak to him about adding a few Democrats to his rogues-gallery.

"Jimmy Carter is back," Eddie reported nervously, "but he lost the car in traffic."

"Did he get the license-plate number?" I asked, frustration sounding in my voice.

"Yes," said Eddie.

"Who's the car belong to? We should at least contact her family and let them know what happened."

"It's a rented car," said Eddie, "and the car rental office refuses to tell me who rented it…they say that they can't give out that kind of information."

"That's ridiculous! Did you tell them what happened?"

"No sir. You told me not to tell anyone."

"Call them again and get the manager on the phone. Tell him the sheriff's calling and it's an emergency—but first, get Jimmy Carter in here so he can tell me what happened." Eddie ran into the outer office and buzzed for Jimmy Carter as I paced Ryan's office. It was a nice office. How the hell did Billy Ryan manage to have: new carpeting, new wood paneling, a leather couch, large oak desk and chair, a padded rocking chair, and air conditioning? It just didn't seem fair that I sweated through summers, froze in the winters, lived with makeshift furniture and hand-me-down decorations, while Ryan lounged in the lap of luxury.

Jimmy Carter knocked lightly on the open door and entered He had a dejected hangdog look. Like his younger brother Joe, the Lawrence deputy master, Jimmy oozed toughness. He had a swarthy, well-worn, athletic face and a brawny body. And like his brother, he had a heart of gold, and was always willing to help anyone in a jam.

"That poor old woman," he mumbled as he sat down in the leather couch. He bowed his head into his gnarled hands. "I'm sorry,

Sheriff, I almost had him, damn it! I almost had him."

"You can't win them all, Jimmy," I sighed, folding myself into Ryan's rocker. "Tell me everything that happened, right from the beginning."

He looked up, hurt crowding his stepped-on face. "Well, I was coming to work—my wife had just dropped me off—when I heard old Jacobs shoutin' from the kitchen gate that Grayson had escaped and had managed to jump to the street from the granite wall. Well, I set out after him, and when I get to the wall, I see this old white-haired lady drivin' slowly down the street in a new white Ford, and Grayson jumps in front of her car. When she stops, he opens the door on the passenger side and dives in. Then the car takes off, but the old lady is still only going about twenty miles an hour—"

"Only twenty miles an hour?" Jimmy nodded. "And what was Grayson wearing?" I asked

"Just blue jeans and a tee-shirt...plus he had on his wig— Grayson is as bald as an eagle, Sheriff, and he wears this Prince Valiant wig that hangs down over his ears and makes him look about twenty years old when he's actually in his mid-thirties. Well, anyway, I run back to Jacobs, tell him what happened, then I flag down my wife who hasn't left the parking lot yet. I jump in the car, tell her to move over and I take the wheel. Now, my car is pretty old and doesn't run too good, but I figure if that old lady is only doin' twenty, I might catch up with her...and I do. Sure enough, I spot the white Ford still putt-puttin' along, heading into Methuen, so I step on it! I see Grayson's head peekin' out of the back window at me. I tried to sideswipe the car, Sheriff, but I can tell that the old lady is petrified, and of course I don't know if Grayson's got a gun or not, so I back off..."

"You did the right thing, Jimmy," I assured him.

"Then Grayson had the old lady turnin' down one side-street after another," Jimmy continued, "but now she's slowin' down to about ten miles per hour. So, I just follow along behind her. In fact, I stopped once to let my wife out so's she could call the Methuen police, but here's where the tough part comes, Sheriff," Jimmy banged his fist into the seat cushion. "We comes to a red light and the lady stops her car. I can see Grayson waving his hands, ordering her to go through the red light. It's obvious she's scared, 'cause she's screaming and wavin' her hands, too. I can't hear her 'cause all her windows were closed, but she was screamin' all right. I pulled my car along side hers and I can see her eyes bulgin' and her mouth movin' like sixty. Now here's where I make my mistake. I got out of my car with traffic all around me, and I run to her car. I point my finger at Grayson and or- der him to get out of the car or I'll shoot, I didn't have a gun or any- thing, but I was so pissed, I had to do something. I'm sure he thought I was crazy, pointing my finger through the window at him and sayin' I was gonna shoot, but anyway, Sheriff, as I'm doin' this, the light changes and the old lady drives off. I ran back to my car, but the old shit-box won't start. People are shoutin' at me and I'm tryin' to jump in other cars to follow the old lady, but they all thought I was a nut- cake. Boy, was I mad!" Jimmy's body trembled as he spoke. "I tried like hell to hitch a ride, but all the drivers were bullshit at me for holdin' up traffic at the light. So, all I got was a couple of fingers. Now that I think of it, I must have looked like a mad man dancin' around and wavin' in the middle of the street. But anyway, about twenty minutes later, a Methuen cop car comes along, and I jump in. We looked everywhere, but we can't find the white Ford again. Damn, Sheriff, I ain't—"

"Mister Peterson is on the phone, Sheriff," Eddie Talbert inter- rupted from the outer office.

"Who the hell is Mister Peterson?" I shouted back at Eddie.

"The manager of the car rental agency."

"Give me the license plate number you got off the old lady's car," I asked Jimmy as I picked up the phone. "Mister Peterson, this is Sheriff Cahill. I'm interested in a car you rented, possibly this morn- ing, a white Ford, registration number five, seven..."

"Yes, well there's no problem there, Sheriff," interrupted Mister Peterson. "That vehicle is being returned right this minute."

"It is? By an elderly woman?"

"Yes, Sheriff. Would you like to speak with her?"

"Would I?! Please, put her on."

A crackly old voice came on the line. "Hello! Who's this?" she asked.

"Hello, ma'am," says I, "this is the county sheriff, Bob Cahill. Are you all right?"

"I'm fine," she replied sweetly. "Do you have anything to do with the jail in Lawrence, Sheriff?" she asked.

"Yes, I do," I replied, "and that's why I wanted to talk to you—"

"I've got a bone to pick with you!" she interrupted, her pleasant voice turning to anger.

"A bone? With me?" Jimmy Carter stared at me with anticipation.

"Yes," she said. "You have a man working for you, a guard of some sort. A gruff, evil-looking fellow." I looked over at Jimmy's pug face.

"Yes, I think I know who you mean."

"Well," she huffed over the phone; "he just tried to push me off the road in his car. He's a madman! He got out of his car and banged on my windows. He followed me in his car for miles. He petrified Marvin, Berry and myself. You should do something about him, Sheriff. He's a menace. I'm thinking very seriously of suing..."

"May I ask you your name, Ma'am?" I interrupted.

"Edith Parsons," she replied.

"And might I ask who Marvin and Berry are?"

"Marvin's my son and Berry is my dog. He's just a wee little poodle who gets extremely agitated, very easily, and your man frightened him half to death."

"And is Marvin's last name Grayson?" I asked, in an attempt to unravel this mystery.

"Why, yes!" she said, seemingly startled that I knew. "You see, I was married before, and my first husband died of cancer nine years ago. He was Marvin's first father, poor dear. Then I remarried Francis Parsons and—"

"Do you know that your son escaped from the Lawrence Jail this morning?"

"Escaped? Oh no!" She started to cry.

"That old broad helped Grayson escape!" Jimmy shouted in my ear.

"Calm down, calm down," I said to Jimmy, but Mrs. Parsons thought I was talking to her.

"I'm all right now," she said, still sobbing. "He told me that he was going on a furlough. He had me waiting outside the jail for him for hours..."

"Why were you waiting behind the jail and not out front?" I asked.

"Marvin told me that some guard was out to beat him up, and he wanted to get away from there fast. He said that the guard would be waiting out front for him... and when that big, ugly man came after us in his car, I thought he was after him to beat him up." She started crying again.

"Where is your son now?" I asked.

"I left him on the highway where some of his friends met him. Marvin said he was going on a hunting trip somewhere up north." Mrs. Parsons couldn't remember the kind of car Grayson and his friends were in, or its color. Nor did she know where they were going hunting. I assumed it was somewhere in Canada. I thanked Mrs. Parsons for her troubles and assured her that I would reprimand my over-zealous guard.

"She's full of shit, Sheriff," shouted Jimmy as I hung up the phone. "It was a setup! She knew what she was doing!" Jimmy was shaking with anger and frustration again.

"Forget it, Jim. She's a Gracie Allen type. She'd so confuse a judge and jury, that if you took her to court, you and I would probably end up behind bars." I explained to Jim that in a way I was relieved. At least we didn't have a kidnapping on our hands. Jimmy Carter insisted, however, that he would find Marvin Grayson and return him to jail if it was the last thing he ever did in this world. That autumn, Jimmy took his vacation in Canada, spending all his time looking for Grayson. He didn't find him.

CHAPTER X

The Diddler

It was a hot humid afternoon in July and I found myself constantly leaving my desk to air out at the open window facing St. Peter Street. Eight barebacked inmates were on their knees weeding a small vegetable garden that flanked the grammar school playground. The children were at recess, yelling, laughing, and romping about the hot top, paying no attention to the inmates who were separated from them by only a chain-link fence. The inmates also seemed aloof to the almost unbearable screeching of the young boys and girls at play. All eight of the inmates were trustees, men whom Warren Bethune and his three-man board of our best correctional officers agreed could be trusted to work around the small front yard and in the sheriff's house, cleaning and doing other odd jobs. Trustees had certain special freedoms, even though they remained confined, and most inmates coveted the privilege. It was a position of respect with added benefits. While these men puttered about the new garden they created and planted, their fellow inmates were stuck inside the jail, away from the sun but feeling the stale heat and humidity. The trustees moved slowly, allowing the sun to burn their white skin, hoping to prolong their labor so they wouldn't have to return too soon to the stuffy cellblock. After years behind bars, with very little daylight, this respite was pure heaven to them. As I stood there watching, I could feel their joy and contentment as they occasionally squinted up into the sun and smiled.

The front screen door of my office squeaked open and slapped shut. Warren Bethune stood before my desk, droplets of sweat trickling down his cheeks. He dropped a stack of bills onto my desk and handed me a payroll sheet to sign.

"It's hot as hell in there," he said, pointing to the jail, "and it's low tide on the North River, sending a smell through the place you wouldn't believe."

"Oh, I believe it," I told Warren. "I've lived on the river long enough to know how bad it can get." We only got a slight rotten-egg whiff of it at the sheriff's house, depending on the wind, but sometimes, all you'd need is a whiff of the river to have your stomach churn all day. Warren lingered in my office and it was obvious that he wasn't in a hurry to go back to the jail. I turned back to the window.

"Who's the little chubby guy weeding out there?" I asked. "I've never seen him before."

"That's Ralph," said Warren, squinting out the window. "We got him from Walpole a few months ago."

I had been noticing that, unlike the others in the garden, Ralph was squatting on his haunches rather than kneeling as he worked, and he shot occasional sideways glances at the children playing. He seemed to be older than the other trustees by a good few years. He had a hard roll of flesh bulging from just below his chest and hanging over the top of his khaki pants. He was short, only a few inches over five feet, and his peppery hair was stringy, half hiding his face as he dug around in the dirt.

I was somewhat surprised that Warren had accepted a prisoner out of Walpole, and doubly so that he would allow a state prison felon to work as a trustee.

"How long was he at Walpole?" I asked Warren.

"Sixteen years," he replied matter-of-factly.

"Sixteen years?" I shouted. "What the hell is he doing here, and how come he's a trustee?"

"Don't get excited, Sheriff," said Warren, wearing his characteristic impish smile. "He's harmless, and he won't run away. He's only got one year to go, and I'd trust him more than any other guy out there."

"The state shouldn't be sending us guys who've been in that long," I barked at Warren. "What the hell's he in for?"

"Diddling," said Warren.

I had been in office for over a year, but I had not heard the word "diddling" before. I had no idea what it meant. I didn't want to reveal my ignorance to Warren, but Loretta, my secretary who had been typing quietly behind us, came to my aid. "What's diddling?" she asked.

"It's like sodomy," Warren replied, his face blushing slightly as he faced Loretta. "Many years ago, Ralph got caught playing around with little boys."

"That's awful," said Loretta, and she returned to her typing.

"He's been eyeing those kids in the playground since the recess bell rang," I said to Warren. "It's like putting a kid in a candy factory."

"No, no, no," replied Warren, "he's cured. The psychiatrist at Walpole says that he has no more problems like that. Remember, that was sixteen years ago."

"What exactly did he do sixteen years ago?" I asked.

"I don't know exactly," said Warren, "but he was caught in a hotel room playing around with a fourteen year old kid."

"How gross!" piped in Loretta.

"Seventeen years in jail for doing that doesn't seem too long," I said, staring at the little fat man more intently now, "I guess he looks harmless enough. You sure he is?"

"Positive," Warren replied with his little grin.

"Okay, but I'll feel better when those kids are back in the classroom. I'm not too happy about giving any guy from Walpole that much freedom."

"Hell, he's up for furlough in a few weeks anyway," said Warren, heading for the screen door, "and he'll be a free man within a year."

I was somewhat surprised at my usually conservative deputy master, but if he trusted Ralph to roam around outside the jail, I supposed I could too. Ralph soon became a fixture around the yard and sheriff's house, making Loretta feel somewhat uncomfortable. He'd go about his business slowly and silently, dusting and sweeping, washing windows and emptying wastebaskets. One day I met him face to face at the stairwell. "Good morning, Ralph" I said cheerfully. "How's it going?" His normally placid face brightened, and presenting me a cherub smile, he grunted, "Good morning!"

Two weeks later, I had the opportunity to speak to Ralph again. It was a hot, humid day, and Ralph had assisted the jail steward in preparing lunch for newly sworn in deputies and their proud families after a long courthouse ceremony. Clam chowder, salad, and sandwiches were served at the sheriff's house, and after they had all gone back home or to work, Ralph sat on the door stoop of the kitchen to cool off. He was sweating profusely, and strands of his graying hair were stuck to his forehead. I handed Ralph a piece of cake and stood in the doorway.

"How's it going?" I asked.

"Fine," he replied, lighting a damp cigarette.

"We sure picked a hot day for a swearing in." He didn't reply. "I hear you're going off on a two day furlough tomorrow."

"Yeah," he sighed, staring out toward the street. "I'm looking forward to it."

"Where do you plan to go?"

"Rockport. I have friends in Rockport."

"Have a good time," I said, walking back to my office. I almost added, "behave yourself," but I bit my tongue. I tried to imagine going out into the world after being cooped-up behind bars for over sixteen years. The changes he'd confront would be phenomenal. I found myself worrying about whether or not he'd have enough money, prices having probably tripled since he was sent away. The anxiety and emotions he had to be feeling were far beyond my imagination, and for the next two days, I found myself constantly thinking of Ralph. What was the first thing he'd do? How would his friends treat him? How is he coping with the modern world? I couldn't wait for him to get back to the jail so that I could quiz him about his experiences. Of course, as is the case with all first time furloughs, there is always the question, will he return? But then, like Warren, I had confidence in Ralph. His crime disgusted me, yet I felt sorry for him—I liked him, and for some unknown reason, I was cheering him on. I wanted him to make it in the outside world. There were many instances of men who couldn't make it on the outside, not just those that were enticed to return to crime, but also the ones who, having been in jail so long, became institutionalized. The jail became home and the rest of the world frightened them. Ralph seemed vulnerable in that way, and I wondered if he had been in too long to return to society.

Ralph arrived back at the jail one hour before his furlough was up. I hoped it was not because he couldn't cope with the outside any longer, but just a wise precaution to make sure he wasn't delayed en route, causing him to miss his curfew.

When he entered my office the next morning to empty the wastebaskets, I was anxious to begin my questioning.

"How did you enjoy your furlough?"

"Fine," he replied.

"Did you have a good time?"

"Sure did, and I didn't have one drink."

"That's good…. Did you see any old friends?"

"A couple," he said, and he left the room with the plastic bag filled with trash before I could get in another question. I would have liked to spend all morning asking about his two days of exploration in the much-changed free world. What did he notice as different after all those years? What did he and his old friends do and talk about? Obviously, I had no right to delve into Ralph's private life and deep feelings, but I was curious—maybe "nosy" is the right word. Ralph did seem happier after his two days on the town, so I figured that he had found some use and pleasure in his freedom. I also guessed that he had survived, if not adapted to, this fast-moving society that had moved at a much slower pace when he left it back in the 1950s; this was a good sign, as soon Ralph would be out on his own for good.

Next morning, Warren came bursting into my office just as I was having my first sip of coffee. "Ralph's dead!" he said. His words momentarily boggled my brain. "He died of a heart attack in his cell last night... there was nothing anyone could do. He never made a sound. He just died quietly."

I was upset. I could feel tears welling into my eyes and a burning in my chest as I tried to hold them back. I'm probably the only one in the world who'll be shedding a tear for Ralph, I thought. Was the furlough too much for him, I wondered? Did the thought of getting

out for good frighten him to death? I would never know. Poor little
chubby Ralph.

We began the process of locating and informing Ralph's next of
kin and making the arrangements for transporting the body. His
family apparently would have nothing to do with him, and Warren
informed me that even though he said he had friends in Rockport,
local police couldn't find anyone that even knew him. Ralph's body
remained in county cold storage for five days, and no one came to
claim him.

"We'll just have to do something ourselves," I told Warren. "The
county will have to pay for his funeral. Call Reverend Webster."

"He did leave a last will and testament," said Warren, which surprised me. "He knew he had a weak heart, and although he didn't
own anything of value to leave to anyone, he did say that he wanted
to be cremated."

"Cremated?" I knew of only one other person who had stipulated
that he wanted to be cremated. For some reason it sent chills up my
spine. Cremation was foreign to me. "Where on earth does a person
get cremated?" I asked Warren.

"Right here in Salem," he replied. "Harmony Grove Cemetery
has a crematorium."

Warren and I set the date for the funeral and cremation, and
since there would be no one at the funeral but the minister, I was determined to go and to pay my last respects to Ralph, and I made
Warren promise that he'd attend too. How sad that a man should die
without a friend or relative to bid him farewell. Unfortunately, the
daughter of a friend of mine was killed in a car accident, and her funeral was the same morning as Ralph's. Warren had a conflict as well,
meaning neither of us could attend the cremation. When Special
Sheriff Charlie Reardon arrived at my office on the morning of the
funeral, I informed him that he must attend Ralph's cremation. We
were Ralph's last caretakers, so I truly believed that the sheriff's department should be represented at his service, and I considered it a
sacrilege if the minister performed the funeral ceremony to an empty
house. Charlie reluctantly agreed to attend.

As skilled and efficient as my special sheriff was, Charlie had an excess of phobias that I was slowly but surely discovering. One was a fear of bridges. Charlie hated to cross over a bridge and sometimes refused to do so. He also disliked crowds and did his best to avoid them. I couldn't fault Charlie because I had phobias of my own—of heights most of all—but when I explained that Ralph was going to be cremated, a funny, twisted look came over Charlie's face. Could he be fearful of funerals or cremation, I wondered? I knew from George Hollum that Charlie had a terrible fear of death; would that mean a fear of funerals as well?

I returned to the office after attending my friend's daughter's funeral, a very sad and tearful event. It was almost one p.m. and Loretta informed me that Charlie Reardon hadn't yet returned from Ralph's funeral. How, I wondered, could Ralph's funeral be longer than the one I attended, where there were hundreds of mourners and a long eulogy? Almost an hour later, Charlie arrived. His face was pale and he seemed nervous and upset. I asked him what was wrong.

"Have you ever been to a cremation?" he asked me.

"No," I replied, "but I was actually looking forward to going to Ralph's to see what they were all about."

"Don't ever go to one," said Charlie, seating himself heavily on the chair beside my desk. "It's gruesome," he said, sighing. "First of all, you have to sit in this tomb-like room, facing a furnace, and the only people in attendance, of course, were the reverend and me. The cemetery caretaker, or whoever he was, wheels in this big cardboard box with Ralph in it. The reverend says a few words, and then the caretaker stuffs Ralph, box and all, into the furnace. This caretaker guy, who looks just like Boris Karloff, shows me these windows on the side of the furnace and tells me I can watch if I want to. I'm tellin' ya, Sheriff, I almost got sick to my stomach right then and there. I didn't look in the window, but just the thought of it made me sick." Looking at his frowning pale face, I held back a chuckle and was quite pleased that it was Charlie that went to Ralph's funeral and not me.

"Then this caretaker takes me around to the back of the furnace,"

Charlie continued in a wavering voice. "There's a little door attached to the furnace, like the kind you see on a gumball machine, only bigger. He tells me I have to wait at this door until some guy breaks up Ralph's bones with a hammer, 'cause the bones won't burn. Then he hands me a cardboard box, a little smaller than a breadbox, and has me hold it open to the door, and out comes ashes and bone chips, still quite warm, which go into the box. By this time, Sheriff" says Charlie, "I'm almost puking in the little box."

I couldn't hold back the tickle to laugh any longer. Charlie looked surprised that I found it funny.

I told him that for some unknown reason, gruesome stories always give me the giggles. "Did your Boris Karloff sprinkle the ashes over the cemetery garden?" I asked.

"No," said Charlie. "The caretaker said that they used to do that, but sometimes relatives show up later to claim the remains, so now they put the boxes of ashes on shelves at the crematorium and save them for a few months. He showed me the shelf with about twenty boxes on it, all tagged, so they don't get the people all mixed up. It really was a spooky place."

"So you left Ralph on the shelf with Boris Karloff?"

"No, Sheriff" said Charlie, "I was sure that no one would ever come to pick Ralph up."

"Then what the hell did you do with Ralph's ashes, Charlie?"

"Didn't you know that Ralph left a last will and testament?" Charlie asked.

"Yes, I did know that. Why?"

"Well," said Charlie, "I followed Ralph's instructions. It was his last request."

"I didn't read the testament," I confessed. "What were his instructions?"

"He wanted his remains spread over the nearest playground," said Charlie.

I was speechless. Was this the final act of repentance, I wondered, or was Ralph still plagued by his sickness, and even in death, wanted to be near little boys?

"So, I took the box up to Mack Park," said Charlie, "and spread the ashes over the baseball field."

I like to believe that Ralph was free of his problem and spreading his ashes over the playground was a final gesture of desiring forgiveness for his crimes. But it does make one wonder if Ralph was really cured of diddling.

May he rest in peace.

The Salem Jail as seen from St. Peter's Street.

CHAPTER XI

The Great Escape

Less than two months from Paul Fitzpatrick's escape from the Paddy wagon in downtown Salem, another young, rambunctious inmate, still wearing his handcuffs, jumped through a plate glass window while awaiting trial at the Superior Court House. He landed on the pavement of Federal Street, six-feet down, amidst broken glass, only a few feet from where Fitzpatrick had begun his marathon with Billy Cox. Deputy Eddie Mees, a left over from Sheriff Wells' court officers, told reporters that he recaptured the escapee, Raymond Sutherland, age 21 of Gloucester, fifteen minutes later, three blocks from the courthouse. His statement to the newspapers would have been fine, except for the fact that Sutherland broke both his ankles in the fall. "How did the escapee manage to get three blocks away with two broken ankles, and why did it take Mees so long to catch up to him?" asked the reporters. My department, once again, became the butt of local jokes and innuendo from Jim Shea and his employees at the *Salem Evening News.*

After these escapes and another attempt at the Lawrence Jail, it was obvious that we had to tighten security. We needed money from the county to do so, but it was not forthcoming. I went before the county commissioners and the 34-member advisory board, made up of all the mayors and selectmen of the county's cities and towns, begging my case: We need metal-detectors for both jails to search everyone coming in and out—inmates, visitors, even guards; we need proper fencing around the jails, and not just a couple of strands of barbwire over a high wooden fence like we have now; I also need vehicles to transport inmates here and there—we can't keep using our own cars like Sheriff Wells and his deputies did. I carefully explained it all to the commissioners. My pleas fell on deaf ears. The answer was, "No. Wait until next year's budget."

Three weeks later, three inmates walked out the front door of the Salem Jail. Two carried ice picks and the third had a gun. The instigator of the escape was Arthur Massei, age 30, from New York, who had been placed with us temporarily because he had managed to escape from a federal penitentiary, where he awaited trial for armed robbery. Massei was considered "extremely dangerous." He was tough, and in my opinion, one of the cleverest and meanest inmates ever housed in the Salem Jail. With Massei was Norman Longval, age 30, of Lynn, also awaiting trial for armed robbery, and Daniel Kerivan, who came to us from Bridgewater State Prison, where he was serving time for armed robbery. He had seven more years to serve in Salem.

It was early evening in late October. It was dark out and the lights had just been turned on in the jail. Massei asked the guard, Walter McGrath, a new man whom I had just hired to replace an old guard who had died, if he could make a phone call. McGrath led Massei outside the cellblock to the only payphone. At the phone, Massei pulled a 38-caliber revolver from under his shirt and pointed it at McGrath's head. Surprisingly, McGrath punched Massei on the side of the head and knocked him to the floor. Two other guards came running, but Massei quickly jumped to his feet and put the barrel of the gun to McGrath's temple. He threatened to shoot McGrath if anyone moved. The other guards backed off. He then ordered the block-officer to unlock the gate and let Longval and Kerivan out. All correctional officers on duty now rushed to the scene and were confronted with three armed inmates. The actions of the guards were in direct contradiction to my recent order that "no matter what the emergency or dilemma, one correctional officer must remain in the office, locked in, to contact police and inform them of the emergency." The escapees took all keys, tied up the guards, and locked them into a cell. Massei even had the presence of mind to steal McGrath's leather, fur-collared coat—it had started to spit snow. Over an hour passed, during which time the locked up guards screamed their voices raw without response, before an off duty guard on his way to work for the late shift found the front door of the jail open. The inmates who were left behind were laughing and singing. Massei, of course, could have let the entire one hundred plus, out onto the street. I was thankful to him that he didn't.

The question was, how did Massei get a gun inside the jail, and was it real or fake—whittled out of soap or wood and blackened with coal dust or soot. All the guards on duty, including McGrath, swore it was a real 38-caliber. The only way it seemed that Massei could have acquired a gun is if a friend of his had climbed the fence from the street, handed the gun into the cell-block through a barred, but open window, and then climbed back over the fence to the street. Actually, it was a simple enough task to accomplish in the evening when there is little traffic and few pedestrians on the streets flanking two sides of the jail. The intruder could also have easily climbed the jail fence from the adjoining, dark, and gloomy Howard Street Cemetery. It hadn't occurred to me until this escape that there were probably just as many shady characters trying to break into the Salem Jail as there were those trying to break out. These interlopers were not only providing weapons, but narcotics, marijuana, and other illicit supplies as well. I definitely needed sufficient high security barbwire fencing to stop both escapes and break-ins.

Like a reoccurring nightmare, I was shaken awake at home to be told that there was another escape at the Salem Jail. When I arrived across the river, there was pandemonium inside the jail: correctional officers either sulking, or shouting at each other, and the inmates screaming with ecstasy. Through the din I tried to accumulate details about the escapees so I could make my 34 phone calls to police stations throughout the county to alert them about my three dangerous fugitives.

This was my All Points Bulletin, as best as I could gather:

Massei, the ringleader, six-feet tall, weighing 175 lbs., fairly good looking, with closely cropped, black hair, wearing McGrath's black leather coat with fur collar. Longval, about six-feet, eight inches tall, 160 lbs., long, light brown hair. And Kerivan, a wiry 19 years old, long, blond hair hanging over his shoulders, sporting a scraggly blond goatee, wearing blue jeans and a tee-shirt, armed with an ice pick.

"Are you sure about the goatee?" I double-checked, not wanting a second serving of crow.

"Yes, sir," replied Deputy Bethune with his typical wry smile.

Bethune had the guards go through all the personal belongings in their cells and in storage. Usually, a letter from a girlfriend with an address on the envelope is a good clue to the whereabouts of an escapee. It's either to her house, a friend's place, or home to Ma and Pa that an escapee heads first while "on the lam." Also, the names and addresses of those who recently visited them in jail can sometimes help lead to recapture. Charlie Geary was the first deputy to arrive at the jail. I sent him, with a loaded shotgun, to stake out the home of Kerivan's parents in neighboring Lynn. Charlie Reardon then doled out assignments to the deputies as they arrived—two here, two there, to various homes in cities and towns where friends or relatives of the escapees lived. It was going to be a long, chilly night. After making all my phone calls to the police, I contacted the radio stations with details of the escape and the escapees. Almost immediately the calls started coming in on our one phone. As soon as I got off the phone with one eager citizen, the phone would ring again with another sighting. It went on for hours.

"I saw Kerivan sitting under a tree in Lynn Common." The caller slurred his words and was obviously intoxicated.

"Third Chestnut tree from the left, as you come from Salem?" I tried nicely, if a bit sarcastically, to get him off the phone.

"You don't believe me?" he shouted. "What kind of a department are you running there anyway?"

"I'm beginning to wonder myself," I replied. "How do you know Kerivan escaped?" I asked.

"I just heard it on the radio at Al's Bar," he said, "and I walked out of the door and there he is, Kerivan, sitting under a tree—who the hell else would be sitting under a tree wearing nothing but a tee-shirt on such a cold night."

The drunk was making sense. "We'll check it out, " I told him and hung up.

"Massei is hiding in his girlfriend's house," says the next caller, and then there was a "click" as he hangs up. What girlfriend? Where? Was it another kook call? How does one decide which calls are real and which are hoaxes? We checked most of them out, so I had thirty deputies running all over the place—most in the city of Lynn. The problem was that neither Charlie Reardon nor myself had any way of knowing where anyone was or how to get in touch with them. They didn't cover this part of the job in the swearing in ceremony. This is when a bit of law enforcement training would have come in handy— if they even teach that kind of thing. After some four hours on the phone in an attempt to keep everyone informed and to keep some semblance of order, I turned the phone over to Bob Curran and let him deal with the confusion. Bob then got a seemingly legitimate call from an anonymous caller who said that Kerivan was hiding with a friend at a boarding house on Prince Street in Lynn.

"I'm a boarder here myself, "said the crackly voice of an obviously old man. "And I saw a young man fitting Kerivan's description enter room twelve. Please come at once. I'm very nervous and I'm sure it's him."

To work out some of my nervous energy and to get some fresh air, I decided to join Charlie Reardon and four other deputies in their assault on the boarding house. Our two vehicles skidded up to the curb on Prince Street, and we jumped out to face a square, four storied, old brick building with a heavy wooden door. I was the only one of the six not carrying a revolver or shotgun. Charlie sent Deputy Dave Lonergan, a Lynn boy, around to the back of the building to watch the rear door as the rest of us tried to get in the front door. It was locked. Charlie rang the buzzer, but there was no immediate response.

"Maybe the escapee has taken everybody in there hostage," suggested Deputy Dobson.

"George, you have a real wild imagination," I told him. He shrugged his shoulders.

"Anything's possible, Sheriff," he mumbled, turning up his coat collar against the cold wind, "remember Fitzpatrick and the phone booth."

Charlie pushed the buzzer until he woke up a janitor who came to the door, sleepy-eyed and yawning. When he saw all the guns, his eyes widened in disbelief, and he stopped yawning. The janitor tried to close the door, but Charlie forced his way in, explaining to the frightened old man that we weren't trying to rob him, but rather were sheriffs looking for a jail escapee. The old man stood aside, dumbfounded, as we tiptoed, one by one, up the stairs to the second floor, leaving Mario Landolphi on the first floor landing with a shotgun. I was pushed to the rear of the line as the deputies approached room twelve. Reardon knocked gingerly at the door. Silence. The hallway was dark and we stood with our backs pressed to the walls. Charlie knocked again, louder.

"Yes, who is it?" It was a man's voice.

"Police," replied Charlie," Open up!"

"Oh my! .... Wait a minute," came a timid voice from within. The door opened a crack, and a gray-haired man eyed us suspiciously.

"If you're really police, show me some identification," he said, in a distinctly effeminate voice.

Charlie showed his badge. "Sheriff's department...we're looking for a jail escapee."

"Here? What makes you think he's here?"

"Can we search your room?" asked Charlie

Four of us squeezed into the small dingy room that contained nothing more in furniture than a bed, bureau and chair—no trap door, no secret compartment, no escapees.

"Do you have any enemies who might call us to say that you were harboring a fugitive?" I asked the little, pale-faced man.

"Only that crude old bastard next door in room ten. He's always pounding on the wall, shouting that my radio is too loud."

Charley Reardon walked back out into the corridor and pounded on the door of room ten. He pounded for over a minute without an answer.

"Get that janitor up here," he said to one of the deputies, "and have him open this door for us." The words were just out of his mouth, when the door to room ten opened, and a prunish, bespectacled face appeared. He yawned and squinted his eyes as if we had awakened him out of a sound sleep.

"Can I help you gentlemen?" he asked, and I immediately recognized the voice. I asked him if he had happened to make a call to the sheriff's department about an hour earlier. He, of course, denied having made a phone call to my office, and said he knew nothing about a jail escape or hiding fugitive.

"He's a liar!" snapped the effeminate one from room twelve. We searched room ten anyway, just for spite, and left the two neighbors shouting at each other from their respective doorways.

What we didn't expect, however, was what greeted us on the first floor landing of the boarding house: Three armed policemen pointing their weapons at us, with correctional officer Mario Landolphi standing in a corner with his hands up. Charley, being first down the stairs, showed his badge: "Essex County Sheriff's Department," he announced. The police were slow to lower their weapons, and the police sergeant was livid. "We got a call that this was a Mafia hit...six plain clothed guys entering a boarding house with shotguns...what's the matter with you guys?" Embarrassed, I explained to the sergeant that I had called his chief about the escape, but forgot to call about our assault on the boarding house.

"We could have had a good old fashioned shootout here, ya' know, Sheriff?"

The street was lit up with rotating blue lights of police cruisers and the nasty looks of Lynn policemen as we slipped into the seats of our vehicles and slowly crept away. I just hoped the press wouldn't get wind of such a fiasco, and thankfully they never did.

It was, however, another black mark against my relationship with local police, and Lynn had the largest force in the county. I'm sure that the sheriff's department's boarding house folly spread quickly through police headquarters. The deputies drove me back to the jail—where I belonged. I enjoyed the excitement of the hunt as much as any man, but I felt like a fifth wheel on the streets; the deputies were always protecting me in one way or another. My job was coordinating the command post, and without saying it, that's where my deputies wanted me to stay.

Back at escape-headquarters, things were heating up while I was away. Curran informed me that Charlie Geary believed Kerivan was hiding in his father's Lynn home, which Charlie had been guarding for hours. I sent Reardon and the rest of the boarding-house crew, plus Bob Curran, to help Geary. A neighbor told Geary that she thought she saw Kerivan sneak in the back door of the house just before Geary arrived. Reardon acquired permission from a judge to search the premises, and before we made a move, I was sure to call the Lynn police department to tell them that we intended to search the Kerivan home. When Reardon and the boys showed up, the local police were hard on their heals to backup them in the search. Reardon was knocking on the front door when the police arrived, and when Kerivan's father wouldn't open the locked door, the police knocked it down. Police and deputies scoured the house, looking in every shadowy nook and cranny, but there was no sign of the escapee. Within two hours the deputies were on their way back to Salem, leaving Kerivan's father to repair his front door.

"I know he's in there somewhere," Charlie Geary kept saying over and over again. "He's got to be in there—the neighbor saw him go in."

"That's it," shouted Reardon who had been pacing the office floor. "Let's go back. That house had three stories, but there was no way to get to an attic that we could see. There must be a secret way up, and we missed it."

I called the Lynn police again. "We're going back in," I announced.

"Wait for us," said the desk sergeant.

At this point I couldn't control myself. I left Deputy Hollum on phone duty, and I joined Reardon and the gang in a second assault on Kerivan's father's home. The Lynn police had beaten us to the house and had already knocked in the repaired door.

The father was frothing with anger at the Lynn police. A more thorough investigation this time revealed a second floor bedroom closet with a hidden stairway, which obviously led to the attic.

"He's armed and dangerous," a Lynn policeman reminded us as my deputies started climbing the stairs.

"Who volunteers to go first?" I smiled at my wide-eyed deputies. Without hesitation, George Dobson, my devil-may-care, ex-registry cop, bounded the stairs two at a time, his pistol drawn and ready to fire. There was an audible gasp from my deputies. Reardon whispered "holy shit" and was up the stairs after him with a flashlight and pistol in hand.

"Come out of there you punk," I heard Dobson yell as he stomped across the attic like a raging bull. Reardon had his light on a crouching figure, trying to hide behind an old steamer trunk. The escapee had a revolver, but one look at the charging Dobson made him drop his weapon, throw up his arms, and surrender.

On the way back to the Salem Jail, Reardon drove, Geary and Smith sat in the back seat flanking the prisoner, and I sat in the front passenger seat staring back at our captive. He looked like a twelve year old, squeezed in between the two burly deputies, blond hair disheveled and falling over his eyes, his tee shirt soiled and torn, his skinny arms splotched with goose bumps.

"Don't worry," I told him, "You'll be back in your nice warm cell before you know it." He gave me the evil eye and said nothing.

"At least six more months of fun time with us for your little trip to Daddy's house, and maybe, because you armed yourself, you'll add two years to your stay. Was it worth it?" I asked. He intensified his stare. "Tell us where the other two guys are and we may be able to reduce that time for you."

All I got in response was a few foul words better left to the imagination. When we arrived back at the jail, we dragged him out of the car and up the stairs to the front gate. Strangely, however, when we rang the buzzer for the guards to open the great steel front door of the jail, there was no response. Charlie shouted through the door, "Open up," but still no one came.

"What the hell is going on?" I asked Charlie, thinking he might have an answer, but he just shrugged his shoulders.

"They're sleeping," said Kerivan, standing now, but still squeezed between the two deputies. He smiled at the look of surprise on my face. "It's the late shift. They just sleep all night...didn't you know that, Sheriff?" I looked at Charlie Reardon for confirmation. He just shrugged his shoulders and returned to pounding on the door.

"I hope to hell they're not sleeping," I said loudly, "or some heads will role."

A quiet voice came from the other side of the door. "Who is it?"

"It's the sheriff," I shouted, "open this fuckin' door." There was the sound of shuffling and muffled murmuring from behind the door, but I didn't hear the large brass key go into the door lock. "Open this door now!" I boomed, and I finally heard the key clanking into the lock and turning. An older guard who I didn't recognize opened the door, but I did notice that he was wearing long johns and no uniform.

As the door opened, I could see through the glass panel of the thick inner door, and saw two guards inside, one scurrying to put on his pants, and the other quickly unbuttoning pajama tops.

"What the hell is going on here?" I snarled at the bespectacled, gray-haired guard trying to hide behind the great door. "We just had an escape and you bastards are sleeping while on duty?"

"But we always sleep on the third shift, Sheriff. Wells said we could."

"You're not getting paid for sleeping," I barked, loud enough for the other two guards to hear. As I entered the jail ahead of Reardon and our captured escapee, I could see that the guards had spread three folding cots in the office with sheets and blankets to cover them. I could hardly believe my eyes. I turned to face Charlie.

"They're right," he said, again shrugging his shoulders, "the old sheriff allowed it."

"Well, those days are over," I shouted at the half-dressed correctional officers that stood before me. They all just stood there with that same hangdog look that Kerivan had when we captured him, but now Kerivan was smiling wryly. "You tell 'em, Sheriff," he called out

The Salem Jail as seen from Bridge Street and the Parker Brothers Game Company, producers of Monopoly.

as he was led back into the cellblock. I returned to the house next door where Deputy Hollum was voluntarily holding down our communications network—the one phone.

"A lot of calls from the newspapers and a few crank calls, but that's it," said George. He was happy we had captured Kerivan, but felt Longval and Massei were the real dangerous ones. We had no good leads on either one. It was now 5:00 a.m. and we were all worn to a frazzle. As we were about to call it a day, close shop, and go home for needed sleep, George Hollum mentioned that Longval's best friend, one Jere Keene of Amesbury, had been let out of Salem Jail the day before, after serving nine months.

"Keene and Longval were cellmates—like brothers," said George.

"Bingo!" I shouted and reached for the phone.

"Who you callin' at this hour?" asked George.

"Our new deputy, Henry Fournier of Amesbury," I replied, dialing the number from my little black book of addresses. I hardly knew Fournier when I swore him in, but he was an Amesbury selectman of good standing and a fun fellow well met, who promised to help me in the next election. I told him all the rules: buy your own uniform, be available for training and parades, volunteer for emergencies. He agreed. I woke him out of a sound sleep.

"Put on your new shinny badge," I said to the half-awake man, "and call down to the Amesbury Police Department and tell them you believe a jail escapee is hiding at Rowell Court, the home of Jere Keene. I want you to capture him and bring him here."

"Now!"

"Yes, but don't go to the door of the house without the police with you."

"I wouldn't think of it," said Henry.

Fournier followed orders, and within an hour, I got a call back from him. "We went to the house, Sheriff, but I don't mind telling you that I was pretty nervous. Two local policemen and I searched the house, top to bottom, and it was I who found him hiding under an overturned rowboat in the cellar. He came peaceably. I didn't even have a gun you know…pretty hairy stuff…does this stuff happen often?"

I was elated. "Just think," I told Fournier, "together, you and I captured an escapee. And we will charge Jere Keene, too, for being an accessory."

"Keene says that Longval forced him at gunpoint to take him in."

"Let's charge him anyway," I said. "Good work, Henry. You can go back to bed now."

"Great," said Henry. "But tell me, Sheriff," he added, "just what are the advantages to being a deputy?"

Months went by before I heard anything about Massei, the instigator of the great escape. State police informed me that he was found floating out in the Atlantic off Florida–"a body without a head." He must have got in with the wrong crowd, or maybe he was in the wrong crowd to begin with. I believed the floating head story until Deputy Terry Marks informed me, a few years later, that Massei was seen by a reliable source alive and kicking, working in neighboring Marblehead under an assumed name. I don't know which story to believe, but I never saw Massei again.

CHAPTER XII

Here Comes The Judge

Peter Perron, a short, balding man in his late forties, walked into one of New England's finest restaurants at noon, its busiest hour. He wore light slacks, and his loudly colored Hawaiian shirt hung loosely outside his belt. He strolled to the manager's office off the main dining room, knocked on the door and entered. Once inside the cramped office, he pulled a 38-magnum from under his shirt, pointed it at the frightened manager sitting at his desk, and demanded the day's cash receipts. The manager obliged by opening the safe and providing Perron with large bundles of paper money and a bag to carry it in. Perron, displaying no signs of nervousness, then told the manager to lie down on the office floor and to count to sixty, after which he could get up. Carrying the bag of cash, Perron left the office, closing the door behind him, and started walking nonchalantly out of the restaurant. The manager didn't wait to count to sixty. He was up and out of his office at the count of five.

The dining room was filled with over a hundred patrons ordering and eating lunch. Perron hadn't quite made the front door when the manager burst into the room screaming, "Help! Police! I've been robbed!" People screamed; some ducked under their tables. The manager was pointing at Perron and shouting, "Thief! Thief! Thief!" A man rushed toward Perron and threw a plate of salad at him. Perron panicked, reached under his shirt for his gun, and moved quickly as he dodged customers, tables, and chairs, looking for a side exit. An off-duty policeman sitting with his wife near the entrance, waiting for a table, reached for his revolver, which he carried in a belt-holster. They were there to celebrate their wedding anniversary, having often come to this restaurant when they were courting. The policeman stood and took careful aim at Perron. He shot him twice in the legs. Perron reeled, and the paper bag tore open, sending bills flurrying into the air. As Perron fell to the carpet, he fired back at the police-man, hitting him in the chest, and sending him sprawling over neatly set tables. Everyone was yelling and screaming as Perron tried to crawl to the exit, but the pain in his legs was too much for him to get very far. He fired his gun wildly into the air in an attempt to keep others away from him. Finally, he spent all of his bullets and lay there on the money-strewn carpet, moaning and sobbing.

Perron and the policeman were rushed to a Boston hospital by ambulance, but the policeman was declared dead on arrival. At the hospital, Perron was officially arrested, charged with second-degree murder and armed robbery, and placed in my custody. He was my prisoner because the restaurant he robbed was in Essex County; if he had been uninjured, he would have been held at the Salem Jail. His leg wounds were so severe, however, that he had to remain in the Boston hospital. Usually when inmates were hospitalized, unarmed correctional officers would keep constant vigils outside the hospital room, but in this case, I placed two armed deputy sheriffs over Per-ron, one in his room, and the other outside in the corridor. The mur-der charge alone was enough to warrant such tight security, but there was also a credible rumor circulating at the jail that the Mafia was out to get Perron for a large sum of money he supposedly owed them. Thus, I surmised, was the reason for the robbery.

The county commissioners were furious, for not only did the cost of Perron's hospital stay and doctor bills come out of county coffers, but so did the extra expense of my deputy guards. The commission-ers were anxious that I get him behind bars as soon as possible, as was I, though for different reasons. While in the hospital, I was fearful he would escape, or worse, be the subject of a hit by the Mafia—which put my deputies at risk as well. After a few days of rest, his leg wounds began to heal, so I ordered my deputies to handcuff him to his bed. Perron's attorney was furious about the shackles and phoned me in a rage, demanding that I "remove the cuffs immediately." I ex-plained to him that Perron's doctor informed me that he was now able to walk to the bathroom, and to me, that meant he could also walk out the front door. I refused to take off the cuffs. His attorney took Polaroid photos of his client shackled to the bed and brought them to Judge Mitchell at the Suffolk County Superior Courthouse in Boston. The judge ruled that it was "cruel and unusual punishment" and had the attorney deliver an order to my deputies at the hospital, instructing them to remove the handcuffs. My deputies called me, and I ordered them to keep the shackles on. I reasoned that Perron's security was my responsibility, not the judge's, and so I would be the one to make decisions regarding the conditions of his custody.

I was in the middle of an important budget hearing with the county clerk, Jack Barry, and all the county commissioners when Bob Curran rushed in and whispered to me—loud enough for all present to hear—"Judge Mitchell wants you in his courtroom in Boston, forthwith. And he says that if you don't show up within the hour, he'll have you arrested." Bob looked frightened for me, as did Jack and the commissioners.

"We can postpone your budget, Sheriff," said Barry.

"No need," I replied, "the good judge can wait to arrest me." I was unnerved by Mitchell's threat, but also furious that this overzealous judge would demand my world should stop to appease him. This was the crucial budget conference allocating jail expenditures for the coming year; at stake was the possibility of a spanking new sheriff's car, and maybe even a new paddy wagon. I wasn't about to leave this meeting for any reason. "Tell the judge I'm in a budget meeting and I'll phone him when I'm out," I told Bob. Jack Barry's eyes danced in his head and he pursed his lips as if to whistle—county folks weren't used to anyone, let alone a new sheriff, telling an all-mighty judge to wait. I stayed with the commissioners all afternoon, and we didn't finish hammering out the budget until 6 p.m.—too late to call the judge, I supposed, for judges usually left work early.

I went home to eat and to call my old state house colleague, Jerry Bowes, the High Sheriff of Cape Cod, for some much needed advice. A good fellow well met, Jerry was my mentor, about twelve years my senior; he was also an expert on the rules and regulations governing sheriffs, jails, and courts. We had become close while serving together

as representatives at the state house, and he was always willing and
able to advise me. "Judge Mitchell is after my hide," I told Jerry. "He
wants to arrest me and he's ordering me to his court in Boston. Is
there a way out for me?" As usual, Jerry came to my rescue and provided me with some old Massachusetts laws regarding judge/sheriff
disputes, which I decided to resurrect for my inevitable showdown
with Mitchell the next day. The judge, however, threw me an unexpected curve.

Later that same evening, two of my deputies, Norman "Dugie"
Russell and Jake Ricci, who had been guarding Perron in Boston,
knocked at my front door. Dugie Russell, who was an old friend from
my scuba diving days, was noticeably upset. "I have a subpoena here
for your arrest, Sheriff," said Dugie. "From Judge Mitchell. He wants
you in his court, forthwith." Dugie offered me the subpoena, but I refused to take it.

"Under no circumstances can my own deputies serve me a subpoena," I told Dugie and Jake. "I would think Judge Mitchell would
know that."

"But a Suffolk County deputy served it to us," said Dugie. "What
do we do with it?" I smiled meaningfully at him, imagining a few
things that I'd like to see done with it. "I never should have asked
that, should I?" he said with a half smile.

"Give it back to Judge Mitchell. Neither my deputies, nor the
Suffolk County deputies can serve me a subpoena. In fact, no county
deputy can serve a sheriff. Have Mitchell look that one up in his
funkenwagnel." My confused deputies left, and like me, wondered
what horrible fate waited us the next day.

At 10:15 am the next morning, the call came. The tone of Judge
Mitchell's voice was anything but pleasant. "Sheriff Cahill, you are to
be in my court by noon, or I'll hold you in contempt, and I will personally see to it that you end up in jail."

I have to admit that his threat gave me the jitters, but thanks to
Sheriff Bowes, I was more informed on what the laws were than
Judge Mitchell was.

"I can't do that, Judge," I replied. "For you to order me to your court, I have to be properly served, and I can't accept service from my own deputies, nor from any other deputy sheriff—that's the law." There was a moment of silence.

"What do you mean?" he asked, his voice mellowing somewhat.

"There's a law in the books, Judge," I replied, trying not to sound overly pompous, "that says that a high sheriff can only be summoned to court if another high sheriff of an adjoining county serves him in hand. Therefore, only Sheriff Eisenstadt from Suffolk County, or Sheriff Buckley from Middlesex County can deliver your summons to me."

"Are you sure of that?" His voice was getting weaker.

"Yes sir!"

"Well, no matter," his voice became defiant again. "I've already arrested two of your deputies, Mr. Russell and Mr. Ricci. So, you'll have to come and get them. And I'd bring a lawyer with you."

"How can you arrest my deputies? They've done nothing..."

"They are following your orders, handcuffing a man to his hospital bed."

"The reason is that his doctor tells me that Perron is able to get up and walk now, and I don't want him to walk away. He is my responsibility."

"It's cruel punishment. He's too injured to walk away."

"He's a murderer and armed robber, and I think he's well enough to walk."

"*Alleged* murderer and armed robber," the judge corrected me. "Unless the shackles come off, your deputies remain in jail. Bring a lawyer."

"Judge, this county is so poor, we don't have a lawyer. Nor do I have a vehicle to get to Boston. I guess my boys will just have to rot in jail. But you really didn't have a right to arrest them in the first place."

"That's up to you, Sheriff," he said, his voice quite mellow now. "But I don't think you should shackle a man to his bed when the doctors tell me he can't walk more than five steps without falling down. How could he possibly escape?"

"Looks like we're at an impasse, Judge."

"It does," he agreed.

There was silence.

"Tell you what," I said. "I'll take the cuffs off, but only for the next couple days, if you let my deputies go."

"It's a deal," said the judge. "But before I hang up, were you telling me the truth about how only a sheriff can summon another sheriff to court?"

"Only a sheriff whose county is contiguous to the other sheriff's county," I replied.

"That's ridiculous," said the judge.

"Yes," I replied, "but it's the law."

Two hours later, Dugie Russell and Jake Ricci, in uniform, gunbelts strapped to their waists, appeared in my office. They were furious. Two Suffolk County Deputy Sheriffs had arrested them as they came on duty at the hospital, and they were taken to the courthouse where they appeared before Judge Mitchell.

"It was humiliating," said Dugie, his face still flush from the experience. "He put us in a cell for over an hour."

"With our guns still in our holsters!" added Jake.

"Imagine that!" piped in Dugie. "Here we are in jail, behind bars, and we're both carrying loaded guns."

"I hope you didn't say anything off-color to the judge when he held you," I said, having witnessed Dugie Russell's temper in the past.

"No, but I felt like it," said Dugie. "I was so embarrassed and shocked that I was dumbfounded. Can't we sue him for doing that?"

"Probably," I replied. "He was wrong, but we're not going to sue, we're going to forget it."

"Forget it?!" Dugie shouted, his face now red with rage.

"You could have been kept overnight, instead of for just an hour or so—or maybe even for days." I could tell Dugie wanted to interrupt me, but I kept on talking. "I wasn't coming after you, I can tell you that, 'cause he would have arrested me, and what a story that would have made for the Boston Globe. It's a damned good thing that the judge and I came to an agreement or you'd still be there."

Dugie and Jake looked at each other, a little befuddled. They had expected me to be as mad as they were. "And what about Perron when we relieve the others at the hospital tonight?" asked Dugie.

"Tonight he remains uncuffed, but tomorrow night, cuff him again. I'm sure that will piss off the lawyer and the judge to no end. But this time, I'm sure the judge will leave you guys alone. We'll see if he summons me to court properly this time. But I'll tell you boys in deepest secrecy, he ain't never going to get me there."

I had provided the judge a way not to lose face with Perron's lawyer, a way to get my deputies out of jail, and a way to keep a minor legal disagreement from becoming a constitutional brawl, but it was only temporary because I wasn't about to leave him uncuffed for long. It wasn't only a matter of principle, but also a matter of security. Two days later when Perron's lawyer came to call at the hospital, he once again found his client cuffed to the bedpost. Dugie reported that the lawyer went "absolutely berserk." Dugie said that the scene he witnessed made up for the time he had spent in jail. It wasn't long before I got a call from my fellow sheriff from Boston, Tom Eisenstadt.

"Bob, I've got a summons for you to appear, forthwith, before Judge Mitchell."

"Well, you'll have to deliver it then, Tom," I said. "It must be in hand, you know, that's the law. You have to place the summons in my hand."

"Bob, it will take me an hour to get to your jail and an hour to get back. I've got an important meeting I have to attend within an hour. Can't you come here and pick it up?"

"Sorry, Tom," I replied. "I can't leave here today. Why don't you drive down after your meeting? Traffic might be lighter then."

"Bob, just this one time, would you allow one of my deputies to serve you?"

"Nope. You know the law, Tom. Either you or Buckley must serve me, you lazy bastard."

"Well then, I won't be able to get down your way until dinner time. Can't you meet me half way?"

"Sorry, Tom, and you probably won't find me here after four, anyway. I have an important engagement."

"Mitchell's bullshit, Bob."

"I'm sure he is, but so am I, Tom. He's trying to tell me how to run my business. Are you aware that two of your deputies arrested two of my deputies the other day?"

"Yes I am, but Mitchell only held them awhile."

"He had no right to do that. And did you know that your boys put my boys into locked cells while they were still carrying firearms—loaded firearms?"

"My boys were just as upset about it as your boys were," said Eisenstadt. "But Bob, Mitchell wants you in his courtroom. If he doesn't get you today, he'll get you tomorrow."

"Not today and not tomorrow, Tom, 'cause the inmate in question will be back in my jail tomorrow. His doctor says he can be moved, so I'm moving him out of your jurisdiction, where Mitchell seems to rule with an iron fist, and into mine. Perron's lawyer obviously has the judge's ear, but if Perron escapes, it'll be my ass and not the judge's."

"Does the judge know you're moving him tomorrow?"

"Nope, but he'll find out soon enough, and there's not a damned thing he can do about that, is there?"

"Not a damned thing," Tom agreed. "But you don't want to come to Boston to tell him that yourself?"

"No way, Tom. I don't intend to set foot in your county for some time."

"I'll tell the judge, Bob. He won't like it, but I guess he'll just have to drop the summons."

"I would think so. As of tomorrow, Perron won't be cuffed to a bedpost; he'll be in jail, securely behind bars."

"I thought you were an easy-going guy," said Tom.

"I *was*. This job is making me tough…and I'm starting to like it," I replied.

An ambulance arrived early the next morning at the hospital to bring Perron to jail. I sent two correctional officers to accompany him. The one who would sit in the back of the ambulance with Perron was unarmed, and the other who would sit in the front seat with the ambulance driver and his assistant, was armed. Perron was drugged and strapped into a cot. Hardly out of the parking lot, Officer Chanel Houle, who was in back with Perron, noticed that a blue Ford sedan was following them down the winding streets of Boston. Houle asked the driver to take a few shortcuts to the Mystic River Bridge, to make sure the car was really tailing them. Sure enough, the car followed to the bridge. Houle could see six men in the car, but it wasn't driving close enough for him to get the license plate number. He alerted the armed guard, Tom Corriveau, sitting in the front seat, to be prepared for anything. The ambulance driver and his assistant were extremely nervous; they had never experienced anything like this before. Houle asked the driver to "step on it" in an attempt to lose the pursuers. He concluded that they were either Mafia men out to kill Perron, or they were friends of Perron who wanted to free him. The ambulance sped down the highway, but the blue sedan kept up, staying about fifty yards behind. Even when the driver blared the siren in order to speed their progress through traffic, the Ford followed without hesitation. When the ambulance was confronted with a red light, Houle suggested to the driver that he race right through it, hoping that the pursuers would be forced to stop for traffic, but they also sped right through.

Houle knew that there was a four-mile stretch of wide roadway ahead called the Lynnway that was sparsely settled and lightly traveled during the day—a perfect place to overtake a vehicle and force it off the road, if that was their intent.

"You got a radio or telephone in this thing?" Tom asked the driver through the screen. The pale-faced driver said that he did. "Then call the state police quick, and tell them we're being followed and we're about to hit the Lynn Marsh Road. Tell them we have Perron in the vehicle—that will make them move even quicker, I'm sure." The driver complied. As they hit the long stretch of road, Houle asked the driver to slow down, hoping the blue Ford might slow down too. The Ford did slow down, but it seemed to be advancing on the ambulance little by little. At one point, Houle could almost make out the license plate and discern facial features of the men in the car. Even the sedated Perron sensed that something was about to happen and opened his eyes wide.

When the roadway cleared of all traffic, the driver of the blue sedan started to make his move. The sedan sped into the passing lane and attempted to pass the ambulance.

"Step on it!" shouted Houle to the ambulance driver.

As the ambulance and the sedan raced down the road side by side, Houle could see the swarthy face of the man sitting in the front passenger seat. He looked out the window at an angle, careful not to present a large target, expecting to see the flash of a revolver or the barrel of a sawed-off shotgun at any moment. Both vehicles were now moving at over 90 miles per hour. Corriveau had his revolver poised and ready to shoot when, all of a sudden, the blue sedan jumped the meridian strip and spun around on the opposite side of the road, almost tipping over in the process. Once it righted itself, there was a spinning of wheels, and the gray smoke and smell of rubber left billowed in their wake as they sped off in the opposite direction. The guards and the ambulance boys were relieved but baffled.

The reason for the hasty retreat of the pursuers, Houle and Corriveau soon discovered, was a roadblock of two state police cruisers up ahead. The gangsters, or whoever they were, had spotted the flashing blue lights before the guards and ambulance driver had.

"Well, your friends have left us," Houle smiled down at the groggy Perron.

"I don't think they were friends," Perron slurred in response.

Within minutes, my wounded guest was behind bars at Salem Jail, and Perron's creditors would have to wait a long time to collect. And in Suffolk County Superior Court, Judge Mitchell would have to find some other sheriff to torment.

CHAPTER XIII

Deputy Dawgs

The thought that Judge Joseph Mitchell—the same Joseph Mitchell that had wanted to lock me up for contempt of court and had my deputies thrown in prison—was presiding over sessions only two blocks away at the Salem Superior Courthouse made me somewhat apprehensive. Unlike my predecessor Roger Wells, however, I seldom went near the courthouses, and felt sure that I would avoid any contact with him. He was rotating from court to court throughout the state, and in September he was assigned to Essex County and serving in Salem. If it hadn't been for Bob Curran warning me that Mitchell was here, I wouldn't have known it. Surely Judge Mitchell was still fuming about our standoff over the cuffing of a wounded inmate in the hospital and my refusal to accept a summons to his courtroom. Judges were use to getting their way, and I had truly agitated Mitchell, who was notoriously quick to anger.

My plan was to avoid him like the plague. Little did I know that a disaster of a different sort was erupting at the courthouse that would force me to Judge Mitchell's bench "forthwith." Over 800 Lynn schoolteachers had decided to go on strike and Judge Mitchell ruled the strike illegal. Deputy Joe Ross called me from the courthouse.

"The Judge wants to see you immediately, Sheriff," he said in an excited tone. "It looks like he's going to send all eight hundred teachers to jail."

"That's impossible!" I shouted into the phone, but Joe had already hung up.

I hurried out the door into a pouring rain, rushing to the courthouse. As I hoofed it down the wet streets, I wondered if I was walking so fast because of the rain or my fear of Mitchell? I had never seen the man—didn't even know what he looked like—and I had hoped it would stay that way. As I walked, I remembered Sheriff Jerry Bowes' words of wisdom, "don't confront or argue with a judge in the courtroom because his word is law there, but you can say anything to him in his chambers." Mitchell hadn't invited me to his chambers; he wanted me in his courtroom. Would he be vindictive over our prior feud, I wondered? Of course he would. When I reached the court-house, I was wet with rain, chilled to the bone, and full of anticipa-tion. I slipped into his courtroom, dripping like a drowned rat. Court reporters, cameramen, television personalities, teachers with mem-bers of their families, and curious citizens were all packed into the courtroom, making it difficult to find a way through. All eyes and ears were focused on the black man in the black robe towering above everyone else, his right hand poised to slam the gavel. The teacher standing before him looked like he had just been plucked from the golf course—white shorts, striped knit shirt, and tanned face.

"I need more time to confer with my attorney," he said

"I need four or five hours to confer with each of my clients," added the young well-dressed attorney standing next to the teacher.

"All right," boomed Mitchell, "I'll give you 'til Monday morning, ten a.m., but you are held on five thousand dollars cash bail due now, or you'll spend the weekend in the Salem Jail." The man audibly gasped. Mitchell then turned his attention to the lawyer. "I will give you fifteen minutes to talk to all of your teachers on hand, as a group. They have been instructed to return to work, and my order has been ignored. I will show you that I mean business."

"I am a lawyer," shouted a teacher from one of the pews, "and I will see that justice is done here."

There was cheering and Mitchell slammed the gavel. "Justice is always dispensed in this court," he bellowed. "That's what I'm here for."

The man wearing shorts reached into his back pocket, pulled out his wallet and counted out $28.00. "That's all I have your honor," he said to giggles from the audience, "just twenty-eight bucks."

Mitchell signaled to Court Officer Joe Ross. "Take him to jail," said Mitchell. So Ross carefully but deliberately took the teacher by the arm and escorted him out to a holding room. The jovial mood of the teachers in the courtroom became somber. They now realized, as did I, that the judge did indeed mean business. As the teachers filed out to meet with their lawyer in a separate room, upstairs in the courthouse, Judge Mitchell, with a wave of his finger, motioned me to follow him into his chambers. He wouldn't allow a court-officer to be with us, which made me think that maybe he wanted to have it out with me, one on one, face to face. I was wrong. The moment we were alone in the room, he closed and locked the door, then turned to me and asked, "How many of these teachers can you keep in the jail for the weekend?"

"Not many," I replied. "We're over crowded now, and I can't take any women. The last female inmates burned out that section of the facility. For the weekend…I can probably take no more than ten men."

Mitchell moved toward me and in a near whisper said, "Call all the sheriffs in the state and find out how much room we've got, especially for females. I really need places to house the women," he said, "and keep this to yourself, don't even mention my words to your deputies. And I want you to call out more of your deputies, because we're going to summon all the teachers to court, and those who do not respond before Saturday will be arrested. I'll stay in this courtroom 'til 2:00 a.m. if I have to," he said. "I'll order them held. All you have to do is find a place to hold them," Mitchell concluded. Surprisingly, he mentioned nothing of our previous disagreement.

Before I made calls to my ten fellow Massachusetts sheriffs, I joined the teachers at the meeting on the floor above. "I'd like to talk to all the women, if I might," I said. The female teachers, who were by far the majority in the room, all smiled and nodded. They had regained their happy-go-lucky mood and announced to me that they were ready and willing to go to jail.

"Please don't be so anxious" I told them. "I cannot put you at the Salem Jail, nor in Lawrence, and at the moment, I don't know where you'll go, but you'll surely be split up, and you may travel to the other end of the state, handcuffed and in a paddy wagon. Accommodations may not be too good, and you'll probably be bunking in with armed robbers and murderers. I don't mean to frighten you, but this isn't going to be a picnic."

They looked at me suspiciously. "I'm telling you the truth, so those of you who can make bail, please do so. Otherwise, you won't have a very enjoyable weekend."

"The Judge can't split us up," declared one enthusiastic but misinformed teacher.

"He can and he will," I replied. "We don't have the room, so you can bet that you won't be staying in Essex County." Now they were somber again, but I felt it was my duty to warn them, for there were few county jails that took in female inmates, and the one state prison that housed females wasn't a place you'd want to have your sister, wife, mother, daughter, or teacher spend the weekend.

When I reported back to Judge Mitchell after calling the sheriffs around the state, he wasn't too pleased either. There was enough room to accommodate possibly fifty of the male teachers, but only ten openings throughout the state for females, and they were divided between seven different penal institutions, some of which were over two hours away from Salem—a frightening prospect for innocent, naive schoolteachers. But Mitchell was adamant that unless they made bail, they were going to jail.

The judge was clever, and only I realized what he was doing. He would sentence five men for each woman, and when he had sent five females to jail, he concentrated only on the male teachers. He was trying to make it look like he was going to run through the entire teacher's union to see if he could get them to break before he ran out of room. It was late Friday afternoon, and the courthouse hallway was lined with teachers, all having been served summonses to appear before Judge Mitchell to be charged and jailed. At least twenty of my deputies were at work under the direction of Curran and Reardon and being paid for their efforts by the court system, which was a new and welcome experience for most of them. Although Mitchell wanted those thirty Lynn schools up and operating Monday morning, it was increasingly becoming an impossibility. Within five hours

*Deputy Sheriffs
Bill Cox and
Jim Walsh
exchange barbs
at a county
meeting.*

*Court Officers
Bob Brown and
Norman "Dugie"
Russell.*

on the bench, the judge had sent twenty-two teachers to jail for not making bail, and another 200 were to appear in his court on Monday morning. One teacher, Fred Latour, was also a Lynn City Councilor and was given a choice by Mitchell: either return to his job as a high school math teacher on Monday morning or go to jail. Latour promised to go back to work, so Mitchell's tough tactics were beginning to make some progress. Joe Gauvin, the Lynn Teachers Union President, immediately received ten days in the Salem House of Correction for contempt of court.

Mitchell had me call in more deputies to deliver contempt citations to the teachers who had not shown up at the Salem Courthouse. At a nearby office, Bob Curran had his mother, wife, and daughter, plus Charlie Readon's wife typing out citations and summonses late into Friday night. Many of the deputies weren't given time to put on their uniforms, and had to pin their badges to dripping raincoats. It was a messy day and night, with children crying and husbands and fathers screaming in protest as their mothers, wives and daughters were handcuffed, placed inside the paddy wagon or a deputy's personal vehicle, and carted away to some distant prison. You could see the fear in their eyes, and Boston TV stations were carrying the sad sight to the citizens of New England as they sat down for Friday night supper.

Whether it was my speech to the female teachers, or Mitchell's tenacity, I don't know, but some of the females reluctantly announced to the judge that they didn't want to go to jail and were willing to go back to work on Monday morning. Surprisingly, the dilemma was over some twelve hours after it began. I left the courthouse and trudged back though the rain to the jail. I did not wait to see if Mitchell had any last minute instructions for me. Now that the teachers' strike was over, he might have time to reflect on our inmate confrontation; I wasn't about to hang around the courthouse to find out. Then it dawned on me that perhaps he didn't realize that I was the sheriff that he had battled with some months ago over the phone. Whether he remembered or not, I had no desire to ever have dealings with Judge Mitchell again, and I never did. But I will always admire the tenacity and dogged determination of the man.

Unbeknownst to me, while I was away from the Salem Jail that Friday, there was a rally of some 200 teachers outside the prison walls, protesting the arrest and jailing of their president, Joseph Gauvin. He waved to them from his third tier cell window, causing them to cheer louder. The sight and sound of those gathered outside unnerved and excited the rest of the jail population, and the correctional officers were having problems controlling the uproar inside the jail. Darby McGhee, the guard who had caused me aggravation in the past, left the jail to talk to the picketing teachers outside the jail. He persuaded them to move away from the building because of the problems they were causing on the inside. Darby's Lynn connections and persuasiveness in dispersing the crowd probably avoided a serious disturbance, maybe even a riot. After such a hard day at court, I was indebted to McGhee for helping me avoid a disastrous day at the jail.

❋ ❋ ❋

That November, I once again collided with a Massachusetts labor union—this time the Beverly Police Patrolmen's Union. They refused an order from their police chief to guard the cities voting stations on Election Day. The police union argued that they had a contractual right to refuse overtime assignments, which included guarding the polls. The chief of police and mayor disagreed, as did the Beverly Chamber of Commerce, who passed an order asking for the immediate police protection of the city's business community. Mayor Jim Vitale first contacted the state police to have troopers cover the polls, but their response was that they could not serve the city unless there was a disturbance. The Federal Marshals would not guard the polls either, even though it was a national election. Jimmy Vitale then called me as a last resort and pleaded his case.

"The attorney general tells me that the election results can be challenged here if we have no law enforcement officers at the polls, and our city could be in big trouble."

"Sure, we'll help out Jimmy. How many men do you need?"

Special Sheriff Charles Reardon and "Deputy of the Year," George Mackinnon.

Above: Cartoon-strip that appeared in the Beverly Times Newspaper, *after the Sheriff started his harbor patrols. (Courtesy* The Beverly Times)

Below: Court Officers Bill Cox and Ed Mees assist Judge McNaught in a mock trial at Newburyport for Andover students.

The mayor was surprised and thrilled at my offer. I, of course, didn't know what I was getting into. Jimmy would need about twenty deputies for day and night shifts, and they would be well paid, which I thought would be enough incentive to inspire sufficient volunteers. I was wrong. Apparently, to many of my deputies, there were more important things than money. Three of them were Beverly police officers, and I heard from them first, condemning me for offering the department's help to the mayor and chief. Not being able to dissuade me, they called other deputies, asking them to refuse my offer to serve as polling guards. Even my special sheriff, Charley Reardon, scolded me for accepting the assignment from Mayor Vitale. Most of my deputies were union men in one form or another and refused my request for their service at the polls. Finally, after many phone calls, some serious arm-twisting, and a few angry conversations with my Beverly deputies to cease and desist their calls to other deputies, I had twenty somewhat willing deputies to serve our department in the city of Beverly.

Early morning on Election Day, we arrived at the Beverly police station to get assignments for poll-duty. I inspected them all in their spiffy green uniforms, spit shined and polished—they all looked surprisingly neat and alert for that hour of the morning. Beverly Police Chief Angelini, who planned to take disciplinary action against his patrolmen, told me he would remain on duty day and night in case there was any confrontation between his patrolmen and my deputies. There were a couple of police lieutenants in the police station on duty when the chief gave me the list of assignments, and they didn't look too friendly.

First in line for an assignment was Charlie Geary, my Irish-American friend who was a constant rebel, occasionally with a cause.

"We shouldn't be doing this," he blurted out. "We shouldn't go against the union."

"Get out!" I shouted at him. "If you don't want to do this, get the hell out of here and stop wasting my time. You were told what this was all about, and if you didn't want to be here, you didn't have to, but you're here now," I shouted at him. "Do you want to serve or not?"

"I just don't think we should–"

"Yes or no, Charlie?" I barked, "you're holding up the line." Charlie reluctantly took his polling assignment and left.

"If any others here have qualms about serving today," I said loudly and angrily, "then leave now or forever hold your peace." They all remained silent and went their way to serve the electorate. The Beverly press was good to us. At end of day they reported that, "The sheriff's deputies, in particular, received high praise from voters and poll workers alike for their neat dress and courteous manner. And City Clerk Walter Doyle said he was extremely pleased with the performance of these men." There were no ugly incidents with the striking Beverly patrolmen. When the Beverly Times Reporter asked me why I volunteered my men, I answered by saying, "This is a national election; we have an obligation and I really had no choice."

I wanted our department to provide any needed service to any of the 34 cities and towns we represented, and I resented the reluctance of my deputies to share that goal. I understood that union members had union rules and fellow union members to take into account, but I felt that their allegiance should be to the sheriff's department first and foremost. If we were going to be called on by the community, I knew we needed to be prepared. To that end, I provided my deputies with training opportunities in shooting, scuba diving, and emergency search and rescue, so they could be ready in every conceivable situation with all the skills necessary. North Shore Community College offered law enforcement associates degrees for all deputies, with classes held in the sheriff's house two nights a week, all free of charge to the deputies. When the Sportsmen's Center in Dedham, through deputy George Dobson, offered our department a twenty-foot boat with a 200-horse power outboard engine, we started a sea-patrol out of Salem harbor, training volunteer deputies in boat operation, navigation, safety and rescue. Simultaneously, we began a scuba rescue team with six deputies who were experienced professional divers, trained at New England Divers of Beverly, which was owned and operated by my brother Jim. The Coast Guard had abandoned their base at Salem and stopped patrolling Beverly and Salem waters two years earlier. I announced that our department would assist Salem and Beverly harbormasters in patrolling the waters at night, and that we would provide emergency service with our new dive team. The two city harbormasters and the Civil Defense Director, John Smedile, all welcomed our help, mainly because there had been a recent increase in boat thefts in the harbors. Jim Shea at the *Salem News*, however, believed that I was "creating a new little empire here," and that I "initiated the patrol to combat sharks." Yet, not withstanding the editorial thrashing, the boat patrols worked well, and the dive-team, under Deputy Dick Paverada, was constantly active recovering bodies, sunken vehicles, and lost articles within the harbors, rivers, and lakes of Essex County.

One active member of the scuba diving rescue team was Deputy Norman "Dugie" Russell of Beverly, a spark plug of creativity, a good outdoorsman, and a fun guy. He was a noted gardener, mushroom picker, boatman, underwater enthusiast, sculptor, birdhouse builder, special events speaker, and artist. I got a call from him on Labor Day. He was in jail. It was late afternoon and he had been placed under arrest at the Salem police station. With his one given phone call, instead of contacting his wife or attorney, he called me. It was only per chance that he got me at home, for I had been at a neighbor's picnic all day and had only returned home for a pack of cigarettes I had hidden in the freezer.

"This asshole assistant harbormaster arrested me for spearing lobsters," said Dugie over the phone. "Imagine a scuba diver spearing lobsters? That's ridiculous! And he said I was drunk-driving a boat under the influence, but I only had two beers... Can you get down here and get me out of this jam?"

"Sure," I replied. The Salem police station was only a mile from my home, and I drove directly there. I was met inside the station by the Assistant Harbormaster Everett Buckley, a husky man, who I was told took his job very seriously and would stand no foolishness when it came to unruly activities on the high seas. Buckley seemed amiable enough, and since he knew that Dugie was a member of my boat patrol team, he realized that I was in a somewhat embarrassing position.

"He was diving in a restricted zone near the Willows Pier," said Buckley, "and he and his two-man crew were acting up, with open beer cans in the boat. When I told him he was under arrest, he called me names not worth repeating and said that if I set foot in his boat he would sue me. He was so belligerent that I was forced to call for backup." Buckley relayed this information in a calm mater-of-fact voice, "and he resisted arrest until I brought in a second squad car. You can imagine what a disturbance it made on the pier. Hundreds came to watch. He was fuming when we brought him here."

It sounded like Dugie. As much as I liked and admired him, once riled up, it was difficult to talk sense into him. The police had him sitting in a locked room, but I could here his raspy voice of protest from where I was sitting in the police booking office.

"So, what can I do to take him off your hands?" I asked the assistant harbormaster. Buckley mused my question for a moment, skewing his face into contortions and said, "Well, I guess I can let him go, but only if I can get an apology from him—an honest apology for what he said and did—before he leaves here."

"That seems fair," I said. "Can I see him now?" I was led into the room by a patrolman, and Buckley stayed behind in the outer room. Dugie glanced up at me with a glare. He was wearing the bottom half of a wetsuit and a tee shirt. He was without shoes or socks.

"Can you get me out of here?"

"Sure I can, but only if you apologize to Buckley...to his face. Now!"

"Bull! I ain't apologizing to him. I'll rot in here before I do that."

"Then you will rot in here, 'cause you're not getting out 'til you say you're sorry."

"But I'm not sorry," he shouted. "He had no right to arrest me. I'm an officer of the law, for crissake."

"Come on Dugie, just apologize and you're out of here. I'll drive you back to the pier and you'll be out to sea again. Stop being so stubborn."

He gave me another angry glare, stood up and followed me into the next room to face Buckley. "He's ready to apologize," I told Buckley. They were nose to nose, except that Dugie's nose came to about Buckley's chin.

"You asshole" Dugie shouted into his face, "I ain't apologizing to you." I dragged Dugie back into the holding room. Buckley just walked away. Dugie sat down again, his head in his hands. "I just can't apologize to him."

"Please, Dugie. We can't stay here all day, and I'm sure Buckley isn't going to hang around here to be insulted every two minutes."

We tried it again as I pushed and nudged Dugie to stand in front of Buckley. Dugie bowed his head. "I just can't do it," he whispered, as if talking to himself. Buckley walked away again, his face still expressionless.

I dragged Dugie back into the room, sat him down and looked him right in the eyes. "Dugie," I pleaded, "This is your last chance. The guy is not pressing charges and he'll let you go if you'll just apologize. I'm not sticking around here all day either. I've got better things to do. Apologize now, or I'm out of here, and I'm sure Buckley is ready to leave too…it's up to you, you are welcome to enjoy a long nap on this bench, or probably in a stinky cell behind bars, if that's what you want."

Dugie stood again and slumped into the next room. He glared at Buckley with fire in his eyes and said through clenched teeth. "I apologize." Then he paused. "But I don't think you had the right to—"

"Thank you, Everett, for being so lenient," I interrupted, muffling Dugie's mouth with my hand, and I walked him to the other side of the room. I could see that Buckley was ready to give Dugie a lecture. I shook my head "no" and Everett Buckley again walked away.

"Let him go," he shouted to the booking officer, and Dugie and I were soon back out into the sunlight, Dugie still arguing his cause all the way to the Salem Willows Pier.

His boat was tied up to the pier, and in it, waiting patiently for Dugie's return, was Deputy Dicky Geary and a well-built bespectacled man with a large nose and tight kinky hair. Dugie introduced him as George MacKinnon, originally from Prince Edward Island,

Canada, who had spent most of his life in Salem. I sat at the stern of
the boat as Dugie, still in a fuss, straightened out his equipment and
sucked on a beer. I told MacKinnon that it seemed strange that both
of us grew up in Salem, yet I had never met him before. Mackinnon
had a deep hearty laugh.

"How old do you think I am?" he asked.

"About my age," I replied, "late thirties, early forties."

"I'm fifty-four," he replied with a whimsical smile.

"He was a commando in World War II," piped up Dicky Geary,
"one of Carlson's Raiders."

"I was at Guadalcanal, Bogenville, and Guam," said George, "finally wounded after most of my squad got wiped up by the Japs."

"He really got shot up," said Dicky with pride, as if it was his experience rather than MacKinnon's, "and he lost an eye," Dicky added
with effect, pointing to MacKinnon's right eye. I found myself staring at George's eye, trying to find any difference in it from his good
eye.

Dugie started the engine. "Are you coming with us, Sheriff, or do
you have better things to do?" he asked sarcastically.

"Of course. I'll have to be the helmsman, 'cause Buckley told me
not to let you drive," I said. So, off we went out to sea, the four of us,
to enjoy the remainder of Labor Day. Before the day was over, I hired
George MacKinnon as a deputy sheriff, and he proved to be one of
my best. Dugie Russell was surprised that I hired his buddy George,
but he was shocked that at the end of the year, at the department's
annual dinner, I announced that I had selected George MacKinnon
as "Deputy Sheriff of the Year." George had a perfect record of service in the jail and courts, and many times contributed services beyond
the call of duty. That being said, his new career as deputy didn't start
out promising. His first assignment, as Dugie is quick to remind both
George and me, "was a disaster."

In his new green uniform and Smokey-the-Bear hat, (which sat
atop George's fuzzy hairdo "like a dish on a Brillo-Pad," Dugie
would say) George was assigned to the Newburyport Courthouse.
His duties on his first day as a rookie placed him outside the front

door of the courthouse, not far from a traffic signal for vehicles and pedestrians on crowded High Street. His orders were to remain at the courthouse door. A young woman pushing a baby carriage and holding the hand of a toddler in tow waited in front of the courthouse for the light to change so that she and her children could cross the street. George MacKinnon, forever a courteous gentleman, leaped from his assigned station and rushed to the side of the over burdened woman.

"May I help madam?" asked George in his booming voice.

"Thank you, yes," said the woman. "This light doesn't seem to change to allow pedestrians to cross. I keep pushing the button but nothing happens."

"Follow me," said George, stepping out into the street with both hands stretched out to stop traffic. There was the screeching of brakes from vehicles heading in both directions...a thud and an enormous crash. The pedestrian way was clear for the woman and her child and carriage to pass, but two automobiles and a pickup truck had slammed into each other. The truck was spitting hot water and steam from its radiator into the street. A crowd began to gather. The woman driver in the nearest car to George had a look of shocked panic on her face. "Are you all right Madam?" asked George. She nodded that she was, but needed a moment to compose herself. The truck driver was furious.

"What the hell are you doing, walking out into the middle of traffic to stop everyone. What do you think we have traffic lights for?"

"It wasn't working," said George. The man pointed up at the light, now turned green for pedestrians.

"You caused this accident, buster! What the hell outfit you work for anyway?"

"You're overreacting," said George and he quickly walked back into the courthouse and closed the door behind him; he refused to speak of the incident again.

Deputy Dicky Geary, the other member of Dugie's Labor Day boat crew, wasn't without incident either, causing great consternation on a number of occasions once he was appointed deputy sheriff. I had already appointed his brother Charlie a deputy months before, and it was Charlie who approached me to hire his younger brother, who he said was a tireless worker. I had everyone checked out before hiring, so there was usually a few weeks time delay from when I put in someone's papers, to when he began serving. I asked Charlie if his brother had ever been in trouble. "Just typical kid stuff," Charlie replied. I needed a good tough deputy right away to transport inmates to and from court, and I felt that if Dicky Geary was as tough as his older brother, he'd be a good addition to the team. I began the process of checking Dicky Geary's record, but on Charlie's word, I broke policy and hired him on the spot. For the first two weeks he worked out well. From my office window, I could watch him barking orders to long lines of cuffed prisoners heading off to court early in the morning. We didn't have any disturbances, and we didn't have any attempted escapes from the paddy wagon. But soon after, his rising star fell fast when Deputy Bethune came into my office with a photo of Dicky with a long list of numbers under it. It was on one of our old jail inmate cards – Dicky Geary had been an inmate at the Salem Jail. Now I was in big trouble; the people that Dicky was guarding each day were his old pals—possibly even his old cellmates.

"What on earth do I do now?" I cried, not knowing if my question was to Warren or to God.

"Well," said Warren, "his brother wasn't too far off when he told you it was typical kid stuff, 'cause he was only seventeen when he got in trouble, and in the old days, kids came to jail for a variety of petty crimes. And since they're all things he did before he became an adult, maybe we can seal his record. Do you know any of the Governor's Councilors?"

"Yes, I know two," I said. "What can they do?"

"They can seal Dicky's old record if you ask them to, and no one will be the wiser."

And so, Warren Bethune's wisdom and experience came to my aid once again. I called in Charlie and Dicky Geary and gave them both hell for not telling me that Dicky had been a guest at our hotel. I called in an old political debt and had Dicky's record sealed by the

Governor's Council. Then I moved him to the Lawrence jail. I would later realize how big a mistake this was, but not before I had to also question his brother Charlie's actions on the job.

Charlie Geary caused me some real discomfort when he teamed up with the overly aggressive George Dobson and volunteered to patrol the little country town of Hamilton during the night shifts with our new/old police cruiser. The city of Peabody gave the sheriff's department a discarded vehicle from their police department. Peabody was getting new cruisers, and we were more than happy to receive one of their hand-me-downs. During the day, we would use the cruiser to transport inmates to and from court appearances, but at night it would remain idle. Then the Hamilton police chief asked for our help in patrolling the many county roads within our jurisdiction. The chief was alone but for one patrolman at night and he welcomed our assistance. It is, in fact, a county sheriff's duty to assist rural police at every opportunity, and this gesture of help seemed fitting and appropriate. I was truly pleased to have Dobson and Geary representing the department on a volunteer basis and made the mistake of mentioning to them that possibly other small towns and villages in the county might call on us for assistance. I should have kept my mouth shut.

After our third evening of helping out on the road, the *Salem Evening News* headlined on its front page: "Sheriff's Men Irk Town Chiefs." I knew nothing of the problem until seeing the article by Carl Johnson, one of Jim Shea's reporters. The lead paragraph read:

> That green and white cruiser with its flashing lights that has been whizzing around in various North Shore communities with the county sheriff's seal emblazoned on it has stirred up a hornet's nest among smaller town police chiefs and their residents. The cruiser was highly visible in Gloucester this week with its lights flashing, and Tuesday night it stopped at Essex emergency communications center and left a message for the chief from its two uniformed occupants that, 'We are in town to help out with the police work'...With the exception of the

Hamilton chief, most police chiefs said emphatically that they
did not want or need a sheriff's department highway patrol, and
in fact, they had no knowledge that Sheriff Robert E. Cahill
was providing such a service....

I, of course, was not providing such a service to the other small town
chiefs, Dobson and Geary had obviously overstepped their bounds by
leaving the note for The Essex police chief, but so did Editor Jim
Shea by exaggerating the situation. The reporter had interviewed all
the town police chiefs and reported each of their comments. The
Chief of Rowley said, "I know nothing about it and I think it would
just be a duplication of service...." The Chief of Middleton said, "I
was never informed of such a service and I wonder how well trained
the patrol would be. I don't need the sheriff's help at this time." The
Chief of Ipswich said, "I see no need for it," and the Manchester Police Chief said, "I'm not keen about the idea. I thought the sheriff
needed all of his men to confront his own problems." The Wenham
chief commented, "How can they lend meaningful assistance to us? If
there are funds available for such a patrol, they should be funneled
into the towns and allow them to beef up their own patrols." Chief
Jim Platt of Essex, who received the note from Dobson, stated he was
"surprised" and "had not been informed by the sheriff that such a
program was under way or was going to be instituted without confer-
ring with the chiefs first...but I see no need for such a service at this
time." The Danvers Chief Ed Farley said that he "did not need or
want any aid from the sheriff's department," but added, "the sheriff is
technically the chief law enforcement officer of the county and can
institute a highway patrol if he wants to." Only the Hamilton Chief,
Bob Poole, said that the patrol had been a help to him.

I told the *News* reporter that I thought my deputies were
overzealous in approaching the Essex Police Chief, and that I would
have most certainly called for a meeting of all the chiefs before attempting to instigate such a program. Besides, all I had was one old
beat-up cruiser and we needed it for our own purposes. "No permission was granted by me to use this car in any other town or city other

than Hamilton. From now on the cruiser will only be used to transport prisoners," I told Johnson. The *News* printed my statement in a small column the next day, under the headline: "Unwanted Cruiser Grounded By Cahill." The damage was done and Jim Shea, as usual, had undermined my attempts to be of service and to improve my department. He had all these chiefs interviewed in a front-page story published before he or his reporter even spoke to me to get my side of the story. Of course, I was an easy target for Shea; I was an inexperienced law enforcement man trying to drag Essex County's correctional system out of the Dark Ages, and from time to time, with the willing help of my deputies, I unwittingly undermined myself.

One side note that came out of Carl Johnson's article was a statement made about George Dobson that I felt obliged to check out. In the article, Johnson wrote, "Dobson of Danvers had shot himself while serving as a member of the Registry of Motor Vehicles motorboat division...." The article went on to quote Manchester Police chief Felix Radack, saying, "He was surprised that 'Red' Dobson is still with the sheriff's office because of previous problems." What previous problems? What shooting? Of course, there were a lot of things going on in my department that I didn't know about and some I didn't care about, but this seemed like something I should know. I called Dobson into my office. He admitted that while he was with the registry, he had accidentally shot himself in the foot with his revolver. Others said that he had blamed the shooting on two members of a motorcycle gang, who were falsely arrested for the alleged crime but were later released when Dobson embarrassingly admitted that he had been a victim of his own misfiring.

While I contemplated what to do with Dobson, he unexpectedly turned his revolver over to another deputy sheriff of mine, John "Jumbo" Haley, a tall, lanky, amiable guy. Haley was on duty at the Holiday Inn in Peabody, secretly guarding key witnesses in a kidnapping case that was being heard in Essex County Superior Court. Charlie Geary was in charge of hiding these special witnesses who were watched day and night until they testified in court. He placed them in various hotels or motels in and around Essex County until the court cases came up for trial and the witnesses were called into court. Geary came to me once and said, "How will I ever know if the place where we are hiding them is compromised or someone recognizes a witness in a lobby or something like that?"

"I will let you know," I told Charlie.

"How will you know?" he asked. "There's no way you'll ever find out where we're hiding," he scoffed.

"Remain where you are with the witnesses under constant guard until you hear from me."

Inevitably, I would get a phone call or a tip saying someone saw Charlie Geary here or there and I'd call Charlie on the phone. "Move!" I'd shout over the speaker. "You've been found out. Find another hiding place." Charlie never could figure out how I knew he was compromised, but it seemed that people would always tell me if they saw one of my deputies somewhere, and if they saw Geary or one of the other guards of a protected witness, I would have them move quickly to another spot, usually from one hotel, motel or inn to another. If I could compromise their location, certainly anyone who wanted to do away with a key witness could do so as well.

Jumbo Haley and my old outspoken pal Jim Walsh were secretly guarding two key witnesses at the Holiday Inn and had been doing so for over a week, day and night, throughout a crucial trial. Even though Jimmy Walsh had a gun, Dobson, who was on day guard duty, thought Jumbo Haley should carry one at night…just in case. Jumbo hadn't handled a gun since his army days some twenty years earlier. Unfortunately, Dobson gave Jumbo a loader revolver. Curious about his new toy, Jumbo cocked the hammer.

"How do I uncock this thing?" he asked Jim Walsh. Jim's gun was not a revolver and he didn't know how to place the hammer back down without pulling the trigger and having the gun go off. So Jumbo tried uncocking it by placing a pencil under the hammer. "Bam!" Jumbo shot himself in the leg. Jim immediately tied a tourniquet to Jumbo's bleeding right leg and called for an ambulance. Jumbo was rushed to emergency at J.B. Thomas Hospital and placed in intensive care. The leg was saved. As the police filled the Holiday

Inn, Jim Walsh had to rush out a side door with the undercover witnesses to find another secure hideaway. When I went to visit Jumbo Haley in the hospital, he was more worried about whether I was going to fire him for shooting himself than he was about his wounds. I assured him I was not, but I was looking for Dobson who was lying low. I soon instituted a mandatory gun instruction and training program, and although I never carried a gun, I attended the classes. I feared that had I been in Jumbo's shoes that night at the Holiday Inn, I probably would have done the same thing he did. Like Jumbo, I'm an old army man, but we never learned the ins and outs of a revolver at boot camp. My instruction had been in the M-1 and 45 calibers, long outdated and of no use to law enforcement agencies. The only discipline I dispensed at the time was against Dobson. I took away his badge.

✳ ✳ ✳

It was at about this same time that our department was having problems with dope getting into the jails; it was especially a problem at the Lawrence Jail where Ryan was catching whiffs of marijuana smoke almost every night. As much as we all tried, we couldn't catch the smokers or seem to figure out how it was getting to them. Ryan thought it was coming in through the visitor's center and, in some unknown way, being passed on to inmates. Guards kept a sharp eye out during visiting hours and everyone who entered the hall was searched without success. Yet, marijuana was somehow getting into the cellblocks. Ryan's office had a series of peepholes, created when the jail was built, allowing the jail keeper to keep an eye on all sections of the building, including the visitor's waiting room. Ryan and I decided to station a trusted guard at the visitor's room peephole in his office so that he could spy on the visitors as they waited to enter the main hall to visit with their incarcerated loved ones. No one knew about our sneaky peeper except for me, Ryan, and The Peeper himself, whose name remains anonymous. Ryan had to be in Boston on the day of our sting, so The

Peeper was to call me in Salem if he spotted anything unusual. When I hadn't heard from him by 2:00 p.m., I called him. He reported that he had seen nothing unusual.

"Have you checked the bathroom?" I asked.

"No," he replied, "Only two visiting women have used it since early morning, but no one else."

"Go check it," I said. "Look everywhere—in the bowl, behind the crapper, the ceiling. Everywhere. I'll wait."

The Peeper returned within four minutes. "There's a hefty bag of marijuana taped to the back of the toilet tank," reported The Peeper, excited and out of breath. "What should I do now?" he asked.

"Nothing," I replied, "just keep peeping, and if anyone else goes into that bathroom, let me know immediately."

I waited impatiently at the phone until 4:30 p.m. and called The Peeper again. "No one has gone in there?" I asked, thinking it strange that our unknown "bagman" had not yet picked up the package of marijuana in an attempt to secrete it into the cellblock. "Check the bathroom again," I told The Peeper. "I'll wait."

Three minutes later The Peeper returned to the phone, gasping. "Sheriff, the stuff is gone...disappeared."

I couldn't believe it. "Are you sure nobody has entered the bathroom since those visiting ladies were in there?"

"No one, Sheriff, I swear...that is, no one but your cousin who went in there to clean and tidy the place up about a half hour ago."

"My cousin???" I shouted at The Peeper. "I have no cousin working up there!!!"

"The guy who you sent up to us a couple of months ago. He tells everyone that he's your cousin."

"Well, he isn't. What's his name?"

"Geary, I think...Dick Geary."

"You go into the jail and drag Dicky Geary back to Ryan's office, and I want you to strip search him immediately, then call me back."

Five minutes later, Dicky Geary was on the phone, stating that he knew nothing about what was going on. I didn't want to discuss such an issue over the phone, so I told him to get in his car and drive down here as fast as he could. "I will be waiting for you in my office," I told him.

Almost an hour later, he walked in as nonchalantly as he might walk into a barroom.

"What did you do with the package of marijuana?" I asked him. He looked shocked and stammered. He began to deny seeing or touching it. "You were the only one who entered that bathroom after the package was dropped off there. We have been watching that bathroom all day."

He bowed his head, then said that he had discovered the marijuana while cleaning the bathroom, and got so nervous about it that he flushed it down the toilet.

"I don't buy your story," I told Dicky, "but I'll tell you what. You and I can walk the couple of blocks to the district attorney's office, right now, and you can tell him that story, or you can hand me your badge and resign from the department right now." Dicky hesitated, then unclipped the badge from off his chest, handed it to me, bowed his head again and walked away.

Once Dicky had left the department, wild stories about his on duty escapades circulated back to me. One such story was that while transporting three just-convicted men from the Newburyport court-house to Walpole, he stopped at a liquor store and bought them cans of beer to sip on during the hour-long ride to the prison.

Another tale relayed to me by Dugie Russell, sometime later, was that while he and Dicky Geary were transporting prisoners to Walpole State Prison in Dugie's old convertible, they took one convicted inmate to a last supper before being locked up. "He was a young guy, well dressed," explained Dugie, "and the judge gave him twenty-five years, which means he'd have to serve about seven. There were three older guys, equally well dressed, who had sat through the whole trial. Henchmen types who had flown up from Florida to give the convicted guy moral support. After the sentencing, one of these henchmen palms Dicky Geary a one hundred dollar bill, and whispers to him. 'Please see that the kid gets a good meal before he gets to Walpole.' We headed for Concord State Prison first, where we had to drop off another convicted guy. But then Dicky springs it on me that we have to take this young, well-dressed guy to dinner. Geary has me pull up in front of the Concord Inn. Keep in mind, Sheriff, this guy didn't act like a thug, and a good meal did sound good. Dicky convinced me it would be alright, and he starts to take the handcuffs off this guy. 'Hold it,' I tell him, but Dicky explains that he can't eat with handcuffs on, and the guy swears that he won't try to escape. We went in, got a table in a dark corner. The guy's a wine connoisseur, so we ate steak and drank good wine, spending all the hundred bucks. I'm telling you this, Sheriff, 'cause I know stories have been floating around about Dicky's exploits...believe me, the dinner was all Dicky's idea, not mine."

"And what made you so sure you could trust this guy?" I asked. "He could have easily run off on you or at least given it a try."

"I had my gun on my lap under the table," said Dugie, "and I told the prisoner, 'If you make a move to leave or even look like you're making a move, I'll snuff you out, and then I'll turn the gun on me and snuff myself out.' Dicky jumped half out of his seat and said, 'And where's that leave me.' 'Just where you belong,' I snapped, 'up the creek.'"

Fortunately, the prisoner was successfully delivered to Walpole later that evening to serve his time. And Dicky Geary did finally find himself up the creek—South Creek, Georgia, where soon after leaving the department, he moved, to become a preacher.

Newburyport Courthouse

CHAPTER XIV

The Bombers

Hugging New Hampshire's southern border on the Atlantic, Newburyport is one of New England's quaintest towns. At the center of this lovely town is the Newburyport Superior Courthouse, a small, elegant redbrick building that overlooks the downtown and the Merrimack River. It was one of three courthouses under my jurisdiction as high sheriff. The other two—neither as handsome nor as old—are in Salem and Lawrence. The Newburyport Courthouse is an antique, built in 1805, designed by noted Boston architect Charles Bulfinch. It has wood-pegged floors, brass chandeliers, hand-hewn ceiling beams, thumb-nail chairs built in 1740, a vintage crier's desk, and old tables with tops made concave by the tapping and pounding of attorneys over the centuries. One advocate who did a lot of pounding and eloquent pleading here in the mid-1800s was America's great orator, Senator Daniel Webster. The courthouse holds the distinction of being the nation's oldest working courthouse. Forty-six judges of the Massachusetts Superior Court sit there, one at a time, in rotation, to hear major cases. But court is only in session in the summer and early autumn, for the Newburyport Courthouse has only one courtroom, and it has no heating unit. There is no air-conditioning either, but Bulfinch designed it to stand in front of a large pond, facing the river, high up on a hill, where there is almost always a good breeze. Unlike the decrepit old Salem Jail, built only seven years later, this ancient brick gem was declared a National Historic Landmark long before I came onto the scene.

Like the judges who rotated to various courthouses throughout the state of Massachusetts, my deputies and court officers also rotated between the three county courthouses. My old college pal Billy Cox, however, lived in Newburyport, so he became my key deputy for the little courthouse. He was content to run the courtroom every day that a court justice sat to conduct county business.

In the morning, Billy's voice would echo across the large frog pond: "Hear ye, hear ye, hear ye, all those having anything to do before the honorable justices of the Superior Court, now sitting at Newburyport, within and for the County of Essex, give your attendance, draw nigh, and you shall be heard. God save the Commonwealth of Massachusetts."

That same traditional salutation sounded from the crier's bench at Suffolk Superior Court in Boston on the morning of April 22, 1976—followed by a loud explosion. Pandemonium broke out in the court, and when the smoke cleared, twenty-six people were lying on the floor of the courtroom and the corridors. No one was dead, but all were seriously injured, and one fellow had his foot blown off. A man saying he represented the "United Freedom Front" and advocating for another revolution had made a warning phone call earlier in the day. It was America's bicentennial, and the anniversary, almost to the day, of the famous ride of Paul Revere. Like Revere, the caller to the courthouse said that trouble was coming, but his warning was not heeded. This prompted the judges of every courthouse in the Commonwealth to demand protection for their courtrooms—a demand that I, as sheriff, could not fulfill without additional funds. Unlike most other court officers in the state who were salaried, my court officers were paid per diem—by the day—and received their eight dollars an hour only when on duty. If a court session lasted only two hours on any given day, the court officer on duty would be paid $16.00. And there were no fringe benefits—no insurance, no retirement, no paid vacation. It was like everything else in Essex County government—hundreds of years behind the times. The judges insisted I protect the courts by stationing deputies and metal detectors at the doors of the courthouses when the courts were in session. I told the judges that I simply could not comply. Director of County Offices, Jack Barry, stated that the county "is unable to find the money, so the sheriff should go to the Chief Justice of the Superior Court to get relief."

I estimated the cost for detectors and personnel to be approximately $65,000 for three months at the three courthouses. "I will need one officer for every entrance and exit to the courts," I told the Chief Justice. "They will have to work in three eight-hour shifts. I assume you want them there even when court is not in session, and when the courthouse is closed for the day, as well as at night, which is probably when those bombers got into the Suffolk County Court without being detected." He wasn't pleased. It seemed like people were never pleased when I informed them that what they wanted to do would cost money.

In May, the process of funding was hurried along when a jet airplane was blown up on a runway at Boston's Logan Airport– the plane was empty and no one hurt. And things became even more urgent when another bomb, less damaging, but just as frightening, exploded in a Middlesex County courthouse in Lowell. The Chief Justice got most of the money I requested through an emergency bill passed in the legislature. My deputies were pleased as punch. They would finally be making adequate money. The detectors were set up in Lawrence and Salem Superior Court Houses, and the question of whether deputies would guard the courthouses after daily court sessions was left up to the discretion of the sitting judges. I would constantly press the judges, as I did Charlie Reardon, to keep the deputies on the three-shift watch, at least until the culprits of the so-called "United Freedom Front" were caught.

There was one bomb-threat phoned into the Salem Superior Court in June, and the entire court and the county offices next door were evacuated during lunch hour. It was a hoax, and all county employees had a two-hour lunch. Two weeks later, the same thing happened at the Lawrence Court House, also at noontime. It too was a false alarm. These hoaxsters were never caught, but their dastardly deeds added considerably to the fear felt by judges, juries, county employees, and all those who had to visit the courthouses for any reason.

During peak hours of court sessions in Salem, I had two deputies at the front door of Superior Court working the metal detector and frisking all who entered. They also searched all briefcases and packages being carried in, and stopped any suspicious characters from entering the building. I had one judge, however, who insisted that I put an additional armed deputy in the courtroom with him for protection before and during court sessions. I told this judge, as politely as possible, that I could not spare an extra man for such personal service. Some judges acted like prima donnas before the bomb scare, used to being waited on hand and foot by court officers; but now, some of them, like this one judge at Salem Superior Court, had become paranoid and seriously feared for their lives every moment in the courthouse. I was adamant that special arrangements just couldn't be made. I didn't have the manpower, and I didn't have extra money to pay for such service. I found out that he had ordered one of the deputies who were assigned to the front door to stand by him in court. I called my colleague, Cape Cod Sheriff Jerry Bowes, the truly learned one amongst sheriffs. He knew all the rules and regulations of Sheriffdom.

"I want to kick this pansy-assed judge in the ass. How do I go about it?" I asked.

"You can call the Chief Justice and complain," said Jerry, "or you can call the judge into his own chambers for a discussion and then read him the riot act. But don't say anything to him while he's in the courtroom, or he'll get you for contempt, and you may end up behind your own bars. Just remember, he's fair game for battle in his private chambers, but not in the courtroom."

I rushed down to the court complex, only a couple of blocks away. The court was in recess, and the judge was in chambers. Deputy Sheriff Joe Ross was there to greet me outside the Judge's chambers with a sickly smile. I didn't even knock on the judge's door, but burst in on him as he nibbled on a sandwich.

" Judge, you return that armed deputy to the front door of the courthouse and do not take him into your courtroom again."

"Or what?" said the surprised but indignant judge.

"Or I'll close down the courthouse," I said, my nose almost in his sandwich.

"Get this man out of my chambers," the judge ordered Ross, whose lips had turned pale. Joe's eyes widened in horror. As a deputy sheriff and court officer, Joe Ross had spent most of his life reacting to any and all whims of the judges, but I was his real boss, and he knew it. As the judge and I stared daggers at each other, Ross tried to appease us both.

"I'm staying right here," I told the judge, "and unless you release the deputy from the courtroom and return him to the front door, you will leave these chambers, and everyone else, including you, will leave the courthouse. I am in charge of all security and safety here, and I deem this building insecure without two qualified deputies at the front door during court sessions. I'll give you two minutes, Judge, to release my man, or you will be responsible for this closing."

Ross tried to break us up again, afraid one of us might take a punch at the other. I ordered Ross to leave the room, and the judge ordered him to stay. Poor Joe Ross didn't know what to do; he just stood at the door, mouth agape. I turned to let him see the angry expression on my face, and he left, closing the door quietly behind him. The judge, just as angry as I was, grabbed his phone and quickly dialed the Chief Justice. He told his boss that I was a madman, and that I threatened to close the courthouse. I grabbed the phone from the judge's hand, and explained my dilemma to the Chief Justice: without proper security at the front door, I would have to close down the courthouse. Like Jerry Bowes, the Chief Justice knew the laws of the Commonwealth well. He asked me to hand the phone back to his Superior Court Judge, who returned my deputy to the front door within five minutes.

I walked back to the jail, surprised that my legs were shaky, and that I felt jittery. The feeling sent my mind traveling back to the time I had been scuba diving alone in the Red Sea, and came face to face with a gray shark. I was more surprised than nervous when I saw it, and it sent a rush of adrenaline through my veins. When I got out of the water, I felt the same shaky energy I felt at this moment. I had confronted one of those overly pampered black-robed sharks and had survived the conflict.

After three months of protecting the courthouses from these phantom bombers, the money was getting tight again. The Chief Justice asked me to cut back the number of guards at the Lawrence Courthouse, and to completely forget Newburyport when court wasn't in session. But the Fourth of July was coming up over a long four-day holiday, and these bombers seemed to like American holidays; significant dates in Revolutionary War history seemed to light their fuses—literally and figuratively. I had just enough special fund money and willing personnel to cover the holiday weekend in Salem with two men around the clock, and in Lawrence with two men at night, and one during the day. But I didn't have enough to cover Newburyport; I called the Chief Justice.

"It's an antique," I told him. "It's significantly historic, and if it blows, we could never replace it." The Chief Justice was apparently sick and tired of spending so much money at the courthouses, and he refused to cover Newburyport.

As the evening of the Fourth of July holiday began, I was at my brother Jim's house, situated on the North River, across from the Salem Jail, awaiting a fireworks display, when the phone rang. It was an FBI agent, or so the caller said. "Are all the courthouses covered?" he asked. "We've had a warning call that Essex County courthouses are due for action on the Fourth."

"All but one," I replied.

"Better cover it," he replied and hung up.

Now I was in a quandary. I had to find deputies who would be willing, on short notice, to spend their holiday guarding vacant buildings from mad bombers. I called the Chief Justice again and told him about the call from the FBI, but again, he told me he couldn't pay the deputies. I needed volunteers, but I couldn't find anybody at home. Everybody was out celebrating the fourth. As a last resort, I called Bill Cox, hoping that he might volunteer. He was in the midst of a big house party—it was his birthday. Bill was a real Yankee Doodle Dandy—the image of James Cagney born on the Fourth of July. Billy was willing, but he was also loaded and slurring his words; I couldn't have him guard the courthouse in that condition. "I have a premonition," said Coxy, and he hung up. Four hours later, Billy's premonition became reality. The pretty little Newburyport Courthouse exploded into the night. Coxy heard the "boom," but thought it was just part of the on-going bicentennial celebrations.

The courthouse wasn't completely destroyed, but there was considerable damage to this rare antique. The bombers had used seventeen sticks of dynamite for the job. High Street was cordoned off, and money became miraculously available for my deputies to guard the charred rubble. It was like guarding the barn after the horses had escaped, but necessary to prevent the ransacking of the portion of the building that remained standing and undamaged. The following evening, across the river from Newburyport, in Seabrook, New Hampshire, the post office exploded, leaving it in near ruins. An unidentified man called the Seabrook Fire department that evening and told the chief that he was the bomber, and that his plan was to return to Newburyport the next night to finish off the old courthouse. Apparently, the bomber was disappointed that he hadn't completely destroyed the ancient building. Now, everyone felt that what was left of the courthouse should be guarded day and night, and the legislature provided the funds.

FBI Boston agent Joe Yablonsky told me that he and his men were in close pursuit of two men for the Newburyport Courthouse bombing, Dick Picariello and Ed Gullion, both of Maine. They were considered suspects in eleven bombings, and were thought to have stolen 600 pounds of dynamite from a New Hampshire drilling company. Plus they were implicated in the attempted kidnapping of Polaroid Corporation President William McCune. These were obviously bad boys we were dealing with.

Two months went by, and the culprits still hadn't been captured. The money to guard all three courthouses in Essex was now coming from the county's general fund, and it was costing the county a near fortune—about $6,000 a week. The mayors on the County Advisory Board, charged with cutting spending in county government, were greatly distressed about this unanticipated expense. Leading the concerned mayors was Mayor Byron Mathews of Newburyport, who, at a board meeting stated that, "Its not fair to the taxpayers. The county commissioners should take immediate steps to stop over-protecting and over-reacting. It's been two months since the Newburyport bombing, and we've gone beyond the point of showing our great concern."

Before I could react to the mayors, Jack Barry, the county's administrative assistant did it for me. "Once Picariello is apprehended," he told the press, "we'll take a good look at the situation, but as long as he's at large, the threat is there." I had never considered Jack Barry an ally, for he often disputed my budget requests, but I certainly welcomed his comments. The members of the County Advisory Board and the newspaper columnists continued to squawk about the expenditures well into the following months.

It was during this jittery time of exploding packages and bombers on the loose that I received a package on the front stoop of my Salem home at Forty Felt Street. When I opened the front door, the package was sitting on the top brick step. I had no idea if the mailman had left it there or not. It was a square box, about the size of a milkcrate, covered in brown wrapping paper, and tied up with a knotted rope. There were scribbled block letters in thick black ink all over the outside of the package. I picked up the box—it wasn't very heavy— and read the various notes on either side of my name and address. They looked almost as if a young child had printed them, and there was no return address. There were plenty of stamps, seemingly more than a package of its size and weight needed, and I began to well up with suspicion that gave way to fear. Written on the box in the childish hand were various slogans: "Sorry, Hope this isn't too late," "I'm sure you weren't expecting this," "We've been trying to get you for a long time." I started to imagine disgruntled former inmates writing these little sayings, chuckling to themselves as they pictured me opening the package to a loud awesome blast.

"Not me, fella," I told myself as I placed the box carefully back on the stairs and directed my wife and kids to leave the house out the back door. Then I told them that we might have a bomb on the front stairs. This, of course, electrified my kids, and they raced out of the back yard to alert all the kids in the neighborhood about the bomb, who of course, alerted their parents. I called what I considered my

"Bomb Squad," Deputies Carl Majeskey and George MacKinnon, and asked them to get to my house, pronto. Majeskey, a former Massachusetts state trooper, had been called in on bomb dismantling situations earlier in his career, and MacKinnon, a decorated World War II marine veteran, knew a lot about explosives and was brave as hell.

They arrived to a great gathering of people outside my house, all keeping a good distance from my front stoop; neighbors were semicircled across the street and on their front lawns, gaping at the sloppily wrapped box sitting at my front door. George MacKinnon, in his take-charge manner, motioned for everyone to back up. I opened the front door to meet Majeskey face to face. He asked me every conceivable question about the box.

"Did the mailman deliver it?"

"I don't know."

"Do you know where it came from?"

"I don't know."

It seemed strange having this conversation standing over the box while George pushed others further away.

"Is there a lake or any water nearby where we can dunk it?" asked Carl.

"There's the river down the street, and I've got a little manmade rock pond in my backyard. "

"Good," said Carl. So he broke a long branch from a nearby tree, hooked it under the rope of the box, and with George leading the way through the back gate, Carl carried the box on the branch to the edge of the pond. Kids were hanging off my stockade fence to peek at the proceedings, and neighbors were pushing and shoving their way into my backyard. Some less adventurous ones kept their distance from the box, folded their arms and stood there to watch. George kept raising his arms and motioning them to move back, but nobody moved. I stood at my back door and insisted that my kids stand near me.

"How do we know we're far enough away?" asked Ben Walsh, my next-door neighbor, and the brother of my deputy, Jim Walsh.

"We don't," I replied, "but you might make last call for dinner in heaven if you're wrong." He gave me a sickly smile and moved back to the yard gate. Carl had George lift the box from the edge of the pond and, using the branch, begin dunking it into the water, once, twice, three times. Then Carl had George lift the box, with the branch, back to the rock wall at the edge of the pond. Carl approached the box and began carefully cutting away the paper covering with a jackknife. The crowd was silent. The kids clinging to the top of the stockade fence stared in awe. Holding the dripping box in one hand, Carl cut away the cardboard with the other. If the bomb weren't the type to be diffused by water, it would blow up right in his face. Then something metal appeared, and the crowd sucked in their collective breaths with an "UHHHH" sound. Carl cut further, gingerly, careful not to let the metal object fall to the ground. It was brass…it was a foot…it was a foot kicking something. Carl tore away the box further, and there for all to behold was a small football player made of brass, about eight inches high, kicking a football. Attached was a plaque, which read, "Rams Football, Salem Midget League - In Appreciation to Coach Bob Cahill." Carl and George breathed a sigh of relief. The crowd, especially the kids, giggled, then laughed loudly, then cheered and clapped. I turned red as the ripest apple. I don't think I've ever been so embarrassed.

The bombers were caught a few weeks later. They were tried and convicted of a series of thefts and bombings—a new breed of revolutionaries with senseless destruction their only motive. My deputies went back to their measly eight dollars an hour, paid only when court was in session. The Newburyport Courthouse didn't get back into full service for three years, but the wounds of the July Fourth explosion are well hidden today. She continues on as America's oldest working courthouse.

"Hear ye, hear ye, hear ye, all those having anything to do before the honorable justices of the Superior Court, now sitting at Newburyport, within and for the County of Essex, give your attendance, draw nigh, and you shall be heard. God save the Commonwealth of Massachusetts," cries Billy Cox.

CHAPTER XV

The Pumpkin Patch

I had been in office for over a year and the problems kept piling up, one on top of the other, coming faster than I could find solutions, and some seemed unsolvable. The over crowding in both jails was causing serious problems, especially in Salem. There was just no place to bunk some inmates, so they were forced to sleep on the floors. In order to make up for our shortage of bedding and linens, we needed access to stores of government surplus mattresses, sheets, and blankets. I asked the City of Salem to make the jail an emergency headquarters for civil defense, as Bill Ryan did in Lawrence, which allowed us to acquire free survival surplus items from the federal government. Bill Ryan even picked up two old vehicles out of the deal, which he had the inmates repair and paint for shuttle service back and forth to the courts.

Lack of communication equipment, especially telephone service to the various police departments, was also creating enormous problems. I went before the Massachusetts legislature, with the blessing of all the county police chiefs, to push for the installation of a countywide radio system that we could all use for emergencies and for sharing information on criminals. Not only was the sheriff's department at a loss for quick communications during escapes or other emergencies, but the small towns of the county were as well. There were many examples of bank robberies, murders, and other crimes in tiny towns like Newbury and Boxford where only a single policeman was on duty, leaving nobody else around to pursue criminals as they sped from town to city to town to make good their escape. There also was no communications between the various city police cruisers. It was a nightmare; the left hand never knew what the right hand was doing. I had strong backing from all the police chiefs in the county with the exception of the Lynn chief who, for some unknown reason, didn't

think such communication was necessary. As much as I pleaded with
my old colleagues in the state house for the funding, it didn't look
good. It was expensive, and legislators from the other counties
wanted new systems and equipment for police departments in their
districts as well. I pressed the Democrats and Bill Ryan pressed the
Republicans. Surprisingly, the bulk of state money slated for local police equipment went to our old pal Sheriff Cliff Marshall of Norfolk
County on the south side of Boston. It was explained that his communications plan was simpler and much cheaper than ours. The fact
was that Cliff had more influential pals in the "Old Boy Network"
than Ryan and I had.

※ ※ ※

I was truly disappointed and couldn't see how we would ever get any
positive changes made without the needed funding from the legislature, but Billy Ryan, always the resourceful optimist, quickly switched
his focus to solving other problems and came up with an alternate
source of support. The old Essex County Reform School, located in
Lawrence on the Merrimack River, only a mile from the jail, had
been closed for two years, and the county commissioners, with the
blessing of the county advisory board and a legislative commission,
were putting it up for sale. I had, in fact, opposed the closing of the
school while I was in the legislature, but I was out-voted by my
county colleagues. The school sat on 14 acres and included: two main
buildings, a barn, out buildings, and a brand new, never been used
gymnasium, built at county expense. It had housed only a few boys
from age 6 to 16, but it was considered a white elephant—expensive
to operate and outmoded as a way to discipline and teach delinquent
kids. In the wisdom of the majority of senators and state representatives of Massachusetts, it was closed, and the boys put into local
homes or let free to wander the world. The facility now stood vacant,
costing the county some $90,000 a year to operate—heat, lights,
caretakers. It was a thorn in the side of the new advisory board, made
up of city mayors and town selectmen who were charged with

squeezing every cent of waste out of the county budget. "It must be sold to the highest bidder," cried members of the advisory board in unison, to the dismay of the county commissioners who really wanted to keep it under their jurisdiction. Since the founding of the county advisory board by the state legislature, the three county commissioners were slowly but surely losing power and property and were trying to ebb the tide with the school property. Nobody in the county, however, knew what to do with it. Billy Ryan knew exactly what to do with it.

"Let's ask the commissioners to turn it over to us," said Ryan, full of enthusiasm.

"So, then we'd have another white elephant," I replied. "Don't we have enough problems already?"

"But we need space," said Ryan, "and this place has a lot of space."

"They also want one-million dollars for the place, and they've been offered $750,000—how can we compete with that? We have no money to buy it. Even the city of Lawrence has offered them $500,000.

"We can say that we'll restore the old farm, using inmates on work release to grow vegetables there like the truant kids once did. We'll save the county money on food by feeding fresh vegetables to the inmates. We could even get a couple of cows and pigs..." Ryan kept rattling on. I knew he was a frustrated farmer, and at first it sounded like a crazy and unworkable idea, but the more he talked, the more he made sense. Even though we didn't have enough correctional officers, money, or supplies for the two jails we already had, we figured if we could send our best to run the place and start with a few trusted inmates, we could create a wonderful new work release center that might relieve pressure on our other jails.

"And if we need extra dough, we can bring in federal prisoners. No one heavy," said Ryan, "but tax evaders and crooked politicians, people who are harmless and cause no problems. The Feds will pay us $22.00 a day per prisoner, which I'm sure would please the county commissioners, and the Feds are crying to find places to unload some guys."

"No state prisoners though," I interjected. "The state's always looking for new places to pawn off cons, but they always send real bad bastards, ones that will give you an me trouble—we don't want them."

"But they pay better than the feds," said Ryan.

"I don't care. The state can't be trusted. You never know who they're going to send you. They've sent me a lot of bad-asses who they said were harmless. We've got enough troubles without their shit."

"Agreed," said Ryan. "When do we go to the commissioners with our idea?"

"It won't work, you know," I told him. "No way are the commissioners going to give us a fourteen acre farm with barracks, classrooms, a barn, and a new gymnasium."

"Of course," said Ryan again, "but let's go after it anyway."

I drew up a proposal and hand-carried it down to the commissioners' office at Superior Court. I was hardly back in my office when I had a call from Dan Burke, the chairman of the county commissioners. He liked my idea, mainly because it kept the property in county hands. He asked me to contact the other commissioners and to be ready to attend an advisory board meeting on the subject within a week. I was also to send a copy of my proposal to State Representative Jack Murphy, head of the special legislative committee on county property.

"You know," said Dan Burke, "you don't have a chance in hell of getting this."

"I know," I said.

I decided to do some serious lobbying of the county commissioners ahead of the advisory board meeting. I called Commissioner Katherine Donavan, a Lawrence teacher whose students were already using the gym every week for an annual fee of $1.00—so obviously, she was in favor of the property going to the city of Lawrence.

The third commissioner, Ed Cahill of Lynn (No relation of mine, although my paternal grandparents were also from Lynn. He was descended from the Galway Cahills, and my ancestors were county Cork Cahills, but somewhere in ancient Irish history we surely were related.) had a reputation of being tight with the county dollar, but always fair. He couldn't see how I could make it work at the training Center in Lawrence, and he was determined to sell the property for no less than one million dollars. Commissioner Cahill felt that a local businessman named Kilcoyne might be willing to pay over one million dollars to turn the facility into a residential retirement center. "Besides," he informed me, "the people of Lawrence don't want criminals who aren't locked up as their neighbors."

Ed was right, of course. Who'd want inmates for neighbors, especially with school kids sharing the gymnasium? Why was I wasting time and energy trying to get my hands on property that was way out of reach?

"Keep going," prompted Ryan, my cheerleader, "What have we got to lose, and what a great prize if we get it."

I appeared one stormy Saturday morning before the county commissioners, the advisory board, and my old legislative colleague State Representative Jack Murphy of Peabody, in Peabody city hall. Most of the mayors and selectmen had made it through the sleet and snow to hear my proposal and vote it down. It was nice to see one particular member of the board, Deputy Sheriff Henry Fournier of Amesbury, because I figured I'd get at least one of the 34 votes—until he excused himself from voting because of a conflict of interest. Mayor John Buckley of Lawrence was there too and was first to plead his case. He wanted the property desperately, and I figured he would get it. Not only was Buckley offering $500,000 for the Lawrence property, but he reminded the group that this very property had been sold to the county by his city of Lawrence in 1898, for $15,000. "Plus the fact that my city has paid fourteen percent of all county taxes since the beginning of time, we have some equity in that property. We have also paid $10,000 in rent over the past two years for using the property." Buckley also intimated that Commission Chairman Dan Burke to stifle the Lawrence takeover of the property for no ~~on~~ than to keep the property in the counties hands. Burke ~~his~~, and reminded all present that county taxpayers were still p~~ ~~ for the recently built $500,000 gymnasium building. The gym opened only a few days before the legislature closed down this school for delinquent boys. Burke mentioned that maybe Mayor Buckley could work something out with the sheriff.

"Absolutely," I was quick to agree. "We can work it so that no inmates are out or around while the children are at the gym. But you must remember as well, that any inmates who would be housed at this facility would be on work release and would be re-entering society within a few weeks anyway. If this becomes a work release center, most, if not all, will be away at work during the day. And if we do have a few federal prisoners to help pay the bills, these are men who are in for such crimes as tax evasion and pose no physical threat to society. The place is now a mess, with piles of trash and weeds covering the fourteen acres. We will clean this up immediately at no cost to the county, and will restore the old farm, producing vegetables that will cut our jail food costs to the county taxpayers. In one of the vacant buildings, we will ask the Massachusetts County Training Academy to move here from the University of Massachusetts in Amherst to train correctional officers. Amherst is inconvenient to most jail guards because it's so far away. The Lawrence property is right off Highway 495 and Route 114. I've already contacted the academy and they're willing to move and pay substantial rent. The other main building will be used for work release, which we've already started at the Salem Jail, with great success—and remember, not only do these men get substantial jobs to prepare them for when they get out, but they begin to pay for their room and board while they're still in jail. The county is now paying some $90,000 just to heat, light and secure the property. I guarantee that the sheriff's department will not only cover those expenses each and every year, but beginning in the second year, we will produce an ever-increasing profit for the county. If I'm not making ends meet within a year, take the property away from me. But I have no doubt that we'll be successful. It will also help alleviate the ever growing and very serious over-crowding problem at both our jails. Turn the Lawrence Training School over to the sheriff's department, and we will work hand-in-hand with the city of Lawrence and their schools," I concluded, smiling at Commissioner Katherine Donavan, "and it won't cost them a cent in rent more than they're paying now." After some questions and wrangling, Commissioner Cahill motioned that the sheriff's department should be allowed to develop the Lawrence property for six months, when our progress would be evaluated as to whether or not we could stay. The board voted and we won with two of the three votes. We would have to move fast to make it work, but if Ryan was willing to give it his all, then so was I. We were both pleased, if a little daunted by our acquisition.

My assistant Jail Keep at the Salem Jail, Warren Bethune, was not happy when I told him I was taking away our best correctional officer, Terry Marks, to run our new facility, which we named "The Correctional Alternatives Center" or CAC. Terry Marks was a great officer who would have been my Deputy Keeper of the Salem Jail if I didn't have Bethune, who I inherited, and who had already served for three other high sheriffs. Terry was pleased with his new appointment. He was a tough but fair officer who possessed administrative abilities as well. All seemed to agree that there was no better man for the job. When I said I needed another top guard, John Kuczun, to help Terry at the new facility, Bethune was livid and came close to quitting his post. "Terry can't run the whole place by himself," I told him, "and hopefully the legislature will give me more money to hire new correctional officers to fill his place." Kuczun, a well liked, seemingly easy going guard, could be real tough with an offender if he had to be, and he was the kind of guy I felt I needed at the new center. These were my two guys in charge and I was putting a lot of responsibility on their shoulders.

"I'm going to send only six work release guys there to begin with, but within a month, I want to send six more. This place is yours to run, and I don't want to be bothered about any petty problems." I told them, "just contact me if you have any major problems and there had better not be any of those." They both nodded with understanding. To round out the new staff, Ryan sent one man to help out, though he was as low on correctional officers as I was and couldn't really spare him. His contribution to the center was Phil Corriveau, a six-feet three inch, four hundred pound former football lineman who had a soft voice and a swift backhand. For the overnight shift, to spend each evening alone with the inmates, I chose Harry Healy. Harry was another easygoing nice guy that could get real tough if you riled him.

Now Ryan and I had a carrot to go with our stick—a nice easy place for inmates to live if they were good and industrious compared to the cramped, smelly cells of our outdated jails. Most of the inmates now clambered to signup for the CAC, but we were only interested in the most well behaved and least vicious of our imprisoned guests. We couldn't afford any trouble at the new place, especially during the first six-month trial period.

When Kuczun and Corriveau weren't overseeing our work release inmates at the Center, they were snatching surplus toilets, sinks, chairs, and cots from the Federal Supply Warehouse and installing better bathrooms, bunk facilities, and living cubicles in the new living quarters. Ryan and I even emptied our own wallets to buy wood and nails. We also started bringing in federal prisoners at $22.00 per day to meet our financial responsibilities.

One problem at the Center was the need for a cook. The men at the Center, inmates and guards, were constantly ordering out for pizza and that was getting expensive.

"The kitchen here is great," Terry informed me, "but we need a cook. The guys we have up here have trouble frying an egg, and I really need another correctional officer anyway." I couldn't spare another correctional officer *and* hire a cook, but if I could find one that could do both, maybe I could tear another man away from Bethune. It would mean cutting the number of guards on the Salem Jail day shift, which would bring us well below minimum guard requirements by the state, but the state's Democratic politicians had kept Essex County's Republican sheriffs under minimum standards for decades, so why, thought I, should I worry about being below standard in guard personnel. When I asked for one page resumes from the guards who had experience as cooks for possible transfer to the new CAC, my deputy jail keeper, Warren Bethune, was one of ten who applied, stating that he wanted the new job because he couldn't run the Salem Jail with any less men than he had now. Warren threatened to quit yet again, but I knew he wouldn't because he had too much time in and hoped to retire within a few years. I calmed him down by telling him that there was probably a good chance of getting money in the next county budget for three new correctional officers—an outright lie—and Warren, although still fuming, was appeased. After receiving all the resumes, I began interviewing the potential cooks. A couple of guards had experience as short-order cooks, and one had been a chef at a popular local restaurant in his younger days. One of the guards applying for the job was Jim St. Pierre, a tall, athletic guy in his late thirties who was an excellent correctional officer, respected by his peers and the inmates. In his short resume he indicated that he had been a cook aboard a ship in the Navy. Coincidentally, I knew a person who had served with Jim St. Pierre on the same ship, and being an old friend, I called him about Jim's expertise as a cook. I thought Jim's old Navy pal would never stop laughing long enough for me to get him off the phone. "The only thing we allowed Jim to cook aboard ship was coffee, and he usually screwed that up," he guffawed.

Next morning I had Jim St Pierre before me imploring me to hire him as cook.

"I see by your resume that you were a cook in the Navy, aboard a destroyer"? He nodded, his face turning red. "How long were you a cook?"

"Oh, I don't know," he stammered. "The regular cook got sick and I took his place."

"For a year, for six months, a week, or what?"

Jim fidgeted in his seat. "Weeks," he managed to blurt out.

I burst out laughing. I couldn't hold it in any longer. "I hear you can't even make a cup of coffee."

"That's a lie," he shouted indignantly. "I make good coffee."

"Well, if that's so," I said, "then you're the new cook at the Lawrence Center." His face brightened, "But I want you to know," I added, "All the other guys who applied for this job, I am convinced are better cooks than you."

His eyes widened in disbelief. "Then why me?" he asked.

"Because you're an outstanding correctional officer, and you know how to deal with the inmates. You're fair and firm, and that's what I need at the new facility. Even though we're sending the cream of the crop to that place, we can't afford a major problem, or the commissioners will take the place away from us."

"Terry Marks is the best man you could get," said Jim.

"I know that, but he can't do it alone, and he needs help. So remember, you are on double duty. You are a correctional officer and you are the cook. Maybe you'll find one of the inmates up there who knows how to turn on the stove." I was smiling but Jim wasn't.

"Really, Sheriff, I'm not a half bad cook. I often cook for my kids when Mary has to work late."

"Don't sweat it," I said, shaking his hand, congratulating him on his new job.

"No extra money, and you'll have to travel farther to get to work, but you'll be free—no more bars and bells and angry men. It won't be a waltz, but it will be a different tune" Jimmy pumped my hand.

"Now I know how inmates feel when they're let out of prison," he said. "I was about to go mad living behind those bars every day …you freed me, Sheriff, and I'm grateful."

"Thanks," I said, "but now you can spend the rest of your time in service behind a hot stove."

Warren Bethune wouldn't speak to me for days and was moody for weeks. He knew that Jimmy St. Pierre was no cook, and I had taken him—one of his best officers—and it didn't make his job any easier. Terry Marks, on the other hand, was pleased as punch. He really didn't care that Jimmy could not cook; he just needed another good man. Jimmy, as pleased as he was, continued to insist through all the teasing about his Navy cooking that he was indeed a very good and experienced cook.

Within three months we had 22 inmates, or "residents," as they were called, at the CAC, and things seemed to be running smoothly as a work release center. We hadn't as yet done anything about starting a farm or clearing the land that was covered with every kind of debris. It looked like the city of Lawrence had been using it as a disposal for the last few years, and a road construction company was still dumping their excavated and unwanted material on the land. We had no farm equipment, no heavy machinery, no farmer, and no plan to acquire any. Yet, I had promised the commissioners and the advisory board a farm with plowed fields and fresh vegetables within six months. Spring was approaching and there was no way to hide the mess on the fields beyond the two main buildings, an eyesore to those passing close by on highway 495 on their way to Boston or New Hampshire. Something needed to be done and the window of opportunity for getting a crop in the ground was closing. Would I dare put out another notice to the correctional officers of Lawrence and Salem that we needed a farmer with a strong constitution and a miraculous green thumb to take over the fourteen acres at the CAC, and have it ship-shape within a couple of months. I really thought Warren was going to choke me to death. He knew that there were a couple of good farmers working in the Salem Jail, especially John Hoctor of Middleton, a good guard and renowned as an excellent farmer.

"I can't afford to lose another man," Warren growled at me. "You're taking all my best men."

I explained to Warren that I had to find a farmer or our department would lose its hold on the center, and it would become a retirement home, or a complex of high-rise apartment buildings. "We have to tighten the belt just one more notch," I told him. Warren really believed that our security was at serious risk. "Even if I personally have to take a shift as a guard, I'm willing to do it," I told him, "but I must have my farm in operation within three months." Warren didn't want me as a guard. I think he thought I was too liberal.

The notice went out to employees, and applications for the job as farmer poured in. Everyone, it seemed, wanted a transfer to the CAC. I interviewed all of them, including my two troublemakers,

Ernie Maynos and Leo Lobeo, who Wells and I inherited from the Old work farm in Middleton. Almost all the inmates who had stayed on that farm had been alcoholics, and some of the guards were too. The Massachusetts legislature had closed the old work farm down a few years before the Lawrence Training School, and the old guards remaining were divided between the Lawrence and Salem Jails. McGhee, Maynos and Lobeo were three who went to Salem, and the conflicts between the old farm guards and the Salem guards started almost immediately. Darby McGhee, I discovered, had excellent counseling abilities and he started up our Alcoholics Anonymous chapter at the Salem Jail, which proved quite successful. I found that Maynos and Lobeo were good workers too, as long as they didn't work together. As a tandem, they were troublemakers who caused serious arguments and fights among the rest of the guards and were constantly complaining about petty things. "They are frustrated having to work behind bars," said Warren, "and so they frustrate everyone else around them." As a team, they constantly affected morale in the jail, harassing other guards, and as often as I talked to them in my office—usually one at a time because I couldn't handle both at once—they either wouldn't listen or just didn't care. During one heated session, Maynos got so worked up that he came over the top of my desk, spitting and fuming about his seniority and need for a raise. I could hold my temper no longer and I came up out of my chair to greet him, fists tightened, my teeth filled with curses louder than his. I was ready to bite off his nose and he knew it. I was angry with myself for losing my composure, but it did cause Maynos to back down into his chair and surprisingly he began to behave like a normal human being. After that episode, Maynos and I got along fine. Lobeo, noted for his hot Portuguese temper, didn't seem to let up. He was full of innuendoes and petty complaints, and surprisingly, he put in for the farmer's job at the CAC.

"I'd love you to take care of this one," said Warren and laughed when he handed me his application. "I'd like to listen into your meeting with him." After talking rather cordially for about a half hour, I asked Leo Lobeo to meet me up at the CAC early the next morning.

I had toured the facility with the most likely candidate, John Hoctor, two days before. Hoctor had looked over the piles of dirt, gravel, cement, and other debris piled high on the land and puffed heavily on his pipe. "What do we do with that?" he asked, "How do we get rid of it? Where do we put it?"

"How the hell do I know?" I answered.

Lobeo, by contrast, looked at the piles of debris and scowled. "A lot of this comes from that road construction crew. I'll have this shit out of here in a couple of days," he said, but he wasn't talking to me, he was talking to the earth. "Peas can go over there, squash here," he was pointing, "potatoes way out there, and corn—lots of corn. You like corn, Sheriff?" he smiled at me. I had never seen him smile before. "How about pumpkins, Sheriff. You want pumpkins. Nothin' like a good pumpkin pie."

I agreed. " One of my favorites."

"What about a tractor?" he asked.

"We don't have one," I replied. "I guess all the farm equipment was taken from here long ago…I don't think the delinquent kids who lived here had worked the farm for years."

"What about help?" asked Leo.

"You'd have to use the inmates," I said. "If we have any potential farmers at either jail and we can trust them to live up here, then I'm willing to let them come up."

"And seed?"

"We don't have a dime for seed," I replied—and to be honest, I hadn't even thought of the need for seed—but my answer didn't seem to faze Leo Lobeo in the least.

"I'll get seed," he said. "When do I start?"

I didn't hesitate, even though I knew John Hoctor would be very disappointed, and everyone else back at the jail would be confounded "You can start tomorrow," I said.

Back at the Salem Jail, I didn't know if Warren Bethune was laughing or crying. He was elated at not having to contend with Leo Lobeo ever again, but he was losing another guard. Terry Marks at the Center also had mixed emotions, as did Jim St, Pierre, but they promised that they would work with Leo to make the farm a success. I was convinced I had picked the right man for the job as farmer. If there ever was a frustrated farmer, it was Leo, and now he had a real challenge before him on which to focus all his pent-up emotions.

"I hope you did the right thing," said Terry. "This could be a disaster."

Before I went to sleep that night I said a prayer for Leo Lobeo. I don't think I really believed he could make it work. I didn't think anyone could.

A week didn't go by that I didn't get a call from the Department of Public Works about one problem or another.

"One of your men is stealing our equipment on the highway," I was told. "Taking pieces off our vehicles so's they won't work."

"Are you the guys that have all your junk strewn over our property at the old Lawrence Training Center off Route 495?"

"We were told we could use that land."

"Not anymore you can't…and you'd better clean it up fast or you'll lose more equipment." – not the answer they were expecting. Leo made them and the State Highway Department clear the land of all the debris before he returned any of their missing parts and equipment.

The next series of calls I got were from local mayors; the first was from Mayor Nick Mavroules of Peabody, and the next two from Mayor Buckley of Lawrence and Mayor Levesque of Salem.

"Bob, one of your men just came in to see me and hit me up for fifty dollars…said he needed it for potato seed."

"Did you give it to him" I asked Nick Mavroules.

"Yes," he replied. "He was very convincing, and after all, he's one of my constituents."

"Good for you," I said, laughing at the thought of it.

The next calls were not as easy to deal with. The Essex Agricultural School in Middleton, also operated by the county, announced to local police that their tractor was missing. Leo had asked the director of Essex Agee if he could use it, and was told no. He borrowed it anyway, and used it to turn our new fourteen acres, preparing it for the seed he purchased with the mayors' money. That job done, Leo returned the tractor. Leo also came back to the Salem Jail to borrow shovels, hoes, and rakes, plus other tools and equipment he needed. Warren was about to press charges, but I stopped him. "It's for a good cause," I reminded him, "and the new center needs the stuff more than Salem Jail does." Leo Lobeo was our unofficial county petty thief and conniver, and he was creating a miracle.

I called Terry Marks to see how things were getting on with Leo, and to my surprise they were getting on well, which eased my nerves about the whole thing. "He spends all his time in the fields or out procuring needed supplies," said Terry. "He doesn't bother me at all, and besides he's a changed man...a driven man. My problem is," said Terry. "He's making good progress, and I'm not! I can't proceed unless I get another carpenter up here to help Kuczun build new cubicles to house more inmates. If you want a few more federal guys to pay the bills, and some twenty-two men on work release by the time the commissioners and the advisory board inspect this place, plus beds for Leo Lobeo's farm helpers, we've got to have another carpenter up here. We'd like Don Richards from Salem who's not only fast, but can do finish work. Plus, he and Kuczun work well together."

I knew that Don Richards, a senior guard at the Salem Jail, was just itching to get to the CAC, and I knew that Terry, John Kuczun, and Jim St. Pierre were chomping at the bit to get him up there. I hated to disappoint Terry, and although the new center was a top priority, I told him, "I just can't take another guard out of the Salem Jail."

"Let us have him for just two weeks," said Terry. "That would help immensely."

"I don't think Warren will allow it. He'll go to the State Commission of Corrections and have me impeached," I told Terry, "but I will ask Warren to let Richards go up there to help you for a couple of days." Warren did everything but spit at me, but finally agreed to let Don Richards go up to the CAC for three days. I saw Richards leave the Salem Jail, packing his tools into his beat-up old Chevy, and with a grin on his cherub face, waved to me as he drove by my office on his way to Lawrence. Four days later, Warren Bethune came to me in a huff. "Where is Richards?" he asked. "I need him back here to run a shift."

I called Terry. "Just one more day, Sheriff," Terry pleaded. Richards didn't return to Salem on the next day…or the next. There was an emergency; four Feds didn't have beds or cubicles to sleep in. Richards had to build them. The following week, a wall fell in that had to be rebuilt, and only Richards could repair it. Then there was a leak in the water pipes. "Richards is also a plumber, did you know that, Sheriff? And only Richards can fix the plumbing properly."

Warren saw the ruse before I did. Richards had been gone a month. He had been shanghaied. "We're never going to get him back," said Warren with disgust. "Those guys at the center never intended to send him back here. They planned this right from the beginning, Sheriff…they captured him."

Warren was right. Richards kept collecting his salary, because Terry made sure that it was delivered to the CAC, and neither Warren Bethune nor I ever saw Don Richards again in the Salem Jail. Whenever I visited the center, Terry would hide Richards somewhere within the compound where I wouldn't encounter him.

One surprise call I got from Terry Marks was for help at the Center at the request of the inmates. "They want you to come up here and tell them what they can and can't do during their spare time."

"Okay," I agreed and was up there in their meeting room the next evening.

There were now about thirty men at the Center, and I noticed that they all seemed   energetic and enthusiastic, something you didn't often see in inmates at the county jails. "We want you to give us some rules and regulations, Sheriff," said their inmate spokesman. "We want to know such things as: can we have picnics on the grounds with our families or girlfriends on the weekends? Can we go fishing in the river? Can we–"

"Do you want to go fishing in the river?" I interrupted.

"Some guys do." he replied

"Why not?" I asked. "Do you think the fish are edible?"

"You mean we can go fishing?"

"As far as I'm concerned, you can do just about anything you want up here, as long as it's legal, moral, and it doesn't upset Deputy Master Marks or the citizens of Lawrence." A cheer went up. "I want *you* to make the rules," I said. "Start a three-man committee that rotates a new man in and an old member out every month, and after you set up rules and regulations for yourselves, this committee will enforce the rules and provide punishment for any violator. Deputy Master Marks can be arbitrator, if necessary, but this is *your* show up here. If you screw up, you know that you'll go right back to the Salem or Lawrence Jail. Up here you have freedom and fresh air and better food and free time, a work ethic and a few bucks in your pocket when you get out. Only a fool would mess it up for himself." They were surprised that I put them in charge, but they made rules stricter than I ever would have.

✻ ✻ ✻

The day of judgment finally came. It was a Saturday morning and the three county commissioners, special legislative county committee and 26 of the 34 members of the advisory board were to tour the facility. My six months were up, and after the visit, this enormous joint committee, established by the state legislature, would decide whether or not I would keep control of the new CAC. The inmates and guards worked day and night to clean the place up. Jim St. Pierre provided coffee and doughnuts in the cafeteria, and thanks to old Jim's Navy discipline, the kitchen was spic-and-span.

Big Phil Corriveau stood over the doughnuts awaiting the crowd. I was nervous, but Phil, looking even more nervous, was sweating profusely. It wasn't overly warm in the cafeteria, and I wondered if he was sick. He wavered slightly as he stood at near attention, his hands folded in front of him, sweat now dripping off his nose and cheeks. I got up from where I was sitting and went over to him.

"Are you okay, Phil?" I asked quietly. He nodded. "Why are you sweating?" I asked. "It's not hot in here."

"Look at those doughnuts," he whispered back at me as if we were in church, "ain't they beautiful?"

I looked down at the dishes filled with every different variety of doughnuts you could imagine. "They look great," I replied, "but why are you sweating?"

"I have a problem, Sheriff...I got this thing for sweets...especially donuts and cakes...I take pills for it and everything, but it doesn't help much." He turned to look at me. His face was dripping, and his droopy eyes danced in his head. "It's like being an alcoholic," he said. I took him by the hand and we walked out of the cafeteria into the fresh air. "I guess it's like an eating disorder," said Phil sucking in the crisp fresh air. "The doctors have me on a diet, but its real tough, Sheriff."

"I know," I said with empathy, "I've fought weight all my life."

I looked at Phil, all 400 pounds of him. "Just stop staring at the doughnuts," I advised – knowing it wasn't that simple. Everybody, guards and inmates alike, had some kind of seemingly unsolvable problem or addiction, but Phil couldn't hide his problem; it was right out there where you could see it – 400 pounds of craving for doughnuts wrapped in a tightly fitting deputy's uniform.

It was doughnuts that got Corriveau in trouble earlier in his career at the Lawrence Jail, Bill Ryan later informed me. He and his brother Bob, a Lawrence correctional officer who weighed some 300 pounds, escorted a young inmate to the local Catholic Church one day to attend the funeral of his mother. He was handcuffed to the Corriveau brothers, but asked that the cuffs be taken off so that he might visit with his dead mother at her casket before she was buried. As the young mourner walked with the pallbearers to the front of the church, hands folded in prayer, the Corriveau brothers rushed across the street to a doughnut shop to get coffee and split a dozen jelly filled before re-entering the church. All the pallbearers smiled sheepishly at the two enormous guards as they returned, wiping jelly from their chins. The inmate genuflected at the alter, turned, gave the Corriveau brothers the finger, and raced for a side door. Phil and Bob were too bloated to give a good chase. The inmate left the overweight guards and his dead mother in the dust. He was recaptured a few days later, but the Corriveau brothers never lived down their "dough-nut debacle;" they were teased unmercifully by the other guards. Even though Phil Corriveau was one of his top councilors, Ryan told me that the fallout from the dozen donuts was a good reason for sending him to the CAC.

Phil Corriveau's pale pallor dissipated in the fresh air, and we be-gan greeting the commissioners and advisory council members as they arrived. Before they took a tour of the work release center, the correctional officer's school, and the weed-free garden, personally manicured by Leo Lobeo and eight federal prisoners, I gave a quick summary of our six-month accomplishments and future plans. Then Terry Marks wowed them with the economics of the new facility as they sipped their coffee. "Rent from the Correctional Officers Acad-emy, the Lawrence Catholic Youth League, and the Lawrence School Department, adds up to $27,000 per year. For housing federal in-mates, we have received $20,000 to date and hope to have $60,000 from the Feds by the end of the year. Work release residents have al-ready provided some $3,500.00 in room and board payment, and should return some $10,000 to us by the end of the year. All of these men will leave this facility within a few months, hopefully never to return to jail, and each leaves here with about $1,000.00 in his pocket to begin life anew. And best of all, each has a steady job to keep him from returning to a life of crime. Our most surprising accomplish-ment, however, is our farm. Thanks to our energetic and enthusiastic farmer, Senior Correctional Officer Leo Lobeo, we're already pro-ducing some $8,000.00 worth of vegetables, and have already sub-stantially reduced the food costs at the jails..." Leo was up and at the microphone before Terry could finish.

"We've pulled 3,500 bushels of vegetables so far, and we'll pro-duce twice that in the fall," he shouted, "and I didn't have no budget—not a penny from the county." Terry tried to nudge Leo away from the microphone. We were afraid he would say too much. Some of the mayors, of course, already realized that it was their fifty dollars in the potato field, the corn maze, and the pumpkin patch. "Without Sheriff Cahill we'd all be back inside the jails," announced Leo, unwilling to give up control of the meeting. "He's brought the county system twenty-five years ahead."

"Funny, " I said aloud, "I thought it was more like three hundred years." As my guests laughed, Terry managed to wrestle away the microphone from Leo. It was amazing to me, my biggest troublemaker had become my good will ambassador, and I truly believed it was Leo Lobeo who tipped the scales for Terry, Bill Ryan, and myself, and provided us with a two-thirds vote from the advisory board to keep the Correctional Alternatives Center. The Commissioners and special legislative committee followed suit. The CAC was ours! It would provide both of the jails with breathing room and all inmates with incentive to better themselves. The county commissioners and advisory board members would still be looking over our shoulders, but as long as we kept making money and stayed out of trouble, they would be satisfied. Were our troubles at the CAC over? Not by a long shot.

Not a week had passed after our big meeting when I was contacted by the state police. Leo Lobeo had been arrested for stealing from a public dumpster. That didn't seem like a crime to me, but he had been caught in dumpsters up and down the highway some seven times, usually in the wee hours of the morning before dawn. His reason, so he explained, was the need for boxes to pack the vegetable in when he shipped them off to the jails. After Leo was arrested, we all chipped in to provide him with enough boxes to pack his vegetables; I also allowed Leo to open a vegetable stand at the Center, just off the highway, where passing motorists would stop for fresh produce on their way home from work. It was a successful enterprise, a good public service, and provided more money to defray the costs of the county.

I got a call one day from a correctional officer, who obviously disliked Leo. "He's stealing vegetables and taking them home to his family and relatives," said the informer.

I shouted at the caller. "This guy, who you say is a crook, built that fourteen acre pumpkin patch by working days, nights, weekends, and holidays without getting one minute of overtime pay. He delivers vegetables, fruit, and you-name-it in his own little truck, with no money for gas or for wear and tear on the truck. I personally hope he does take vegetables home…I'd be surprised if he didn't…in fact, I'd be disappointed if he didn't." The caller wasn't happy and threatened to go to the county commissioners. I just laughed and the man hung up, not to be heard from again. Two weeks later, Harry Healy delivered three pumpkins and squashes to my home in Salem—from Leo Lobeo.

One convicted thief that did cause problems at the CAC was not an inmate, but a councilor, Joe O'Rourke. He had spent sixteen years at Walpole State Prison for bank robbery. We hired him under a federal grant, knowing full well that it was illegal to hire an ex-convict into the field of law enforcement or corrections. But O'Rourke was a diamond in the rough. He was an experienced councilor at the Shirley School, so we hired him to interview every inmate who we felt was eligible for work release at the center. After a half-hour or so conversation with a potential worker at the center, Joe could tell better than any experienced guard whether a man was ready for work release. O'Rourke, having been there himself, could talk the inmates' language and became an invaluable asset for us at the CAC. Not only did he screen all applicants, but also ran marriage encounters for the inmates, managed the AA meetings, and arranged all evening activities at the Center.

I was not only warned by other sheriffs that I was risking my position by hiring O'Rourke, but I was approached by an FBI agent who told me the same thing. "It's against the law," said the FBI man, "You can't hire an ex-con."

"I know," I replied, and that was the end of our conversation. O'Rourke stayed on.

What was worse, I wondered, hiring an ex-con to out-con the cons, or hiring an ex-cook, who couldn't cook? I didn't bother Jim St. Pierre for the first few months after he first arrived at the center, for I knew he was nervous about his new position. Just mentioning the fact that his cooking might be suspect would send him raving about, flailing his spatula throughout the kitchen, and babbling to himself. He was a temperamental cook and saw to it that he had inmates surrounding him who excelled at the culinary arts. Jim was especially interested in acquiring federal prisoners who were tax-evading chefs. One day I arrived at the center well after lunchtime, but I was famished. I asked Terry, while sitting at a meeting in his office, if I could call down and have the cook make me something—anything. St. Pierre answered the phone. "All the lunch was eaten up…and I'm alone down here, all my help has gone to work elsewhere."

"Just a sandwich, peanut butter and jelly—anything, I'm starving."

I could tell by his voice that Jim was nervous. "How about ham and cheese?" he asked.

"Good," I replied. "I'll be right down."

When I arrived, Jim had a chair set at a small table in the kitchen, with a sandwich on a plate and a glass of milk. I dug in, but almost immediately realized that something was wrong with the sandwich. Jim stood over me, hands on hips, apparently preparing himself for a compliment. I opened the sandwich up and then looked up at Jim. "What's wrong?" he said, eyeing me suspiciously.

I held up the open sandwich so he could look inside the two pieces of bread. Both bread slices were lathered with mustard and a slice of cheese. There was no ham. "Holy shit!" I shouted, trying hard to hold back my laughter. "I not only hired a cook who can't cook, but he can't even make a ham and cheese sandwich." Jim turned colors as he stood before me, his mouth opened in an attempt to explain, but nothing came out.

CHAPTER XVI

Caped Crusaders of the North

I t will be an adventure," Bill Ryan told his wife Maureen. "We'll just fix up the old granite house attached to the Lawrence Jail and live in it. Just you, me and the kids, rent free, and we'll be right downtown, close to stores, restaurants, the church..." Maureen was reluctant. They were living in a nice house in Haverhill, close to the highway, not far from downtown. "And the grammar school for the kids in Lawrence is only a block away. They can walk to school." That was apparently the deciding factor, for Maureen said yes. She would live in the master's house beside the jail where her husband would only have to take a few steps to be at work, and she could walk her kids to school.

As soon as he got the O.K., Billy assigned those inmates who were most willing to leave their dark and cramped cells to clean up the old house and prepare it for the Ryan family. There was no money for paint or repairs, but Billy, whom I always considered the greatest of procurers, was true to form. He persuaded Sheriff Jerry Bowes of Barnstable County to give him thirty gallons of paint. Where Bowes got the paint, no one seemed to know, but to get so much paint for sprucing up the jail and the house was a welcomed gift. Even the inmates were thrilled, for they had been living with dirty, dingy, pealing paint for years. The problem was that all the new paint was green. I later realized, while heading to Cape Cod for vacation one sunny July day that it was the same color green covering all the outbuildings and barns of the Barnstable County Farm Complex. Bowes, like Billy Ryan, was a stalwart Republican, and since they were of a dying breed in Massachusetts, they were quick to assist one another. Of course I was happy at Billy's acquisition, but I wondered why Jerry Bowes hadn't offered me paint as well. I certainly needed it as much as Billy did, and Bowes and I were good friends. Was I feeling a tinge of jealously?

Billy's problems at the Lawrence Jail were almost as great as my own in Salem. Only a few weeks before he took over the jail, there were two escapes. In the first one, the escaping inmate shot correctional officer Bob Brown in the neck with a gun that had been smuggled into the jail. The shooter walked out the front door only to be captured a few days later. Bob Brown survived, but doctors were afraid to remove the bullet; it was too close to his spine, so it remained in his neck and he returned to work with a little extra hardware. In the second escape, three inmates exercising in the jail's third floor gym managed to bend the window bars with an iron dumbbell. Two men squeezed through, but the weight lifter was too large and couldn't fit. The two thinner ones then climbed an old wooden fence topped with barbed wire that surrounded the jail, but one got hung up on a wire. He was seen dangling there by a neighbor who lived in one of the many tenement houses flanking the jail. She called the jail and the escapee was hauled back down into the jail yard by guards. The other got away for ten minutes and was walking down Main Street when he was recognized and recaptured by police. The bodybuilder who couldn't squeeze between the bent bars was found hiding behind a hot-water tank in the boiler-room. Needless to say, it wasn't a well-run prison when Billy stepped in to take it over.

The day Billy arrived at the Lawrence Jail to begin work, the very fence that the one escapee got hung-up on fell to the ground in pieces and could not immediately be put back together again. The Lawrence Jail was not only falling apart on the outside, but the inside was in tough shape as well, and unlike the Salem Jail, it was filthy dirty. Besides paint brushes, Billy bought buckets and mops out of his own money and had the inmates clean the place from top to bottom. I traded him white and blue paint for some of his green, and he mixed his colors so that the entire interior of the jail wouldn't be all one shade. The inmates and the guards were pleased to clean and brighten up their environment, but like the Salem Jail there was much more structural work needing to be done. Bill Ryan and his new deputy-master, Joe Carter, were unrelenting in their efforts to bring programs and projects into the jail, for the inmates. All the windows were boarded up in their third floor gym, basketball hoops were installed, and pickup teams were organized to keep the men active. "It's cold as hell up there," said Ryan, "but once they get a little sweat going in the games, they don't mind the cold. In fact, it's refreshing." Like Salem, the Lawrence boiler didn't create much heat—it was only recently converted from coal to oil.

The plumbing and other facilities were very outdated. The bathroom consisted of four exposed toilets facing eight showerheads, with no privacy in either direction. The men who washed themselves twice a week in the showers, looked straight at the men on the toilets, making for an uncomfortable experience for bathers and sitters.

"It's quite embarrassing," said Ryan, "almost as bad as Salem." Lawrence did have a few portable chemical toilets that never seemed to work properly and had to be dumped every other day. Like in Salem, the vast majority of inmates used buckets in their cells to defecate and urinate. They were hand carried each morning before breakfast to the basement of the jail and dumped down the drain of a large sink. Billy also had a rat infestation problem, and since the kitchen and dining room were in the basement at Lawrence, river-rats would often join the inmates at mealtimes.

"At least you've got an old paddy wagon to haul prisoners around," Ryan said to me, "but all I've got is a fifteen year old truck—without a working gas gauge—to transport men to court. Carter had to bring three guys to Salem for a court appearance the other day, and the truck ran out of gas on the highway. Joe had no phone, and he couldn't leave the inmates alone, so he lifted the hood and just sat there 'til a Lawrence police cruiser came along. Like you, I have no alarm system in the jail, and nothing to fight fires, not even a hose, and no water hookup to the street hydrant." Billy got the Lawrence fire department to donate an old hose they had lying around, and he found a hose-rack that two guards snatched from a discarded oil truck at the dump. That installed, he rented a backhoe and dug a trench from the jailhouse to the street. Guard Frank Brealey, a pig farmer before he became a correctional officer, had enough pipe at his farm, once used to water the pigs, to run a connection to the city hydrant, tapping into the city's main water supply. Thus, Lawrence Jail now had one piece of fire-fighting equipment, thanks to the ingenuity and persistence of Bill Ryan.

"This place is scandalous," said Ryan, "but my greatest fear here is fire. I sometimes have no more than three guards on duty, and most of them are older men. They lock up over one hundred men each night in ten-foot by eight-foot cells, and they hand lock each cell, tier by tier. One guard carries 135 keys. If there were a fire, he'd never have time enough to open all the cells, and if anything happened to the guard, like being overcome by smoke, they'd all be cooked alive. We need electronically controlled locks. This situation has been ignored for decades and could erupt into a tragedy of major proportions."

Bill Ryan and I filed a bill in the legislature for a sum not exceeding $225,000 for the installation of electrically controlled locking systems at both jails, and the construction of new passage doors and emergency exits. Then Bill started inviting local legislators to tour his jail in hopes they would have sympathy for our plight and designs to upgrade the two facilities. It almost backfired when, after touring the Lawrence Jail, Democratic State Representative David Swartz said that our requests for funds hadn't a chance of passing in the statehouse, and State Representative Bernie Flynn, Democrat from Amesbury, told the press that, " the Lawrence Jail is a brighter institution and more livable than Salem. This place isn't so bad, but Salem Jail should be torn down." Ryan was livid.

Unlike my situation in Salem, Billy had the press on his side in Lawrence and Haverhill. He also had extra room in the jail to build classrooms and new recreational areas, but he needed funds to affect any real changes. He didn't hold his breath for the legislature to help, but instead used the local press to ask for help from local businesses and agencies. Plus, by taking in federal prisoners, he was allowed to raid places like the Fort Devans Army Base to acquire surplus items such as beds, blankets, and even old vehicles to help him improve his lot at Lawrence. Salem was too old to house federal prisoners.

"When the state calls and says they have a prisoner for me, I tell 'em that I don't have room," said Billy, "and sometimes I even do it to the local judges, so's I can take in federal prisoners and get paid $22 a day by the Feds to buy things for my jail. And I constantly use the federal card to get surplus items."

The response from local businesses and citizens to provide equipment, recreational items, and services was excellent, but Ryan's greatest need was staffing. He asked the county commissioners, advisory board, and legislature for twelve new guard positions to meet minimum state standards. The commissioners cut his request to six, the advisory board reduced it to five, and the legislature slashed the request to two. Ryan was told by members of the advisory board to rely on the "Comprehensive Employment Training Act," or CETA to acquire guards. "In Haverhill and Lawrence," said Ryan, "the people under CETA, were those who couldn't get jobs anywhere else...but I needed warm bodies, so I used them. A couple of them turned out to be good employees, but most of them were more trouble than most of the inmates. One young man who came highly recommended by the local clergy," said Ryan, "I found directing traffic in his new guard's uniform in downtown Lawrence, and when I confronted him, he started screaming like a lunatic and wouldn't stop. Two of my real guards subdued him and I had to let him go. Another CETA employee was a hefty woman, who was a blessing to me. She was useful for frisking female visitors who came to visit inmates. These visitors would try to sneak in contraband to their boyfriends, husbands, or brothers. Because our male guards couldn't thoroughly frisk females, we had a hard time stopping this illegal traffic. Our new female CETA officer was an aggressive searcher, and was proving to be an excellent addition to my correctional officers staff, until one day, she and my most valuable senior guard told me that they were leaving the jail together. They eloped and moved to Maine. So, she actually cost me two guard positions."

During this crucial time for Bill Ryan, he had an escape. A trustee walked away while helping the cook, Romeo Emilio, carry meat into the jail from Eddie's Meat Market wagon. The fence was still down, so inmate Peter Pilloti merely stepped over it. He didn't run, he just walked down the street and lost himself in a crowd of downtown shoppers. It was embarrassing for Billy because he had to tell the news reporters that, "the escapee didn't cut through anything, or climb over anything, nor did he run when he hit the street. He just leisurely walked away." He wasn't really dangerous, and he was caught twenty days later in Gloucester. Billy blamed it on the lack of guards. Only three were on duty to watch 110 inmates, and he needed funds to build a fence around the jail, but Billy was embarrassed just the same.

✻ ✻ ✻

The lack of a fence around the outside of the jail and the keeper's house was also causing Ryan problems on the home front. The Ryans, like Sandy and me, had four small children, and they would play outside the granite house attached to the Lawrence Jail almost every day. The first night, they left their scooter, tricycle, and cart on the front lawn, and the next morning, all three items were gone. Maureen told Bill that some strange looking, ragged neighborhood kids were hanging around their front yard the day before the theft. Maureen described them as, "Real Oliver Twist type kids" and said she believed they stole the kids' toys. Billy drove around the neighborhood with his kids in the car, hoping to spot the toys somewhere out in the open, but they saw nothing of their stolen goods. Billy bought his kids new toys to ride on and the next day, the Oliver Twist kids were back, "slinking around the yard." Maureen called Billy at the jail, and as he was heading out the front door, the oldest of the motley gang, a boy of nine, had a new tricycle under his arm. With a little sister and brother trailing behind, he made a run for it up the street. Billy jumped into his car and followed the trio for half a block where they hid the bike under a porch of a triple-decker tenement house. Billy got out of his car and snuck up on the kids, grabbing the ringleader by his long hair, but he quickly let go, for the boy's hair was filled with lice. The culprit then turned on Billy and called him "an asshole." Billy told him that he was going to tell his parents and the

Bill Ryan and wife Maureen with Bob Cahill and wife Sandy, 1975.

kid called him "a fuckin ass-hole." Billy threatened to call the police and the kid laughed. The little dirty-faced girl pulled on Billy's pant leg, and wide-eyed revealed that not only had her brother stolen the new tricycle, but the kids' three other toys as well. Billy knew that they were hidden under the porch, and he soon found them. He knocked on the door of the house, but it was locked, and nobody seemed to be home. The little girl then explained to Billy that she didn't have a father and when the mother worked, she locked the kids out of the house all day to play in the street.

Billy returned home with the new tricycle, leaving the old toys behind. That evening he went to the house to speak to the mother of the wayward kids. He returned home to Maureen fifteen minutes later.

"Did you get the toys?" she asked him.

"No," replied Bill. "I left the toys there for those kids to keep...they were getting old anyway, and if you've got any hand-me-down clothes that our kids don't need, let's send them down to that poor woman and her filthy kids." Ryan is that kind of guy.

To keep strangers from entering his yard, Billy bought a dog. It wasn't a huge dog, but not a small one either; it was just a mongrel that Billy called "Marvin." He bought it to play with and protect the kids as they played in the yard. At night, he'd leave Marvin outside, tied on a long leash, with a makeshift shelter to sleep in when it was raining. Early one morning he was just standing at his kitchen window, looking outside at the rows of tenement houses. He was wearing his "superman outfit," as Maureen called it, a red bathrobe and slippers. As he was looking out, he saw a man on the sidewalk near the jail calling a dog. "I hope the dog isn't shitting on our lawn," he told Maureen who was making breakfast. Then Billy saw his own dog come into view. The man wasn't calling his dog, he was calling Billy's dog. With one swish of a knife, the man cut the leash and he and Marvin went bounding down the street. Billy ran down the stairs as fast as he could to his car, shouting as he went, "Thief! Thief! Thief!" but he had to run back into the house because he had forgotten his car keys. On the way out again, he lost a slipper; so with bathrobe flying in the wind and one bare foot, he made it to the car. He slammed the car into gear and sped off through the narrow streets looking for his dog. He returned an hour later, totally dejected and dogless. The man had escaped with Marvin. The kids were devastated.

"Why?" the caped crusader shouted at the dawning sun as he stood in front of the Lawrence Jail.

It was only a few nights later that Bill and Maureen were awakened in the middle of the night with what Billy could only describe as "the cries of a Banshee." It was an old woman on a bicycle, wearing earmuffs, with a little girl riding behind her, holding onto her waist. She parked the bike in Billy's front yard.

"Hellooo, hellooo," she shouted with a piercing voice. "Stevie, Stevie! We love you. We miss you. Don't let them hurt you Stevie!" She waited two minutes and repeated the lament. This continued on for almost an hour. She returned two nights later and repeated her ritual. Stevie was a teenager, sent to jail for two months for disturbing the peace, and now his mother was disturbing Maureen and Bill's peace. Four nights of every week for the whole two months of Stevie's incarceration, she faithfully returned to Billy's front lawn. "I was going nuts," said Billy, " but Maureen thought it was funny." It was, however, enough to persuade the Ryans to move out of the Jail Master's house and back to their old house in Haverhill, where their kids could walk to school without a bodyguard, their toys didn't need locking up, and a leash was all a dog needed to keep it in the yard.

✷ ✷ ✷

One of Billy Ryan's initial goals—money or no money—was to improve the jail's kitchen facilities and the awful food that inmates were forced to eat each day. Although an inmate delivered a noontime jail meal to Billy in his office each day, unbeknownst to anyone, he never ate it. "Not even a bite," said Billy. "Just in case someone in there wanted to poison me. I'd starve before I ate jail food."

Within a few months of Billy's reign at Lawrence Jail & House Of Correction, the *Lawrence Eagle Tribune* published a half-page article with a photo and the headline: "Jail Kitchen Wins Praise." With the help of Fort Devans surplus, local business sponsors, inmates, and guards, Ryan had transformed the jail kitchen and dining room from a dingy, broken down health risk, into a sparkling, state-of-the art dining facility—a model of beauty and efficiency.

"From a dingy, decrepit and inadequate facility," wrote state prisons inspector John Chmielinski to the county commissioners, "the Lawrence Jail and House of Correction is rapidly being rehabilitated, to the credit of the Sheriff, Master William Ryan, his staff and the inmates." I obviously didn't have anything to do with Billy's kitchen metamorphosis and didn't even see the kitchen until after the remarkable transformation was complete. "I have been the liaison officer between state and county, inspecting the Lawrence structure for the past eight years," Chmielinski continued, "and during that time I have noted deplorable conditions existing in the culinary section. The building lacked basic equipment, such as a dishwasher and washing machine, and the stoves were not working correctly. It is with a great sense of satisfaction that I now find these problems have been resolved, and great progress in refurbishing the area has been made." I would have been more than pleased if Chmielinski stopped there, but he didn't. His letter continued: "However, the Salem Jail and House of Correction has a stove which has been condemned by the Boston Gas Company. Last week there was a flashback explosion in the oven from a gas leak. The inmate who was lighting the oven for the noon meal narrowly escaped serious injury. The gas company repaired the leak but condemned the stove. It said both ovens are dangerous and should not be used. The company warned that continued use of the stove is at the county's own risk." I didn't hear about the incident until I read it in the paper, and I had to admit he was right. I had not made the Salem Jail kitchen one of my priorities. As Ryan smiled with pride for the good press praising his kitchen, I seemed to have egg on my face. My only excuse was that my jail was so old that the federal government refused to send me their prisoners, and therefore I wasn't eligible for federal surplus items, such as stoves and dishwashers. Actually, Chmielinski's letter did benefit the Salem Jail as well, for the commissioners were so pleased with Ryan's little miracle, and so displeased with my kitchen efforts that they gave me $1,250 out of the general fund to "fix your stove or get a new one." The county commissioners always seemed to jump into action when the state inspectors shined a light on the flaws in the county operation.

Ryan didn't stop at just having a clean and efficient kitchen; he became obsessed about providing the inmates with better food. Again, working through the federal system, he was told at a meeting that there was this marvelous pastry cook who had been chef on a luxury liner and had been caught with his hand in the cookie jar. He was serving six months in a federal prison in New Jersey. Billy called the jail keeper in New Jersey. "That man is originally from Massachusetts and he has family here. Wouldn't it be better all around if he serves out the last three or four months of his sentence with us?" The talented inmate was from Indiana and had no relatives in Massachusetts, but the New Jersey jail keeper was more than pleased to send him up to Billy, and the inmate had no say in the matter.

"What a prize'" Billy said to me on the phone. "You've got to get up here and try this guy's muffins and bread and cup cakes. Everybody up here has gained ten pounds—the guards, the inmates and me. He's terrific. Moral has improved one-hundred percent."

"You're actually eating jail food now," I chided him.

"This isn't jail food. This is gourmet cooking. The guy is an artist."

"How about the food budget?"

"Believe me, Bob, this guy can make the most tasty treats out of nothing. If he needs fruit, he steals the raisins from Raisin Brand Cereal."

I did go to the Lawrence Jail and did taste the chef's raisin buns and apple pie. It was delicious food, and it was obvious Billy had done it again.

"Don't have treats down in Salem like these," smiled Deputy Master Joe Carter, sitting before a pan of muffins, still steaming, just out of the oven. "Your boys having gruel again tonight?" he laughed. And as I left Lawrence Jail, I noted a hairline whimsical smile on Bill Ryan's face. Ryan and Carter were far surpassing my expectations for progress at the Lawrence Jail, "but if that is so, Sheriff?" I asked myself, "then why are you feeling a little pissed?"

"Ryan has opened up the doors of the Lawrence Jail and let in a stream of fresh air," the *Lawrence Tribune* quoted the chairman of Turning Point, a human services agency. "Prior to Ryan, jail programs were nearly non-existent, physical conditions primitive, available federal funds ignored and an attitude of brutal neglect reigned…. Ryan has gone into the surrounding community areas and has rounded up groups to come in and counsel inmates. Previously, counseling groups were not allowed to come into prison. Now, two local area groups, projects CASE and EASE, alcoholic and drug counselors and Spanish-speaking job counselors, respectively, have been invited by Ryan to work with the inmates. Massachusetts Rehabilitation counselors are also expected to come in. Ryan goes out into the communities and solicits the help of groups...."

Billy built a new library from scratch on the third floor of the jail. Houghton-Mifflin Publishing Company of Boston donated crates of books, and Western Electric, whose headquarters wasn't far from the jail, provided chairs, reading desks, and wooden bookshelves. It made Salem Jail's makeshift library in the chapel, half filled with tattered, hand-me-down books, look like an outhouse reading-room in comparison. Billy also enrolled his more intelligent inmates in classes at Northern Essex Community College, and he extended furlough times for eligible inmates.

✻ ✻ ✻

All, however, was not coming up roses for my super hero of the North and his balding sidekick, Joe Carter. One of the first problems in the jail was the beating of a new arrival by five other inmates. A "blanketing" they called it; it is when a blanket is thrown over the victim's head so he can't identify his assailants, and then he's beaten to a pulp through the blanket. Ray Crepeau, a 37-year old Haverhill man was arrested for going on a window-breaking spree in downtown Haverhill. He couldn't make $500 bail, so he was put in jail. That night he was beaten so badly that he had to be rushed to the hospital. There were no witnesses to the beating who were talking, and nobody seemed to know why it was done, but the newspapers headlined the incident. "We don't have enough help here to really provide proper security," Ryan told the press. "On any given day we have eight or more alleged murderers and twenty or more alleged armed robbers, mixed in with guys who are drunk and disorderly or go around breaking windows, and these beatings will happen unless we get more guards to watch over our increasing number of dangerous inmates."

A week later, a gruff-voiced anonymous caller informed me that an inmate at the Lawrence Jail was tied to a post in the jail's dungeon and whipped.

"Dungeon? What dungeon?" I asked.

"A dirty, rat-infested hole under the cellar floor of the jail...better check into it, Sheriff," said the informer and he hung up. I had always hoped that there was a dungeon under the floor of the Salem Jail—maybe an old witch hideaway—but no such luck. Now, however, it seemed Lawrence had a secret dungeon. I called Ryan about it, but he knew of no dungeon. "Fairy tale stuff," he said.

"Ask Joe Carter," I said, "and call me back."

The phone rang ten minutes later. "Joe says there is a dungeon here...used only on very special occasions."

I was up to the Lawrence Jail within a half hour, confronting Carter.

"Yes, Sheriff," said Joe. "I've used the dungeon only twice since I've been here, and the last time was only a week ago."

"Why on earth would you tie a guy down in a dungeon?" I asked. "Did you whip him?"

"No, Sheriff," Joe gave me a questioning eye. "I'd never whip a guy. Punch him maybe, or slap him around, but never whip a guy. The guy I put in the dungeon actually tied himself up to the bars with his shirt to keep his feet off the floor."

"Water?" I asked.

"Rats," said Joe, " big ones with red eyes. They'd scare the pants off you, Sheriff."

"The inmate had been screaming at the top of his lungs for three nights straight since the day he arrived," said Joe, "keeping everyone else awake all night. If I hadn't of put him down there, Sheriff, the other inmates would have beaten him to death. I just kept him down there one night...he was quiet after that. He may have screamed all night down there, but we couldn't hear him up here, and when I pulled him out of there in the morning, he was as mild and meek as a pussycat, and I told him that if I heard one peep out of him, he'd spend another night down there. It worked like a charm, Sheriff."

I had Joe Carter show me the dungeon. We entered through a wooden trap door near the laundry room and down a small flight of iron stairs to an entirely bricked in large room with an iron-bared cell in one corner. It was shaped like the inside of a beehive. The brick floor was uneven and wet with dirty water, which in some places was ankle deep. The cell door had an old padlock, and Joe showed me the large black key that locked it.

"The rats come at night," said Joe, "about twenty of them."

"No more, Joe," I said. "Don't you ever put a human being down here again, day or night. I don't care how long or often a man screams or is disorderly."

"Okay, Sheriff, We'll make it off limits…but it sure is a neat place, ain't it?"

"Yes," I had to admit, it was a neat dungeon and one I wished I had in Salem—only for show of course—where witches were held before execution.

Ryan and Carter were a valued team—Mister Inside and Mister Outside, my carrot and my stick in the North. Joe was a constant taskmaster who was always working to improve the morale of the inmates and the abilities of the correctional officers. His guards were always on duty, even when they were off duty. Two of these guards, Howie Camuso and George Hashem were having lunch in downtown Lawrence one day when they saw an inmate walk into a nearby liquor store. They concluded he had somehow broken out of jail, so they waited for him to come out of the store, grabbed him, each by an arm, and stuffed him into Howie's car. The inmate protested vehemently, but the guards dutifully drove him back to jail, where Joe Carter informed them that the inmate had been released from prison a week earlier. He did, however, praise Howie and George for their alertness.

One federal prisoner that Billy and Joe had out in the yard repairing and re-erecting the jail fence fooled the cape crusaders by telling them that the federal marshals had called to say his mother was coming to visit. He asked if he could get off duty with the fence work and dress in his suit to greet Ma when she arrived. Joe agreed.

The federal inmate, named Walter, dressed in his finest, picked up a tray of food from the mess hall to deliver to Master Ryan in his office, or so he told the guards. The food delivered, Walter merely walked out the front door, not recognized by the guards because he left Ryan's office all dressed up looking like a businessman. Walter would have made good his escape, accept that an off duty guard named Conachio, who was walking to work, spotted Walter and recognized him as an inmate on the loose. Conachio walked up behind him, grabbed him by the arm, and escorted him back to jail.

"If we had a fence around this place, none of this would have happened," said Ryan. But only three weeks after guards and inmates reinstalled the Lawrence Jail's wooden fence, there was an escape. Teenager Charlie White had tied and knotted sheets together, cut the window bars of his cell, climbed down two stories, and scaled up and over the wooden fence to freedom—temporary freedom. As soon as the escape was discovered, we put calls out to local police and dispatched deputies all around the area. Charlie White's girlfriend lived in Lowell, so we put a deputy, Charlie Manual, on guard at her house; White's mother lived in Lawrence, so we put two deputies hiding in the bushes near his mother's house; Charlie White's father lived in Reading, Massachusetts, so we sent two deputies there to keep an eye on his apartment. The rest of us scoured the streets of Lawrence and Lowell, armed to the hilt. We followed behind local police who kicked down doors to buildings where they thought White might be hiding, but we had no luck. For some unknown reason, city police liked to go around knocking down doors when members of the sheriff's department were around. What made things worse was the pouring rain. I joined the search for a few hours and then went back to Bill Ryan's office to relieve him at the phone. Finally at midnight, a call came in; it was the North Reading Police. They captured Charlie White breaking into a jewelry store. My deputies went to Reading and returned him to the Lawrence Jail. Special Sheriff Charlie Reardon interrogated him. "But can I still stay here?" he pleadingly asked Reardon. "I want to remain in the Lawrence Jail."

"No way," said Reardon. "You're going back to Walpole where you belong. You've caused too many of us a wet, sleepless night." At that, all the deputies packed up their weapons and belongings and headed home. I was the last out of Ryan's office and had my hand on the doorknob when the phone rang again. It was Charlie Manuel at a payphone.

"How long do you want me to stand out here in the rain at the girlfriend's house?" he asked.

"You can go home now, Charlie," I told him, "We just caught White."

Actually, we had caught White hours before, and I had completely forgotten that Charlie Manual was still standing out there in the rain and cold in Lowell. If he hadn't called he might be standing there still.

✳ ✳ ✳

The greatest fear of any sheriff or jail master is a jail riot, and Ryan and I were faced with one at Lawrence on the day when word spread that I had fired Joe Carter as deputy master of the jail, and that he would have to leave Lawrence Jail at once. Bill Ryan and others had previously warned me about Joe's fondness for gambling. He loved the horses and the dogs, which was his business, as long as it didn't interfere with work at the jail, which was my business. But eventually it did. Joe was not only taking inmates out of the jail to go to meetings or to play flag-football, I was told he took one or more of them out to the racetrack. Joe knew this was against all rules and regulations, and I knew I had to do something more than just disciplining my northern crusader. I first checked with Terry Marks, my director of the new Lawrence Correctional Alternatives Center, and he agreed to take Joe on as work director at the center, a job recently vacated by Mike Menery who became a Lawrence Alderman. With the help of Billy Ryan, I transferred Joe Carter to our CAC facility. Joe took the transfer in stride, but the inmates of the Lawrence Jail did not. A riot broke out, with shouting, swearing, and things being thrown around. Ryan locked all the inmates into their cells and transferred his most rebellious inmates to other jails, but the riot continued. He disallowed any visitations from family, friends, or councilors for two days, but the yelling and screaming continued from the cellblocks. When I arrived at the jail, the inmates were chanting: "We want Carter, we want Carter!" They were throwing anything in their possession onto the polished central wooden floor: cigarettes, cigarette packs, matches, handkerchiefs, playing cards, etc. I stepped out onto the floor and walked to the center of it, waving up to them as if I was a politician running for office. The din grew even louder. Then, out of the shadows, a figure, walking quickly, approached me. It was Jimmy Carter, Joe's brother. The inmates cheered when they saw him. It was like being stuck in a cage with a gorilla, surrounded by an unfriendly audience pelting me with objects and abusive words from above. Jimmy had that bulldog look about him. He wasn't happy, and I thought surely he was going to punch me out, here in the center of the auditorium where his brother's boxing-ring once stood. He faced me toe-to-toe, as close as he could get.

"Why'd you fire my brother?" he snarled.

"I didn't fire your brother. I transferred him, but anyone else would have fired him."

"Are you going to let him back here?"

"No...he'll do a better job where he is, and he'll get the same pay. I know he liked it better here, but you know what his problem is, and I just can't keep him here. Also, you know that there is only one man besides Joe Carter who can stop this rioting, and that's you. These boys shouting above us think that I hurt Joe. I didn't. He'll be better off where he is, but if you want to take a swing at me, go ahead." I stuck out my jaw and silently prayed he wouldn't swing. Instead, Jimmy did an about-face and walked away. He went from cell to cell quelling the riot and within an hour it was over. I felt then, and always will feel that Jimmy Carter's actions that day were a profile in courage. I am forever indebted to him.

A few years later, Jimmy Carter retired from corrections and he came to visit me at my home in Salem. He wanted to tell me that Marvin Grayson, the man who escaped the Lawrence Jail by fleeing with his mother in a rented car, was finally captured, in Boston. The Boston Police had called Jimmy down to identify him. "It was one of the great thrills of my life, Sheriff, " he said in his gruff voice, "just to see that bastard back behind bars." That same day Jimmy also revealed to me that he had always wanted to be a baseball umpire. "As you know, all my family were in sports, and ever since I was a kid, I wanted to be an umpire behind the plate. Well, Sheriff," he continued, "this dream is coming true, 'cause I've been going to baseball umpire school, and I graduate this week." Jimmy's first game as umpire behind the plate was at a well-attended semi-pro game in Lawrence the following week. He was in his hometown, about to live a lifelong dream, thrilled, but surely a bit nervous as he was about to shout "Play ball!" to the players and fans in the stands. He stooped over home plate to sweep it clean with his little whiskbroom. An eyewitness said, "He collapsed face first into home plate, and he never got up again." Jimmy Carter was dead...his dream fulfilled.

Bill Ryan and the Carter brothers were my caped crusaders of the north—tough guys with hearts of gold who, against all odds, made the system work.

CHAPTER XVII

Do Not Pass Go

Some of the young girls walking down Saint Peter's Street would lean against the chain link fence that separated the long jail windows from the sidewalk and would lift their blouses to bare their breasts to the attentive inmates. A whoop and holler would go up from inside the cellblock, and Warren or I would quickly send a guard out to the street to interrupt the girls at their play. Whoever they were, they would show up periodically, and although they often couldn't see the men behind the dark barred windows, they would shout to the boys and then perform to their delight. One inmate told me before he was released that the best part of his stay at my ancient inn was the occasional performances by these young girls.

Other more modest females would walk by the jail to whistles and groans from inmates and ignore the noise. A few, though, would stop to talk if the barred windows were open. In one instance, a friendship developed between a women who passed by the window on the way to and from work at Parker Brothers and a rather talkative, chunky young inmate named Phil Burt. Burt was only in for petty theft, but wouldn't be leaving his home-away-from-home for another two years. Alice Fontaine, who was in charge of millions of dollars in Monopoly money each day, couldn't wait for the end of each workday when she could spend fifteen or more minutes beneath the window talking to her new friend. They talked of many things and discovered that they had mutual interests: hillbilly music, fast cars, gangster movies, cats, and graphic arts. Alice had actually gone to art school for a year in Boston, and Phil was constantly drawing up fancy escape diagrams of the jail for inmate friends, which he did gratis. He used to brag to me about the success his cellmate Paul White had using his escape map to make his getaway from Salem Jail; White hadn't been caught yet. The only reason Burt didn't escape with White that night, squeezing through an old vent system into the yard and over the rickety fence, is that it would have been the end of his daily rendezvous with Alice. White, who led my deputies and police on a wild goose chase, had stolen a car when he left the jail, and being a stockcar racer, outmaneuvered all pursuers. He remained a fugitive and was so bold while on the lam that he called Warren Bethune to tell him that he would return to the jail one night soon to break out his old cellmate Phil Burt. Now my problem wasn't just inmates breaking out of jail, but breaking in as well. White was a wild one and I told Warren not to take his threat too lightly. I also informed him to warn the night crew to be alert, which I realized was a tall order since many of them, I suspected, still slept through their late night work shift. White was the type of guy who might come bursting into the jail with six-guns blazing. It was, I concluded, much easier to break into jail than to break out. And although Warren didn't seem worried about it, I was.

Two weeks after White's departure, the mapmaker Burt approached Reverend Webster, who preached Sunday services at the Jail library/chapel to a near empty house each week. Burt told Webster that he wished to marry Alice Fontaine. Webster's church was close by on Bridge Street, and the Reverend asked me if the marriage ceremony could be held there.

"No!" I responded. "If there is to be a wedding, it must be in the jail, and Phil Burt will not leave the jail, either for a honeymoon or conjugal visit."

"How do they consummate the marriage?" Reverend Webster asked with a sheepish smile.

"A year later," I replied, "when he goes out on furlough."

I told the Reverend that it seemed to me that the entire marriage was being rushed. I also warned him that Burt was adept at mapping out and planning escapes, and that although he hadn't attempted an escape himself...yet...his pal White threatened to break into jail to spring his lovesick cellmate. "What better time than at the wedding. Maybe White has been invited to be the best man." Reverend Webster kept on smiling.

"Isn't it wonderful," he said, "Just think, a wedding in the jail, and they met just through casual conversation and fell in love without ever being close to each other." Reverend Webster was a tall, handsome, grey-haired man with a deep, smooth voice. I always considered him a powerful presence, but now he   was melting before my eyes.

"Reverend, this marriage thing could get out of hand. It could be trouble. Do you really think these two are in love?"

"Without a doubt," he replied. "I'm sure there won't be trouble."

"If I shout 'duck!' will you remember to do so?"

"Why would I duck?" he asked.

"So's you won't get shot...I'm not kidding, Reverend, this wedding bothers me."

It bothered Warren Bethune too, but for different reasons. "A bride, bridesmaids, family, friends, inside the jail? I don't like it. We can't hold it up in the library where most of the inmates can look on...that's just asking for trouble. If one guy calls the bride a dirty name we'll have a riot on our hands."

"Right," I agreed, "we can hold the ceremony in the office near the visitor's screen, and if a few selected inmates, friends of the groom, want to witness it, they can be behind the screen. As for the reception, cake and Coke can be served in the office too. Webster won't like it in the office. He wants the chapel-library, but that could be risky, and Warren, I know you think I'm paranoid about White's returning, but can we put a couple of armed guards outside, on Bridge Street, out front and in the cemetery."

"We just don't have the people to do it," said Warren.

So instead, I called in three of my volunteer deputies, in uniform. I decided to have them escort the bride into the jail, and then take up critical stations outside, in case White showed up in a honeymoon getaway vehicle.

On the morning of the wedding, Reverend Webster was his breezy self, full of love and camaraderie. "Remember what I said," I cautioned him before we entered the jail.

"What's that?" he asked.

"Duck," I replied. He hadn't remembered. "If I shout duck, or you hear strange noises, like gunshots, hit the floor fast."

"You don't really expect trouble, do you?" His face took on a pained expression.

"Reverend, I really don't know what to expect. I've never even heard of anyone getting married in jail before—especially with the best friend threatening to kidnap the groom."

Alice arrived in her bride's dress and veil, with a hefty bridesmaid dressed in yellow holding a bouquet of yellow daisies. My three volunteer deputies escorted them arm in arm into the jail. Reverend Webster and I followed. Behind the visitors' screen, more than a few inmates crowded the benches and stairway to watch the ceremony. There were yelps from the group and I prayed there would be no off-color comments, but when the bride entered and the groom was let out of a barred door to meet his bride-to-be, the gathered inmates began to clap and cheer. Burt wore a tuxedo and bowtie, and his best man, a noted forger serving three years, wore a black suit and red tie. Burt beamed and Alice blushed. They walked arm in arm into the main office and guardroom, facing the visitor's screen. We all followed them in. Warren Bethune stood smiling near the door, but his eyes wandered suspiciously through the crowd. Bluegrass fiddles and banjos played softly in the background as Reverend Webster's velvety voice echoed throughout the ancient building.

"We are gathered here this day to join together…" The on-looking inmates were quiet, and stared unblinkingly in awe throughout the entire ceremony. When Webster said, "I now declare you man and wife," they sent up a cheer that could be heard in downtown Salem. The cheer went up again when Webster said, "You may kiss the bride." It was their first kiss. Then, without moving more than five steps, they cut into a large pan-cake that was baked in the jail kitchen, and poured cups of Coke for the entire wedding party. The inmates behind the screen called for cake and the bride and groom handed little pieces out to each one of them. They shouted congratulations and good luck to the happy groom, who, ten minutes later, was back in the cellblock with them. The bride kissed Burt's mouth and cheeks over and over again as the turnkey guard opened the heavy front door. The best man received a cheer as he attempted to walk out the front door with the bride and maid-of-honor. The Turnkey grabbed him and turned him around, heading him back to the cellblock.

"Well, that went smoothly," said Warren to the minister and me.

"Yes," sighed Reverend Webster, "but it is kind of sad, and yet at the same time, kind of wonderful."

"Too bad you can't get this kind of attendance at your Sunday sermons upstairs in the chapel," Warren said to Webster.

"It would be nice," he mused.

"I bet if you served cake like we did today you'd increase your flock." Warren jokingly suggested.

"Good idea," said the minister. "I'll try it next Sunday."

And so, our in-house wedding went off without a hitch. I truly expected Paul White to appear on the scene when Reverend Webster asked, "If there is anyone here who knows any reason that these two should not be joined in matrimony, come forward now or forever hold your peace," but White was not good to his word, and I was relieved.

He was captured some three weeks after the wedding in Quebec, Canada. My wedding day jitters had been unfounded. White had been hundreds of miles away on the wedding day. I don't know if the marriage itself lasted or not, but I was informed that some years later, Phil Burt was back in jail, as was his best man, for making counterfeit twenty-dollar bills. I wonder if he was inspired by his wife's occupation of making Monopoly money.

Why, I often wondered, do such men become society's failures? Burt and his pals were obviously talented and seemed to have positive attitudes, yet they were dishonest and, in Burt's case, thrived on the accolades of other criminals. Most of them, it seemed, didn't care that they harmed others. They lived in an unstable world like the Dickens characters in Oliver Twist, Fagan and the Artful Dodger, and had become mean, brutal, and destructive. Some were obviously deranged, like one of my inmates who poured creosol over another inmate's face, blinding him for life, in a dispute concerning the sale of four packs of cigarettes. Both were in jail for murder. But this was not true of the majority of the inmates. I am convinced that the majority of criminals in prison can be rehabilitated.

※　※　※

There were two suicides in the Salem Jail while I was sheriff, and in all suicides, the sheriff must go with the coroner to act as witness to the declaration of death. In both these cases the men were young, barely out of their teens. One apparently felt so guilty about committing a sex crime on a child that he tied his bed sheet to the bars and hung himself. Another had been convicted only of a petty crime, but suffered such depression that he too hung himself with his own tee shirt. Another who almost succeeded in hanging himself was an old man who had been living in various jails for a long time and ended up in Salem. He became delusional one night and cried out his own name, shouting that he wanted to visit himself in his cell. Why, I wondered, did he want to see himself? He tried to commit suicide that night, and we shipped him off to Bridgewater state Hospital for observation. He probably suffered from mental illness all his life, but obviously had slipped through the cracks of the education and health systems. The only people that even took notice of him were those in the criminal justice system, and we were the least equipped to deal with his problems. I never saw him again.

Another old-timer lost in the limbo land of corrections was Leo Nolin, age 73. He had been in jail for 51 years and was seeking a new trial through Essex County Superior Court. Leo had been convicted of killing a storeowner back in 1927, in Haverhill, Massachusetts, but was just now appealing his case, claiming that he was innocent. Judge Donahue denied a new trial, mainly because the trial transcript no longer existed, all key witnesses were dead of old age, and as the judge stated, "All evidence against Nolin was overwhelming." Many convicted murderers like Leo Nolin spent their final years of confinement in the county jails to make room in the overcrowded state prisons for the many new murderers and rapists.

County Jails hold accused criminals of all types awaiting trial for their various dastardly deeds, and sometimes the wait is very long, lasting for months. For a while in Salem, we had no less than ten convicted murderers and alleged murderers awaiting trial in our custody. A rumor was spreading around the jail one day, which fortunately caught my ear—all ten of them were planning an escape. Imagine the fear on the streets if ten murderers were at large, and imagine the embarrassment to the High Sheriff of Essex County. I immediately moved nine of them out to other jails throughout the state. When I explained my fear, justified or not, each of my nine fellow sheriffs accepted a murderer from me. I was taking no chances. I had learned that rumors making the rounds in jails often come to fruition, and I was not about to tempt this rumor into reality.

Strangely, I felt a strong affinity towards one Salem man who was awaiting trial at Salem Jail for shooting his mother. James LeMay shot his 66-year-old mother through the head with a .32-caliber Berretta to "relieve her pain." She was lying in bed moaning from the effects of cancer, and she refused to take her pills, which she told her son did not ease the pain.

"I walked over to the bed," testified LeMay, "put the gun near her left temple and pulled the trigger, firing one shot into her head.... I then called the police station and told the officer who answered that I had shot and killed my mother."

Here I was, sitting in my sheriff's office, only a stone's throw from where LeMay sat shivering in his small dark enclosure, and yet I believed that I was guilty of the same crime as he was. I didn't use a gun on my father, who was dying of cancer in a Marblehead nursing home some six years earlier; I used a bottle of vodka. Although he kept up his spirits when my brother and I were around him, my father was in pain, had almost stopped eating, and had lost so much weight that he was skeletal. During the last visit I saw him alive, he asked for a bottle of vodka. I repeated his request to the doctor. "He hasn't eaten in six days," said the doctor, "but I leave the decision to you." I went out, bought the vodka, returned and made my father a stiff drink. I knew exactly why he wanted it, and I knew what I was doing when I gave it to him. He swallowed it with gusto, and within a couple of hours, he was dead. How different was my action from LeMay's? In both cases it was euthanasia, pure and simple. We had both mercifully put an end to our parent's suffering, yet he was behind bars and I was his jailer—it didn't make sense.

Fortunately LeMay was soon out on $25,000 bail. Unfortunately, his trial didn't come up for 52 months, during which time he was probed, examined, and evaluated by every conceivable type of doctor and psychiatrist that the state could conjure up. The conclusion was "a depressive neurosis brought about by stress," meaning that he could not distinguish right from wrong at the time he shot his mother, but that he was no threat to society now. Although the judge at the trial announced that he did not condone mercy killings, he concluded, "I find James R, LeMay not guilty by virtue of insanity at the time." It was a long, grueling, and emotional ordeal for LeMay, but it finally ended with relief and freedom for him, and for me as well. Was I insane when I gave my dad the vodka? I don't think so. How many thousands of people are faced with the same decision every year? And yet our laws don't adequately address the question.

Another emotionally upsetting case quickly followed the LeMay trial. A 13-year old girl from Lynn was raped several times and brutally beaten. She managed to point out, in a police line-up, a middle-aged man who was her next-door neighbor, Willis Redman, an insurance policy collector who went door to door each workday in the black districts of Lynn to collect insurance policy payments. The girl testified that he had cornered her on a stairwell in her apartment house and forced her into the basement, gagged her and had his way with her for hours, then beat her up and left her for dead.

On the afternoon we received Willie Redman at the jail, the deputies were seething, as were the guards, and the inmates were pumping their fists in anticipation of getting their hands on the new arrival. For his own protection, we decided to put him in solitary lockup where they couldn't get at him, but he could still hear their curses and threats. The guards who had to deal with him on a daily basis didn't like touching him. He was dirt, the lowest of the low. Even I felt like popping him one. He remained with us for eight weeks, during which time everyone avoided him like the plague, called him names when close enough to lock-up to do so, and treated Willie Redman like scum. He ate very little, said nothing, and one evening unsuccessfully tried to commit suicide by hanging himself with his tee shirt. Most of us wished he had succeeded.

Then came the trial, and all eyes, inmate's and guard's, were on him as deputies led him to the paddy wagon, hands cuffed in front, wearing a black suit, head bowed. "The Bastard, I hope he gets life," I found myself mumbling under my breath as I watched the procession. Only two hours later, the verdict was announced…"Not guilty!"

I couldn't believe it. The moment the deputies returned to the jail, I met them at the front door of the house.

"What happened?" I shouted.

"Willie Redman didn't do it," smiled MacKinnon. "The little girl confessed that her boyfriend beat her up and raped her, not the insurance salesman."

Willie Redman was now in the jail gathering his belongings to leave. I ordered the deputies to use our old cruiser to drive him home, or anywhere else he might like to go. I lined up every available guard and house worker, Loretta Rainville, Jack Jerdan, and anyone who was anywhere near the jail. We formed a double-line outside from the jail door to our cruiser, and when Willie Redman stepped out the jail door into fresh air, we all began clapping and cheering. Everyone shook his hand and patted him on the shoulder. His clothes were hanging off him and his face was pale. He had lost some thirty pounds while in jail, but he was smiling. Those who had scowled, shouted, and spit at him, now couldn't pump his hand long or hard enough or provide him with enough wishes of good luck. Some guards, I noticed, actually had tears in their eyes, and these were the ones who had treated him the worst while in jail. As the cruiser drove off to Lynn and all returned to their jobs, I realized a terrible truth: Willie Redman hadn't tried to commit suicide out of guilt for committing a crime—he hadn't committed the crime. His attempt was because we were against him: friends, family, society and the sheriff's department, including inmates, and, yes, the sheriff himself. I was guilty of condemning an innocent man and he couldn't stand the pain of our contempt—I didn't feel good about it. I would try to be less judgmental next time, and I knew there would be next times.

✳ ✳ ✳

Because of Redman's failed suicide, which was thwarted mainly as a result of having a guard checking him every few minutes, even when asleep, we decided to begin an organized "Suicide Watch Committee," which Jack Jerdan insisted I be a member of. There were seven members, including one inmate the committee felt was trustworthy and seriously interested in recognizing the symptoms of a potential suicide victim. We interviewed five inmate volunteers for the job of "suicide watcher," and an inmate named Freddie Fields won the position on the committee. I felt Freddie was a con man, but other members of the committee thought he was conscientious and capable of detecting depression in fellow inmates who might be a danger to themselves. In closed session, I told other members of the committee, namely Jerdan, that I believed Freddie's only interest was to flee the premises at any time and anyway he could. I did not trust him. Jack Jerdan and three of his colleagues on the committee did, and so Freddie became our inside man to detect possible suicide victims.

There was one inmate, Arthur Argue, that Freddie believed was truly depressed with life in Jail and should be moved to a cell in the front of the jail, where he would be easier to observe. "I can't live in this atmosphere," Arthur shouted more than once to the guards, so they changed his atmosphere to a second floor cell overlooking the front lawn, the sheriff's house, and street—a scene that certainly wouldn't have lifted me out of depression. Freddie then announced at one of our Suicide Watch Committee meetings that Arthur Argue was "getting real bad," and that maybe he should bunk in with Arthur to keep a closer eye on him. It was a bad idea, I thought, and I was supported by Larry Puleo, one of the guards on the committee. "Let

Freddie sleep in the corridor" said Puelo, "or the cell next door. If he sees Arthur is in trouble, he can call for the guard."

"Too much time would elapse," argued Freddie. "If I'm right there, I can prevent it immediately."

The vote was against Puleo and me. Freddie spent the night with Arthur in his cell…well, not the entire night. When I arrived to work next morning, I saw bed sheets hanging from the second floor window over the jail's front door. They were tied together in knots so that they almost reached the ground. The sheets dangled from Arthur Argue's cell. The suicide boys had cut two bars with a smuggled jewel cutter and made a late night escape by shimmying down the sheets then merrily walking away. Obviously, Arthur found the atmosphere on the outside less depressing. They were caught four days later, and Freddie was of course banned from the committee.

Only a few days after Freddie and Arthur took their little vacation, there was another major breakout at the Salem Jail, and as in the case of the suicide buddies, the break wasn't discovered right away. In making his rounds at 9:00 p.m., Correctional Officer Johnny Blaisdell noticed that a screen in a window facing the recreation yard was awry. Johnny sounded the alarm and immediately took a cellblock check—four men were missing. They had not only neatly cut the bars of the window, but had made a replica of the bars out of cardboard blackened with coal dust, and once through the widow, had placed the cardboard cutout back in the window frame. Only because the cardboard had slipped a little did Johnny discover the ruse. The inmates had been gone for almost half an hour. They were Bruce Balestraci and Wayne Chamberlain, both of Gloucester, and two Lynn boys, Fred Henning and Paul Fitzpatrick. Yes, Fitzpatrick! The same young man who had escaped from the paddy wagon on his way to court and had led me and my deputies on a merry chase through Downtown Salem and the surrounding woods. The Salem Jail could not contain such creative and talented inmates. After cutting the bars, he and his cohorts squeezed through the window, placed their cardboard cut-out back in the open window, dropped down into the recreation yard, climbed the wooden wall facing Bridge Street, picked their way through the rusting strings of barbed wire topping the fence, and jumped down to the street. They then ran through Parker-Brothers' yard to the railroad tracks and disappeared.

I called all my deputies. "Emergency, emergency, get to the streets." I sent half to Lynn and half to Gloucester, and I alerted both police chiefs that my men in green were descending on their territories. The Gloucester police welcomed them, especially when the deputies assisted them in apprehending two teenaged boys who had escaped from a youth detention center. After stealing a car, and speeding past the Gloucester Police Station, local police and sheriff's deputies caught them fleeing through a wooded section near the seashore. My North Shore dynamic duo, Dobson and Geary, had teamed up again, and a homeowner near the woods where the boys were captured complained to the Gloucester police that a bullet was fired through his window during the pursuit. Nobody knew who fired it, but I had my suspicions.

Nearby, Mrs. Mary Murry had called police that her husband Leo was harassing her again, and could they come and pick him up. He had become intoxicated and belligerent. The Gloucester Police had broken up their squabbles many times before. Mrs. Murry walked outside her house to get away from her husband and await the police. Dobson and Geary coincidentally drove by her house at that moment in their hunt for the escapees. Mrs. Murry waved them down. "He's upstairs," she whispered to them as Dobson rolled down the window. Geary and Dobson were into the house and up the stairs in a flash, guns drawn, thinking that they had cornered an escapee. Mr. Murray was watching television, oblivious to what was going on around him. The deputies quietly snuck up on him from behind and stuck the barrels of their guns into his neck.

"Hands in the air and don't move a muscle," were their orders to the startled man. Mrs. Murry had now made it back upstairs and was shocked at how rough these law enforcement men were treating her husband, "just for being a little drunk and belligerent." She couldn't believe it, and as Dobson and Geary cuffed Leo Murry and began dragging him down the stairs, she begged them to stop. It took the two deputies a few minutes to realize that Mr. Murry wasn't one of the escapees and that they had the wrong man. They uncuffed Mr. Murry, who was truly bewildered, and he swore to the deputies that he would never harass his wife again. Mrs. Murry seemed pleased, so Dobson and Geary tiptoed away, also pleased that they weren't sued for false arrest.

While all my deputies were out scouring the escapees' old neighborhoods and frequented haunts, I was filtering the many phone calls from various parts of New England, all swearing to me that they had seen one or more of the escapees, or had a hunch as to where they were hiding. My guess was that Fitzpatrick wouldn't hang around the local area this time. I expected he was long gone, or at least on his way there. One call I got was from an ex-con who lived in Beverly, but was vacationing up in Maine. He had squealed on his fellow inmates before, gathering brownie points for good treatment if he ever returned to our jail. "I saw Fitzy and two of the others at an old summer house near Bangor. It's owned by a pal of mine and theirs. I heard them say they were heading to Canada."

Although I received many kooky calls and even some from friends of the escapees trying to throw me off their trail, I considered the Bangor call a legitimate lead. I would guess Fitzy would head for Canada in the hopes of staying there awhile. I notified the Maine State Police, the Border Patrol, and the Canadian Mounties. Within an hour all entrance stations to Canada were notified. I had spent three days and nights pursuing various leads, and I was exhausted, but I knew Fitzy was heading for the Canadian boarder, and we were ready for him. The problem was that he and his fellow escapees never showed up at the border stations. I waited impatiently for days, expecting a call any minute that they had been caught in their flight north, but word never came.

It came as a surprise to me that three days later I received word from the Boston MDC Police that one of the escapees, 18-year-old Fred Henning, had been arrested in Dorchester, Massachusetts in the process of trying to steal an automobile. He certainly couldn't have been heading for Canada if he was in Dorchester. When he was returned to Salem Jail, now considered a hero by his fellow inmates, I grilled him about the possible whereabouts of the other three. The only information I got was that he went his way, and they went theirs. Another setback for my Canadian theory was that a week later we received a report from North Carolina that three young men fitting the descriptions of our three inmates-at-large had tried to pass off a bogus credit card. Now they were heading south, probably to Florida, after traveling all the way to Maine. Had someone tipped them off that I had the border stations to Canada covered, thus prompting them to turn around and head south? I didn't find out the answer to this until years later. Paul Fitzpatrick had an apprehension as he and his cohorts neared the Canadian border. It was so strong that he feared capture at the border and convinced the others that they should turn directly around and head south to Florida. It was a good intuitive move on his part and provided him with a few extra weeks of freedom, but eventually he was picked up by the Florida police and returned to me in Salem. Wayne Chamberlin met the same fate a little while later, but to my knowledge, Bruce Balestraci was never recaptured.

I placed Fitzpatrick in protective custody, away from the other inmates, and he was a model prisoner for some time. One day he asked to see me.

"When are you going to move me in with the general population?" he asked.

"Never!" I replied. "To be honest, I don't dare to. You've escaped on me twice, and the last time you took three guys with you. I can't afford to lose you again. I'm so impressed with your escape techniques, Fitzy, that I'm not even going to tack on extra jail time for your last escape."

He looked at me wide-eyed, not believing my statement. "You have to take me to court for the escape," he said, a half smile on his face.

"No, I don't," I replied, "and I won't. I'm not going to have you hang around this cheese-box of a jail, trying to find other means of successful escape. You're just doing this so I'll keep tacking an added six months to your jail time here, and you can avoid going to Arkansas where they're waiting to try you for armed robbery."

"You've got to keep me here," he said.

"I don't want you here," I said. "They're coming tomorrow morning to take you back to Arkansas, and the sheriff down there told me that he can't wait to see you." Fitzy gave me a hard stare of disgust. I smiled and waved him goodbye. "So long Fitzy," I said leaving his cell, " I can't say I've enjoyed having you around, but you sure kept me and my deputies on our toes." Next morning, two deputy sheriffs with drawling southern accents came and took Fitzy away.

I begged the county commissioners to give me new perimeter fencing topped with sharp Conestoga wire and a new lockable front gate that could be operated electronically or with keys. The press was emphasizing the frequency of escapes from Salem Jail, and I emphasized to the commissioners that anyone with brains, like Fitzy, could find ways to get out. "That's all some of the inmates do all day is think up ways to get out. Therefore we must devise ways to keep them in. A half decent fence with non-rusting barbed-wire would help." The commissioners and state legislature finally relented, and Salem and Lawrence Jails received security fencing topped with new non-rusting sharp wire that curled about the top of the fencing like tumbleweed. It was so sharp that a worker installing it at Salem lost half a finger, and a bird that came to perch on it lost a foot. "Even Fitzpatrick would have a tough time getting up, over, or around this stuff," I told my secretary Loretta Rainville, who seemed to get paler and paler as the fencing and wire was being erected around us. When the electronic front gate was installed, Loretta, looking as if she was about to faint, walked into my office and announced that she was quitting.

"This can't be," I looked up at her in utter horror. Loretta was the life-blood of the department. She was the one who kept us organized and operational. "Why would you want to leave?" I asked.

She pointed to the new front gate. "I can't be locked in," she said. "I have a phobia about closed-in places. I must have a means of escape." This created an enormous dilemma for me. I couldn't afford to lose Loretta. It would be impossible to find someone with her honed skills and knowledge of the department, yet I was obliged to secure the premises, especially after begging the commissioners and legislature for money to fill the need. I did however understand Loretta's problem, as she wasn't the only one in the department who suffered from "agoraphobia" which Webster describes as "A fear of being in an inescapable situation." After careful thought, I realized that there was only one solution to our dilemma. But I also knew that I could never tell anyone except Loretta of my plan—not the commissioners, not the legislature, not even my deputies or guards. I whispered my solution to Loretta and swore her to secrecy. She agreed to remain as my secretary. I assured her that we would never shut or lock the front gate until she had left work each day, and when she arrived to work in the morning, we would leave the front gate ajar. Loretta could see the gate from where she sat, and therefore could remain calm all day. I was relieved to keep Loretta running my office, but after all my crying and moaning to state legislators, county commissioners, and members of the County Advisory Committee, the Salem Jail remained as vulnerable as ever.

CHAPTER XVIII

Wyatt Earp's Revenge

It wasn't often that I left work before 5:00 P.M., and even less frequent that I would stroll downtown, wander into a restaurant or bar, and order a drink. But after two years of turmoil, the stress of work prompted just such a stroll on this Friday in early spring. I had heard that yet another of my most experienced correctional officers, John Blaisdell, was quitting the department, and that my old college pal Billy Cox was working some sort of black market scam at the Newburyport Court house. To make matters worse, I was informed that, in Lawrence, the writ servers were throwing writs into the sewers because the payments were too menial. On top of all that, I got word that Dugie Russell was putting tadpoles from the pond outside the Newburyport Courthouse into Judge Linscott's water pitcher while he was sitting on the bench. My cup runnith over. And last but not least, the night before I had been awakened just after midnight and called to the jail to quell a riot.

"Please, Sheriff," shouted Correctional Office Larry Puleo over the phone, "the inmates are screaming and trying to breakdown the iron gate."

I arrived within minutes and Larry opened the front door for me. I could hear the yelling when I entered the compound. All the lights were out inside, and it was completely dark but for the waving beams from the guards' flashlights. Only Larry Puleo and two other guards were on duty. They were facing 150 angry, cursing inmates. Larry had just been made a senior guard, and it was his first night in charge of a shift. His face was pale and sweat dripped from his bald head.

"What are they angry about?" I asked him over the din.

"I don't know," replied Larry. "When I shut off the electricity at midnight—which we do every night—there was an uproar, and then they went into a frenzy. They shouted at me—spit at me. It's as if they all went insane at once."

"But you don't know why?" Larry shook his head. "There's no reason for it?" He shook his head again. It didn't make sense. I walked over to the screaming, fuming inmates that crowded the cell-block gate.

"What's the matter?" I asked loudly.

"That bastard shut off the electricity," shouted one. "We was watchin' *White Heat* with Jimmy Cagney, and that asshole shut off all our sets."

I turned to Puleo. "Turn the electricity back on," I said, "and keep it on until the movie is over."

Puleo looked dumbfounded. "But we're supposed to shut off electricity at midnight." Puleo saw I was perturbed and he followed my order. The inmates all ran back to their television sets. The jail was once again quiet. I walked out of the jail without saying another word to Puleo. *White Heat* was an appropriate title, for I was white hot with anger.

Next morning I got the call about Billy Cox before I had my coffee. "He's selling stuff from the Newburyport Courthouse," I was told by an anonymous caller. "Better check it out, Sheriff."

"Eggs," Billy confessed. "I've been selling eggs to the Chinese, and I've been doing it for months. It's become very profitable and helps supplement the shitty salary from you for being a court officer."

"Explain yourself, Billy. You're not making sense."

"What else can I tell you," stuttered my Cagney-like pal. "I'm guilty of trading goose eggs for scotch-on-the-rocks at the local Chinese restaurant. I was taking the goose eggs to my house, but there were too many of them, so Doris made me stop bringing them home."

"And you get these goose eggs from the Newburyport Courthouse?"

"Yes, actually, from the windowsill out back by the pond."

"The geese lay the eggs on the windowsill?"

"Not exactly...the local kids scoop them up by the pond and leave them for me there—and believe me, they really start piling up. No one else wants them, Bob, so I trade them for whiskey."

"Why do the kids leave them for you? What do you give them?"

"Nothin'…well…you see, I caught them breaking the eggs on the rocks out back of the courthouse, so I befriended them and let them touch my gun. I told them to save the eggs for me, which they do religiously. The guy at the Chinese Restaurant considers them a delicacy, and I get free drinks. It works out for everyone. But if it's a crime, Sheriff, I'll wait outside the courthouse, and you can send cops up to cuff me and bring me to jail. You'll have to send someone up here to collect the goose eggs every couple of days, though, or they'll start stinking up the courtroom. But, if you've got nothing better to do than arrest your own deputies, after you arrest me, I suggest you arrest Dugie Russell. He's putting tadpoles from the pond into the drinking water up here. And that's more criminal than selling eggs to the Chinese, don't you think?"

"Top of the world, Ma!" I shouted at him.

"What???"

"Nothing. Go collect your goose eggs." I was happy that all I had on my hands was an entrepreneur egg collector, and that I wouldn't have to discipline and old friend.

I then had to hunt down Dugie Russell to have him explain putting tadpoles in the judge's water. "Just a joke, Sheriff," said Dugie. "The judge thought it was funny." It still amazed me, however, that this was the silly kind of so-called crisis I had to deal with as a sheriff.

It was that kind of a day—all day. But the call from North County lawyers telling me that my deputies were throwing writs into the gutters was serious business. These legal papers were orders for people to appear in court or risk arrest, and were found by a passer-by and turned over to the lawyer whose name was on them. I called Bob Curran, Chief Deputy of Process Serving, who was already aware of the problem.

"You've also got some deputies serving papers for lawyers as constables and doing so wearing their deputy sheriff badges," Bob added to the dilemma.

"The writ serving deputies agreed not to do that," I told Bob.

"But even though they told you that they won't serve process as constables while they are on duty as deputies, four of them are serving as constables and are using the badge you gave them to do constable work. Something they swore they wouldn't do. You're too easy on them." Constables were chosen to serve process for each city and were only able to serve within that city. Deputy sheriffs, on the other hand, were hired to serve writs for lawyers throughout the county, often conflicting with the constables.

"I've told them twice not to do that," I said to Bob.

"Tell them again," urged Bob.

As I sauntered up to the bar at the Beef & Oyster Restaurant in downtown Salem, I mulled over Bob Curran's words: "You're too easy on them." That very week, Charlie Geary had called me a "marshmallow" for being too easy on a wayward deputy. I thought I was being tough on everybody, but maybe I was a marshmallow. Maybe I should become a tough-as-nails sheriff like in the Old West. As I sipped my drink standing at the bar, I heard familiar voices coming from a table behind me.

"Hey! Sheriffs aren't suppose to drink at the bar," said one voice.

"You shouldn't be drinking whiskey at this hour," said another.

I turned to face a table filled with *Salem Evening News* reporters, Rollie Corneau, Carl Johnson, Barb Yagerman, and two others. Johnson was smiling but the others weren't.

"You should sit at a table and not stand at the bar," said Corneau. The comments were ludicrous coming from two of these reporters, who were known heavy drinkers.

"All sheriffs drink," I retorted, "like all news reporters drink."

"Not standing at the bar," said Corneau.

"It's after working hours," I replied. "I'm not in uniform—what's the beef?"

"It don't look right," said Corneau.

"Haven't you ever heard of Wyatt Earp," I said. "He drank at the bar all the time." I had good reason not to be too friendly with Barb

Yagerman or Rollie Corneau, two of Editor Jim Shea's assistants, with whom I had had previous run-ins over articles they wrote when I was a state representative. I turned to face the bartender and didn't look back. I quickly finished my drink and headed off to Peabody and Johnny Blaisdell's going-away party without giving the reporters another look. Next morning there was an article about me in the *Salem News* penned by Barbara Yagerman. The headline read "Sheriff Cahill Thinks He's Wyatt Earp."

I arrived at the little nightclub where the correctional officers were having the party for Johnny, and sat at a table away from the others, silently fuming at the comments by the reporters. I felt like I was being maligned from all directions—the court officers, writ servers, news reporters, and now as I sat at Johnny Blaisdell's retirement party, by the correctional officers. The few who came over to my table to talk came to complain about one thing or the other, and those who were deep into drink, complained the longest and the loudest. I stayed until I could stand it no longer and I walked over to Blaisdell to say goodbye and good luck. I was losing a senior correctional officer with intelligence and common sense, two premium qualities not often found in a correctional officer. Blaisdell's departure added to the foulness of my mood.

"So, you'll be a Marblehead cop now." I shook his hand.

"Only part time," Blaisdell replied.

"You're leaving a fulltime job for a part time job? The pay must be terrific."

"I'll be making much less," said Blaisdell.

"Then why the hell leave us?" I snapped at him.

"I thought you wanted me to go," said Blaisdell.

I was surprised at his comment. "What would make you think I wanted you to leave?"

"Cause I was in charge of the shift at the last big escape, and you were so pissed at me, that I figured you wanted me out of the jail."

"You mean to tell me that the only reason you're leaving the sheriff's department is because you think I'm bullshit at you? I was bullshit at everyone after that escape, not just you!"

Blaisdell managed a slight smile.

"So you really don't want to leave?"

"No, Sheriff, I don't want to go."

"Well then, please don't," I laughed. "I can't afford to lose experienced guys."

He hesitated. "But what about the party, sir, and the presents the guys gave me and everything. I can't just show up to work again, I'd feel like an ass."

"Tell you what," I said. "Take your part time job as a cop and work for me as well! You can do part time as a court officer, and then after about a month, we'll slowly bring you back into the jail. Nobody will ever know."

Johnny Blaisdell and I shook hands on it, and I felt so good about my one successful maneuver of the day, that I stayed at the retirement party and celebrated with the boys, toasting periodically to Johnny Blaisdell and his new job. He never did retire from the sheriff's department while I was in charge.

I awoke the next morning, with a pounding headache, and a resolve to turn over a new leaf. I would no longer be a marshmallow, but a tough don't-tread-on-me sheriff, like Wyatt Earp. I called the writ-office in the north to find out as much as I could about the writ papers found in a Lawrence gutter. "Deputies don't like serving those cheap writs 'cause they only get about two bucks per service," I was told by Bob Curran.

"Whoever was responsible for those writs found in the gutter, I want fired," I said.

"Only you can fire him," said Bob.

While I was in a good cranky mood, I called the northern county writ server who had disposed of his legal papers. "I hate to do this over the phone, but I don't have time to go to Lawrence. You're fired!" I shouted at him. "Turn your badge into the writ office."

Then, I set up a meeting for early that afternoon for the writ-serving deputies from Beverly, Gloucester, and Newburyport. With all seated before me, I asked, "Did we not agree that you as deputy sheriffs would not serve civil process for your cities as constables?"

They all nodded yes. "Did I not call each of you at least twice after I discovered you were serving as constables using the deputy badge?" They nodded yes. "So you've had your warnings. You're all fired. Turn in your badges to Loretta on your way out."

So, in one day I fired four deputies. I still, to this day, cannot figure why those serving writs as deputies insisted on also serving as constables, which they had earlier voted with their fellow writ servers not to do. Was it greed? Was it that they all served under Sheriff Wells, who turned a blind eye? Was it possible that they could not break an old habit? They never offered a word of explanation, but simply walked out of my office in silence.

* * *

The firing of the writ-serving deputies was just the beginning of my problems with that division. Bob Curran had handled complaints for well over a year, and centralizing the writ-service in the southern cities and towns of the county seemed to be working well for the south, but the northern office, although under Bob's jurisdiction, was at times quite unpredictable. Curran informed me that when the northern office secretary and Deputy Charlie Canto of Methuen went on vacation, the office was closed for a week or more, and the Lawrence lawyers could not serve papers or summons for court appearances.

"Also," Bob Curran informed me, "the deputies who serve process in the north have not been paid for months. Something is really afoul up there."

"I'm getting sick and tired of all these old Sheriff Wells deputies trying to pull the wool over my eyes and treating all the new deputies like second rate citizens. Go up to Lawrence, Bob, and bring their operation back to Salem. Close them down and notify the northern lawyers that service will be out of Salem from now on. We should have centralized the whole county in the beginning. That's what I get for trying to be accommodating. Don't even tell them you're coming 'til you get there. That way they won't be able to hide anything."

"Do you want me to pay the deputies who haven't been paid?" asked Bob.

"Yes, if you can, and tell them all to come to Salem for work from now on. Go up there like Gestapo and clean out their office. Bring a truck and move everything south."

"Are you going to fire the office staff?"

"Just the secretary. Everyone else will stay, but they have to work out of your office here in Salem, where you can keep an eye on them. The head guys may quit anyway when they realize what's happening."

I knew Bob Curran would do the job quickly and efficiently. I had no fall-out when I centralized the writ service in other areas throughout the county, so I expected little reaction from the north. I was wrong again.

There was a "wicked witch" in the northland, who prompted the top reporter from the *Lawrence Eagle Tribune*, Norma Nathan, to come visit me for an interview in Salem, and to sit with Chief Deputy of the Writ Service Bob Curran, as well. Her three-part, three-day article was scathing to say the least:

Curran left a $25,000-a-year job he held for 20 years with the General Electric Co. to work at 'streamlining' the legal fees organization. The deputies operation is a private one even though it is under the wing of the sheriff and a patronage operation, and therefore the total fees are hard to ascertain. But Curran is believed to have received checks amounting to approximately $3,000 (from the Lawrence writ-office), a portion of fees deputies received from lawyers for delivering writs, summons or attachments. The fees billed to lawyers are the deputies' pay. Traditionally, the Lawrence fees stayed in the Lawrence office to be split among Lawrence deputies. The checks were mailed to Curran at his home…'I never told anyone to send checks to my home', Curran said, blaming the 'girl' who made out the forms in Lawrence…The Lawrence office was absorbed into a 'consolidated' deputies office, run by Curran from Salem, which is expected to generate about $200,000 in legal paper deliveries.

By his own recollection, Curran had received checks total-
ing 'maybe $2,000 to $3,000.' This is the sum he remembers
when repeatedly questioned during a two-hour interview. He
said the money was for expenses, like mailing and envelopes,
charged against the up-county office by the centralized operation in Salem. Curran said he couldn't produce a total figure for
envelopes and clerical expenses charged by Salem against the
Lawrence office except for a mailing piece for a $544 price to
15,000 lawyers in the state advising them on the new set-up;
$30.00 for a bulk mailing permit and the cost of stamps...Both
Curran and Special Sheriff Charles Reardon collected fees as
deputies last year. Cahill said they were in the $6,000 or $7,000
range. Since the business is private, the figure does not have to
be made public. Reardon's wife and Curran's wife are both em-
ployed in the deputy's office as part of a four woman clerical
staff....

This unfavorable article series on the writ-business, vilifying Bob
Curran, was reprinted verbatim in the *Salem Evening News*. I felt
obliged to reply in both newspapers, realizing full well that the articles were provoked by a disgruntled employee of the North. I started
out by stating:

Your inference that the serving of civil process in this county is
complicated, political and secretive, run loosely by the sheriff, is
right!

If the county or state can run it more efficiently and with
less politics involved, I welcome them to take it over. With the
responsibility of two jails, three courthouses and a growing alternatives in corrections program, the last thing I need or desire
is the running (or overseeing) of a private business. If you and
your staff wish to draft up legislation with me to change this situation, I am more than willing to cooperate, but let me first cor-
rect some errors in your recent articles, and explain as simply as

I can, why I have made certain changes in the writ business. I hope you will be willing to give me space in your newspaper for this purpose. I am a firm believer in 'freedom of the press,' as long as, like all other freedoms, the duty of responsibility to tell both sides of a story is realized. When I became sheriff, I closed down four city writ offices for the following reasons: (A) Writ serving deputies, some good businessmen, some not, were handling service in different ways, charging different fees. (B) When a deputy in charge of a specific city or town decided to take a vacation, leave for a weekend, or was sick, lawyers could not get service. (C) Local deputies had specific areas to cover, but did receive writs to be served outside their areas, which they did serve, angering the deputy of the outside area. As a result, all serving deputies disliked and distrusted each other. (D) Some lawyers, realizing that most serving deputies were at odds with each other, would first use one, not pay him, and then use another and not pay him either, knowing that the two would never compare notes. And (E), the sheriff never had control over these little dynasties, but I did receive all the complaints for sloppy or late service by the deputies. Thus, centralizing was the solution and does seem to be working fine....

I thought my little rebuttal to the newspapers would end the dispute and the innuendoes, but it didn't. The lawyers in the North were up in arms and wanted an open meeting with me in Lawrence as soon as possible. It was an open meeting of the Lawrence Bar Association with over forty attorneys in attendance at the courthouse. All were ready to pounce on me for moving their writ-office to Salem. Even before I reached the podium, escorted by Bill Ryan and Bob Curran, the questions came fast and furious. "You have a county commissioner in Lawrence and a clerk of courts in Lawrence. Why can't we have a deputy sheriff in Lawrence?" shouted Attorney Carmine DiAdamo to the applause of the others.

"You have more than one deputy sheriff here," I replied. "It's just the writ office that has been moved to Salem."

"And most of your deputies up here are also on the county payroll," cried another attorney. "If Ryan is suppose to watch the Lawrence Jail, he can't be out serving papers as well."

"There were no complaints, and we had a good thing going here," said Attorney Mike Tarshi. "Now it's changed. Why?" I tried to explain to them the purpose of centralizing the service and how well it has worked in the south county, but they started booing me in mid-explanation.

"Let's make a deal," shouted DiAdamo over the groans and moans. "You said in the *Eagle Tribune* this week that this business is a headache and you want help with it. Let us help. We want two Greater Lawrence deputy sheriffs, an office, and a secretary in Lawrence." The crowd cheered and the room shook with applause. The only other time that I felt this angry and defeated in Lawrence, was some twenty-five years earlier when I stood in the middle of Lawrence Stadium as their high school football team defeated my Salem Witches, 42 to 6.

"As I view county government, it's always the Lawrence area which turns out to be the ugly step-child of Essex County," said Attorney Angelo Fischella. "It's a banana shaped county and everything is down at the southern end. Our clients in Lawrence are citizens and voters, and they are being put out. If you want to centralize, pay rent in Middleton—halfway between—so Salem is as inconvenienced as Lawrence," he said.

"Five law firms that handle eighty percent of the business here in the north aren't even here today," Bill Ryan whispered in my ear, so I repeated what he said to the crowd, which seemed to make them even more belligerent.

"You don't even know who's here," retorted Attorney DiAdamo, and he called for a show of hands, which indicated that delegates from three of the five firms were in the audience. Finally, in complete frustration, I lifted my hands to quiet the room. I was being verbally pulverized, and I had no intention of giving the Lawrence deputies and lawyers back their unruly and disorganized kingdom of mishandled civil process.

"Gentlemen, I've heard all of your complaints," I heard myself saying, "and most of them are valid, but I ask you to bear with me for six months…just six months," I repeated over the groans. If this new centralized method is not working to your satisfaction, we will return to the old system, with a separate office here or in Middleton. I guarantee there will be no delays in your service, and the same deputies minus one, will be serving you. The deputy who was throwing your low-paying papers into the gutter has been fired. Any questions or complaints with this new centralized service, call Bob Curran or me immediately. Thank for your time, gentlemen, which I know is precious." I walked directly from the podium, out the front door and to my vehicle, with Curran close on my heels.

"Lets get the hell out of here fast," I told Bob, and we sped off to Salem. *The Eagle-Tribune's* headline the next day read: "Angry Attorneys want service – Cahill Asks Lawyers For Time." It was the last time I was ever written up in the Lawrence newspaper, and it was the last time I ever heard from a Lawrence attorney. Apparently centralized writ-service from the south worked for them, for when the six months were up, there wasn't one discouraging word from the north county.

There was, however, more than one discouraging word from the south. While Bob Curran and I were on a lunch break in downtown Salem, we visited Gibley's Clothing Store to look at suits. Gibley's was located across from the Beef & Oyster Restaurant, where I'd been drinking at the bar to the ribbing from the Salem reporters. Two men walked into the clothing store, and the taller, bulkier of the two confronted me, and with an angry stare, said, "I guess you got it good from the lawyers in Lawrence last week."

"Yes," I smiled in agreement. "They got me good." I realized that I knew this man from somewhere, but I couldn't place him or remember his name.

"Don't you have anything better to do than poke around in a clothing store all afternoon."

"I have plenty to do. Just taking a break," I replied, wondering what business it was to this man what I did with my time. I turned to

Curran and he just shrugged his shoulders. He obviously didn't recognize this bold man either.

"What about you?" I asked. "You don't have anything better to do either?" The older man standing with the outspoken one looked shocked, and he put his finger to his lips, signaling me not to say anything else. I took a good look at him and I realized that the older man was Jack Splain, the advertising manager of the *Salem Evening News* and a well-liked man about town. "Hi Jack," I said, "I didn't recognize you at first," and I shook his hand. Then it dawned on me who the big man was. It had to be Cy Newbegin, the publisher of the *Salem Evening News*, who I had only met once before when we sat at the same table at a banquet. It was obvious that he didn't like me, but I didn't know why. I wiped the smile off my face and stared back at Newbegin with the same angry glare he was giving me.

"You don't spend much time at your job as sheriff, do you?" he snarled.

"I spend too much time," I replied. "I don't have a plush job like newspaper publisher with a flunky editor like Shea to do my dirty work."

Jack Splain's mouth opened wide and he almost fell over in disbelief, and Curran's jaw dropped too. Like with judges, it wasn't wise to talk disparagingly to newspaper publishers, but the words just flowed uncontrollably from my lips. I had taken a lot of unjustified crap from this man and his editor, and this was about the only opportunity I had to go directly to the source and give some back.

"You couldn't lick Jim Shea's boots," he shouted, red faced.

"Not while he's lickin' yours every day," I laughed in his face.

I thought the man would explode in front of my eyes. His mouth opened and foam sprang forth. He turned and walked quickly away.

"Don't get into a pissing contest with a skunk," warned Jack Splain.

"And that's really what he is, isn't he," I said loud enough for Newbegin to hear, "A skunk!" He disappeared into hanging rows of suits.

Jack shook his head. "Look," I said to Jack, "this guy has done to me about everything one man can do to another, so even though I will probably pay big time for this, I truly enjoyed the confrontation…and by the way, Jack, he started it, not me."

Curran and I left Jack Splain standing there in disbelief. Was my revenge sweet? Yes! But it wasn't long lasting.

CHAPTER XIX

Who Shot The Sheriff

For the upcoming Fourth of July, the inmates asked if they could paint the outside wooden fence that faced Bridge Street red, white, and blue. The old gray fence that enclosed the small recreation yard was in need of a paint job. On condition that only trusted inmates did the work and a guard was present with them at all times, I acquiesced. Don Clark of Water's & Brown Hardware of Salem donated the paint and brushes.

Throughout most of the hot summer, the barebacked and torn tee-shirted men built their own staging and happily contributed to the patriotic fervor of the anniversary of the American Revolution. In the midst of this spirited effort, I received a letter from the President of Parker Brothers Game Company, Randolph Burton III. The Parker Brothers employees could watch the progress of the colorful red, white, and blue striped fence from their windows, and Randolph Burton III didn't like it. He also explained that he didn't consider inmates American citizens. I didn't know whether to laugh or cry. I contemplated sending the letter on to Cy Newbegin or Jim Shea at the *Salem Evening News*, but decided against it for fear that they wouldn't share my disappointment in such a letter. So I showed it to no one, nor did I reply to it.

With contributions of food from local businesses and individuals, the deputies, guards, and I sponsored an all day cookout in the recreation yard for all the inmates on the Fourth of July. No fireworks or alcoholic beverages, but a lot of volleyball, basketball, good eats, and refreshing camaraderie shared between deputies and inmates. It was a first for the Salem Jail and any anticipated worry about inmate misbehavior was unrealized. Holidays are usually sad days for the incarcerated because of the increased sense of isolation and loneliness, but this bicentennial celebration in the jail yard seemed to be enjoyed by all, me included. I just wished Randolph Barton III could have been there to celebrate with all these other Americans.

The only problem came the next morning as I sat at my desk enjoying my second cup of coffee and not enjoying an expense report. The peacefulness of the morning routine and the melancholy that always follows a party broke with a thunderous explosion from somewhere inside the jail. Stunned, I leapt from behind my desk and made for the door, listening for more noise – another explosion, gunfire, alarms, anything. I heard nothing but muffled screams from deep inside the jail. I ran across the lawn, and as I reached the door, voices came clearer and I could hear a guard shouting that a man was down. I followed two scurrying guards and took the stairs two at a time, trying to keep pace. The strong smell of sulfur hit me at the top of the stairs, but I still couldn't tell what had exploded or who was hurt. I lumbered down the corridor of the second tier, out of breath and sweating, and now could hear the moans of pain from behind a crowd of officers. I shoved my way though and into the cell of an inmate who was on the ground with his left hand and arm torn to shreds. Blood was splattered everywhere. A quick working guard had tied the arm off at the forearm and was applying pressure to the wound. Three of us helped the young inmate off the floor and rushed him out through the back to the parking lot where we stuffed him into the back of a guard's car, and he peeled out toward the hospital. The inmate was in shock and much pain.

He had been making a pipe bomb, stuffing a small length of pipe with match heads that he had been collecting for months from borrowed cardboard matchbooks. He had packed them too tight and his homemade bomb exploded in his hand. It was his own little fireworks display.

The doctors were able to save his hand. He would, however, have a lot of scars and need a lot of rehabilitation. Fortunately the *Salem News* reporters didn't get wind of the homemade bomb explosion at the jail.

✳ ✳ ✳

My expectation of the other shoe dropping after my battle with Newbegin in the clothing store did, however, eventually come to fruition. When my old election campaign committee decided to have a testimonial for me and to have guests pay to attend, as a means to pay off my overdue campaign debts, Jim Shea came at me with a vengeance:

> Most politicians have a massive ego or they wouldn't be in public office to start with. Many have a lot of brass. A few have unmitigated gall. It is bad enough when there is an election campaign in progress to have to endure the fund-raising efforts of office holders and office seekers. It is particularly galling to have them putting the arm on people for money they will not put to use for legitimate campaign purposes. Sheriff Robert E. Cahill appears to fit into that category of 'the public be damned' as he raises political money out of season and engages in a kingdom building campaign in the exercise of his office.... Here is a man who absolutely loves to run parties for himself.... There is no justification for a fundraising party for Cahill. He will probably claim there are some liabilities left over from his non-competitive campaign, but we doubt this.... The thing is a holdup and should be investigated....

Reading the editorial, I cancelled the testimonial and sent off a rebuttal to Shea at the *Salem Evening News*, which he published in part. It read:

> If I deserved the criticism, I'd take it and that would be it, but this was just completely vindictive... .My tendency to give testimonials, as the editor called it, is unfounded. I certainly had fewer testimonials than any other Essex County official.... How else does a politician pay his debts? I still have some $4,000 remaining of campaign debts, and this is after re-mortgaging my home to pay some debts off...

Next, the *Salem Evening News* posse came at me through my
dog. A front-page feature story, titled "Sheriff Cahill In Court Today
Over His Dog," once again, caught me off guard. "Bob Cahill's dog,
as with Bill Grogan's goat, is causing problems for his master," wrote
Peter Homan, one of Jim Shea's reporters. Homan went on to write:

> Cahill, the county's chief law enforcement officer was to be sub-
> poenaed to appear in Salem District Court this morning to an-
> swer a complaint that his dog has been violating the city's leash
> law. The complaint was filed by Mrs. Madeline Michaud, wife
> of Dr. Raymond A. Michaud of Salem Hospital.
>   According to Mrs. Michaud, this is the second court hear-
> ing scheduled for Cahill's dog in nine days, but the first was not
> held because Mrs. Michaud's complaint had disappeared from
> court files. Dog Officer Donald R. Famico confirmed that all
> court records pertaining to the Cahill complaint had disap-
> peared…. Mrs. Michaud said she waited all morning long, sat
> through every case heard that morning, and her complaint never
> came up. At the end of the session that day, she said Judge
> Abraham Ankles asked why she was there and then gave the
> clerk ten minutes to produce the complaint. But, she said, 'there
> was no trace of it'….

I had no idea where my neighbor, Mrs. Michaud's complaint had
gone, but it was obvious to me where this article was going. Although
all this information was news to me, the *Salem News* used Mrs.
Michaud to make me the scapegoat and accused me of stealing court
files. The article continued:

> Mrs. Michaud said she is not a dog hater, she has a dog of her
> own which is 'never, never, never, never on other people's prop-
> erty!' She said 'the dog is running around constantly,' chasing
> cars and snapping at children. The Michauds have a large yard
> that is well maintained by Dr. Michaud. 'I think it's just jeal-

ousy. The sheriff has a great big, fenced in yard,' said Mrs. Michaud, suggesting that the dog need not be loose on the street. According to Famico, at least two $10 violation notices have been sent to the sheriff.

Mrs. Michaud said she has 'nothing against' Cahill but the issue has become a matter of principle, 'if a sheriff can go down and pull complaints out of court.' She also said her husband is tired of cleaning up after neighbors' dogs...

I had never received any violation notices, and my dog, Archie, never snapped at more than a flea, and did a poor job at that. The aging dog was always around kids and wouldn't know how to chase a car. She was just a fine old medium sized mongrel, who all the neighborhood kids loved. I imagined that the boys at the *Salem Evening News* were really chuckling at this one. Homan quickly followed the next day with another front-page article. "Sheriff Told: Tie Up Dog," was the headline for this one:

Judge Ankeles personally telephoned Cahill to request his appearance in the court to respond to a second complaint brought against his dog by Mrs. Madeline Michaud. When Mrs. Michaud, her husband, Dr. Raymond J. Michaud, and Dog Officer Donald R. Famico appeared in court for the scheduled hearing on the complaint, they found that Cahill was not there and that for the second time in two-weeks, records of the complaint had disappeared....

I had never been served with a summons, and when the reporter confronted me, I explained to him that neither I nor any of my employees were in charge of District Court records, and even if I were, I certainly would not snitch a complaint against me or my dog. At the judge's phone call, I walked over to District Court to be confronted by my dog's accusers. When I arrived, I apologized for my tardiness and explained that I had no knowledge of the hearings concerning my dog. Then I turned to Mrs. Michaud, who I knew only slightly, and told her that I wish she would stop referring to my pet as "The Sheriff's Dog." "The dog's name is Archie, a female with long floppy ears and a long crooked nose. Truly a happy-go-lucky dog, that is allowed to play in my fenced in, big back yard. She does occasionally sneak out with my four children and she has been known to visit my brother's son Mark, who lives diagonally across the street from the Michauds. However, if Archie peed on Doctor Michaud's lawn, only a phone call to my wife or me was needed. Mrs. Michaud testified that her daughter saw Archie wee-wee on the lawn, and therefore, I will tie Archie to a long leash in my yard so she won't escape into the neighborhood again."

I took a breath and continued. "Mrs. Michaud's contention that I sneakily slipped into the dog officer's file and lifted Archie's cloudy record," I told the judge and the reporter who stood nearby, "is pure drivel. Neither a sheriff nor a dog would stoop so low. I was not notified of these hearings, it's as simple as that," I concluded. Doc Michaud had a wispy smile on his face, but Mrs. Michaud still looked perturbed.

"By the way," I added, as the Judge agreed that the solution was to tie up the dog, " I think it only befitting that Mrs. Michaud stop calling Archie a mongrel. Now that my dog is notorious, let me set the record straight. Archie is not a mongrel, she is one-third beagle, one-third terrier, and one-third something else."

To add insult to their injury, my brother Jim sent Mrs. Michaud a bouquet of roses. The next day the headline was: "Sheriff Growls Good Naturedly After Judge Puts 'Bite' On Dog." At least I could laugh along with the editor and publisher on this one. But I just had the feeling that Shea and Newbegin weren't done with me.

✹ ✹ ✹

Ten days later, September 14, 1977, the *Lawrence Eagle Tribune* headlined: "New Jail For County Proposed." The article went on to say that "Senate President Kevin Harrington and House Speaker Thomas W. McGee discussed the building of a new jail in Essex

County yesterday at a special meeting called by Harrington...Suggested were sites adjacent to the Lawrence Alternative Center, on or near the present Salem Jail and in Middleton or Danvers..."

This was the opportunity that Editor Jim Shea took to pounce. He apparently did not want the *Lawrence Tribune* to out-scoop him on the issue of a new jail. In the *Salem Evening News*, he suggested in a bold headline: "What's Wrong With County Jail At Danvers." After stating that I seemed out of touch with political and economic realities and that my ideas "proposed for solving the jail situation have no broad-based community support," Shea decided to provide a solution of his own:

> When you are spending millions of dollars in public money on building projects in a county, the public seems to be always looking at the commissioners with a questioning eye. There have been aborted efforts to get the centralized jail concept in motion, including spending of considerable money about 15 years ago on some plans, which were never used.... Knowing that the climate for a new jail with a $10 million to $30 million price tag was unrealistic and had no chance politically, Cahill would instead like to settle for a measly $5 million to patch up the Salem and Lawrence Jails.... I have a possible solution.... Why don't we just close down the Salem and Lawrence Jails and relocate the prisoners on the grounds of Danvers State Hospital... .I think it would be a perfect spot for an Essex County jail without spending millions of dollars....

At first I thought Jim Shea was kidding. The Danvers State Mental Asylum was almost as rundown as the county jails. A massive grouping of brick and wood structures with major wiring, heating, and plumbing problems, plus outdated cell locks. Shea continued:

> The idea came to me recently while looking through a newspaper in Florida. In that state, it apparently is a common practice

to have prisons on the same real estate as mental hospitals. Danvers State is a perfect setting for accommodating a penal colony, and because of the great decline in the population at Danvers State, the time appears to be ripe.... Some years ago, Danvers State had more than 3,000 patients. Today that figure has shrunk to a fifth of that, maybe between 600 and 800 patients, and this total is declining.

Jim Shea persuaded Commissioner Ed Cahill "to have the sheriff at least make a study of the possibilities there." Shea then had his *News* staff pursue these possibilities, following up with headlines like, "County Jail At Hospital Possible." Shea then asked me to join him on a tour of the mental institution to determine its feasibility as a jail, and I reluctantly agreed.

Shea was grinning from ear to ear when I picked him up at the *News* office. On the six mile ride to the Danvers Mental Institution, he filled me with trivia about the prospects of its becoming the new county jail.

"You mean that it would become just another old county jail, don't you?" I corrected him. "There's nothing new about this old creepy place."

"Look at the property here. It's as massive as ever, high on a hill, away from town, with a lot of room for recreation." There was no stopping his enthusiasm, even after touring the interiors of the various rundown brick buildings

"These buildings are not only antiquated, but wouldn't hold our smartest inmates. They'd be out of here in no time."

"Then why don't the inmates who are here escape more often?" said Shea with a wry smile.

"They do," interjected our tour guide, who was a state employee. "We just keep it as quiet as possible. Quite a few just walk away from week to week, but we usually catch up with them before they reach town."

"And I think my inmates are a bit more intelligent than most of these folks," I piled on. "My guys are always looking for a way out, and these brick buildings wouldn't keep them in for long…this place won't do unless you tear these buildings down and start from scratch." Shea didn't like that. His face became stern and he was virtually silent on the way back to the *News* office.

There was no follow up in the newspaper, and not another word was ever written about the editor's proposal. What's wrong with a county jail at Danvers? There was plenty wrong with it and Shea knew it. He also knew I would rebut any article that he or any of his reporters might write to applaud his idea. At any rate, the entire idea of a new jail was once again crushed by the county commissioners who feared a state takeover of county government.

The federal government would provide no more money for jail repairs, and jails were filled to capacity and then some. I announced to the judges that I had no more room for those convicted or those awaiting trial. One judge tried to sneak a 17-year-old convict into the Salem Jail for some petty offense, and I sent him back to the court, telling the judge that not only didn't I have room, but also I refused to take kids into my jail. The judge was furious. As usual, the judges didn't like to be told what to do. I was within my rights not to accept children from the court.

At this juncture it seemed that everyone was angry with me—the press, the judges, the commissioners, the inmates, and then finally Jack Jerdan. I closed down a productive carpentry shop in operation for many months in the old shed and barn attached to the back of the sheriff's house. The Feds and Civil Defense surplus had provided saws, hammers, and wood, plus other equipment needed for our shop, and we discovered that quite a few inmates had carpentry skills. They mostly made coffee tables, which they sold to the public, the money made going into funds to be saved for their release. Everything seemed to be working well until I discovered that they were also making many intricately designed marijuana pipes for all the inmates in the form of little hard penises. I closed down the shop at once to the vehement protests of Jack Jerdan and the inmates.

A sliver of light penetrated my gloom and despair when Shirley

Camper Soman came to visit me at the jail. She is a noted writer whom I had met some 15 years earlier when I was in charge of community relations for the John Hancock Insurance Company in Boston. Shirley, a New York City gal, was writing a book for Hancock then. She was now President of the New York Magazine Writers Association, and she wanted to write an article and book about the Salem Jail. She had decided that the theme of her book would be how the antique bastille had slowly transformed me from a conservative politician to an on-the-job liberal. She was going to title the book, "The Sheriff Without A Gun." Shirley's research didn't last long, however, as she was forced to give up her project on the day she arrived in Salem. The reason was that when she stepped only a few feet into the jail, the steel door closed behind her, and she turned pale and almost fainted.

"I must leave this place," she said to me. "Please, get me out of here, fast."

Did she have claustrophobia, or agoraphobia like my special sheriff, secretary, and wife? Shirley didn't know why she was overcome, but felt she couldn't write the book unless she could interview inmates and find the heartbeat of the institution. Thus I suffered further disappointment. Yet, Christmas loomed on the horizon, and every Christmas Eve we held a party for my family and friends. Jim Shea was right when he boldly stated, "Cahill loves parties" –I do. Shirley Camper Soman's husband, Bob Soman, had recently died of a heart attack, and although Jewish, Shirley and her grown daughter Francie would be alone over the holidays, so I invited them to stay with my family at my house. My brother, two nephews and a niece, a few deputies and their wives, a couple of old college friends, plus my wife and four kids would keep the Somans happy for a few days. Besides turkey, Adam Ricci made spaghetti with squid sauce—something most of us had never tasted. I knew it would be a good time for all, a relief from the grueling day-to-day battles in the jails and at court.

I worked Christmas Eve until 8:00 p.m., then went home to the party, with a gala Christmas the next day. At about 6:00 p.m. that evening, I began having chest pains—little blips in the center of my chest, like someone was poking me with a pencil. I took some Alka-Seltzer, thinking it was indigestion. Shirley Soman and my wife Sandy thought I should go to the hospital. I refused, but the gnawing pain persisted. I decided to go to bed early Christmas night, for all I really needed, I thought, was sleep. In the early morning when I woke up, the pain was still there. I decided to take a bath to calm my body. Shirley Soman was soon pounding at the bathroom door.

"Get out of there," she shouted. "You must go to the hospital right away, without delay." Shirley seemed especially upset and agitated, and I realized that this probably reminded her of her husband's demise only a few months before.

"I'm okay, Shirley, " I said. "I'm sure it's just heart-burn from eating turkey skin. I get it often."

"No it isn't," she shouted. "It's a heart attack. I know it is. You must rush to the hospital. If you don't, I'm calling an ambulance."

I chuckled at her hysteria. "I must take a bath," I shouted at her through the door, "My mother told me to always make sure I was clean if I had to go to the hospital." Shirley was not amused. She banged at the door so loudly that she woke the rest of the family and guests. I quickly dried off and put on clothes before Shirley broke in the door. Shirley bundled me up, my hair still wet, and had Sandy drive me through a heavy snowstorm to Salem Hospital. After a few tests and a bit of probing by doctors in the emergency room, the Cardiologist, Doctor Chester Clarke, announced to Sandy and me that I was having a heart attack—Shirley had been right. I spent a few weeks in the hospital's cardiac unit and was then sent home, where I was told by my doctor to rest quietly for a month. This was near impossible, and in two weeks, I was back on the job. I was not so much devastated by having a " mild heart-attack," as I was in trying to figure out what would have caused it.

"Stress," said Doctor Clarke, "Your job is going to kill you with a fatal shot to the heart, if you don't slow down your pace."

I truly liked Doctor Clarke and considered him an outstanding doctor, but I had to tell him how I felt about his diagnosis. "You're full of shit. I thrive on being sheriff," I said, "and I'm heading back into the game with gusto."

"You're in a job where you can't see any light at the end of the tunnel," said Doctor Clarke, "and that means that something's got to give. I'm afraid that something may be you."

CHAPTER XX

The Last Roundup

I was sitting in my office when Loretta announced that the people from the Civil Liberties Union of Massachusetts (CLUM) were here to see me. CLUM's mandate is to look out for the protection of everybody's civil liberties, especially those who are less able to do it for themselves. It was the meeting I had been dreading, and yet had been looking forward to since the day I took office. The people from CLUM were glum. They were shown into my office, and a well-dressed, middle-aged man and an older, tall, bespectacled woman approached my desk with looks of anger and disgust. As soon as they sat down, they came at me like gangbusters with a verbal tirade that wouldn't allow me to get a word in edgewise. "Tiny cells, poor plumbing, no heat…three inmates bringing suit against me –"

"Hold it!" I shouted at them as they glared at me. "Where have you been?" They were momentarily speechless.

"What do you mean?" the lanky woman finally asked in a huff.

"I've been waiting some three years for the Civil Liberties Union to show up here. You're very late! I'm getting no cooperation from anyone, county or state. So sue me, and let's get this show on the road." I smiled at them.

They were surprised; they had geared themselves for a knock down, drag out fight, but found me more than cooperative.

"We'll have to take you to court you know," said the woman.

"I'm ready and willing to plead my case before a judge," I replied, "but I'm asking you to hurry the process, so we can get things done fast."

"Judge Garrity has already closed down the Charles Street Jail," said the CLUM man, "and he may close down this one."

"We're in worse shape than Charles Street—I can tell you that—and if he closes Salem Jail then we'll just have to build us a new one. The county commissioners, advisory board, and state legislature won't like it, but will have to comply. Or we can put all the jail residents back on the street, and I don't think the police or the public would like that. So please, sue me."

The pair left my office smiling. They had never met a sheriff who wanted to be sued so he could plead the same case as CLUM.

Loretta couldn't believe it. "They were ready to bite-your head off when they arrived and I thought they were going to kiss your hand when they left. What did you say to them?" she asked.

"I just agreed with them," I said. " I told them, 'I will offer no defense. The inmates are right. This place isn't fit for human habitation.' The Civil Liberties Union of Massachusetts is our last resort in saving our two jails." Loretta just smiled and shook her head.

Marcia Brockelman, the Beacon Hill reporter for the Boston newspapers, produced a feature article a few days later that was headlined, "Law Suit Slamming Jail Conditions Has Defendant, Plaintiff Mixed Up." She went on to write:

> I laughed. It was an ironic laugh, because there is nothing very funny about the terrible condition at the Salem Jail. But a Civil Liberties Union of Massachusetts (CLUM) lawsuit naming Essex County Sheriff Robert E. Cahill as defendant, along with the county commissioners, does have its comic side.
>
> When the dramatic blue-headlined legal-sized news release arrived on my State House desk from CLUM, my immediate reaction was, 'C'mon gang, you're slamming the wrong guy.'
>
> Now I realize there have to be plaintiffs and defendants in these legal things, and I think the CLUM suit may serve a good purpose in the long run. But if anything, these defendants should be the plaintiffs in the 'barbaric conditions' case…. A year or so ago, in the course of an interview, Sheriff Cahill commented to me that he almost wished a federal court judge would come look at the Salem Jail…. Cahill at that time was still

clinging to hopes that all the stumbling blocks to a proposed Middleton Jail would somehow be bulldozed away, and that somehow a medium security detention facility could be built.

He had a dream. It included county correctional facilities at three levels: a medium security building in Middleton at the center of the county, the Lawrence House of Correction and the Correctional Alternatives Center....

Cahill has had difficulty squeezing nickels out of the county commissioners who originally planned to sink jail dollars into a new jail, and who are themselves facing outcries from the county advisory board, the officials in the cities and towns, and a ceiling from the governor.

The jails ran out of money in February, and had to ask for money from a reserve fund to put out bread and butter and Spam for the rest of the year. After much pleading, Cahill was able to get $1,066 for some Salem Jail maintenance from the Committee on Counties....

And if Corrections forces closure, or if the courts as the result of the CLUM suit do, or if a federal court judge does wander through Salem some day, what then? The Charles Street Jail is still open, for there is no place for the inmates to go. Lawrence is already over crowed and its facilities only one grade above those in Salem.

Barb Yagerman, one of Jim Shea's reporters at the *Salem News*, wasn't as gracious as Marcia Brockelman. "The conditions and arbitrary treatment of detainees at the Essex County Jail are shocking and outrages and cannot be tolerated by a civilized society," she quoted the CLUM executives as saying. She said that Salem had "poor sanitary conditions" and that we "harassed prisoners." Instead of contacting me, Yagerman got a quote from Special Sheriff Charlie Reardon, which didn't please me, but I'm sure pleased Editor Shea. "This is not a country club," Reardon was quoted as saying. "We never asked these people here and they look for every benefit when they get here."

Another unexpected response to the civil liberties suit came from the inmates themselves. They wrote to the *Salem Evening News* and enclosed a petition signed by 78 "residents of the Salem Jail." They blamed the civil liberties   suit on "two disgruntled inmates," and said that they were rebutting the article by Barbara Yagerman. They wrote:

> Our intention is to make the general public aware of what we, as inmates, believe to be a grave injustice to the administration and all persons concerned named in the 'Class Action' brought upon this institution by mainly two disgruntled inmates who are named as plaintiffs and what we inmates class as a play for their own personal gain....
>
> Taking into effect the age of this institution, there was mainly only outside plumbing when built, there is not much that may be done to correct toilet facilities without the use of jackhammers or perhaps explosives.
>
> It is cruel and injustice in its own right when certain individuals take it upon their own to defame others who are only doing their job and to the best of their ability under the conditions of which this instance are said to exist at the Salem Jail and House of Correction. First of all let us state the fact that the majority of men on the House of Corrections side of this institution have themselves at one time been detained on the jail side. Until a person has been sentenced he has to spend his time in the section of jail of which the main portion for the printed complaint is said to appear. We inmates who have served time, so to speak, on the high court side of the jail have never encountered any of the harassment by any officers of which the Salem News article suggests. In fact, there is not one inmate who may state that he has never seen an instance where a guard has not gone out of his way to help any inmate.... No inmate is locked up without due cause. The administration and its subordinates have shown every due respect for the inmates and their families during visiting hours.... Meals are not deprived for any

inmate, phone calls are not monitored. Every man not in lock-up is allowed out into the yard in fair weather. No one is deprived of this....

Under the conditions that exist here at the Salem Jail and House Of Correction, is no fault of the administration. We inmates believe things run fairly and smoothly.

Since Sheriff Robert E. Cahill has been administrator here there have been many changes...all for the betterment of the inmates and thus for the betterment of society of which these inmates shall one day be re-instated....

Neither Barbara Yagerman nor Jim Shea commented on this inmate petition, but two Boston television stations sent crews and reporters down to see me at the jail. Both reporters found it difficult to understand why the majority of the inmate population would come to my aid. I told them that I never expected the inmates' reaction to it. But the inmates obviously felt like we were a community and wanted to protect that. They, of course, couldn't have realized that I welcomed the suit from CLUM.

Jim Shea received another letter, this time from the mother of an inmate, and the combination of this and the letter from the inmates had a tempering effect on his sharp criticism. Shea's Saturday editorial of May 7, 1977 was, I thought, not only surprising, but also refreshing for a change:

It is pretty easy to criticize conditions at the Salem Jail.... For that reason, it didn't take much ingenuity or originality or courage on the part of the Massachusetts Civil Liberties Union to lambaste conditions at the jail. But it was interesting the following day to see a majority of prisoners at the Salem Jail bounce right back with a strong defense, not of the jail, but of the way they are treated at the House of Correction.

In that same vein, I have received a letter from a Peabody woman whose son is a prisoner at Salem Jail and is also a diabetic. She believes the staff of Sheriff Robert E. Cahill is doing a good job under the circumstances. 'This is a very sick boy and one that is going through a lot of mental and physical stress due to his past habit. I can only say in sincerity,' wrote the woman, 'that every guard and deputy sheriff and those above have helped to keep this boy alive. He was sick enough to be taken out in a box, but through the unselfish efforts of Salem Jail guards, he is on his feet.

'This boy is not unlike any other and he gives backtalk to guards even when they are doing him a kindness. He has been too much of an animal for such a long time and I am sure he has had difficulty adjusting to humane treatment. We all know that the jail is old and its needs are plentiful, but what the public should know is that the sheriff, his assistants and all the guards are doing the best they can and in our case, my son could likely be already dead if not for their help, Respectfully, Mrs. Lawrence King.'

This communication from Mrs. King is an unsolicited testimonial, which brings great credit on Sheriff Cahill and his staff, which is working in impossible conditions....

I was overwhelmed, not just by the testimonials from inmates and their families, but also by Jim Shea's reaction. He apparently had not talked to his boss, Newbegin, and heard of our heated session in the clothing store. Perhaps my brother taking Shea to lunch and confronting him about his shabby treatment of me had done some good. My brother and Shea were fellow Rotarians and had an amiable rapport. Shea told Jim that he only criticized me in the newspaper because it sold more copies. My usual quick and angry rebuttals to the editor, Shea explained, also increased circulation. I was sure that there were other factors involved. The nature of newspaper reporting and editorializing since Nixon's Watergate scandal had hardened journalists on politicians. Also, publisher Newbegin was one of former Sheriff Roger Wells' best friends, and I knew he didn't like my criticisms of how the old sheriff left the jails in such disorder. Whatever the reasons for the criticism, the letters to the editor caused a turn around. His negativity toward me seemed to be subsiding, and for that I was grateful.

※ ※ ※

At the same time as my dealings with CLUM, another hot political issue—new state minimum standards for the jails – kept me busy outside the jail. Governor Mike Dukakis, whom I had served with in the legislature, appointed me, along with his wife Kitty, and eight others to his committee to draft new jail standards. The entire committee was considered ultra-liberal—except for me. Kitty Dukakis and I didn't get along. She thought I was just an old conservative sheriff, but after four years on the job, I had actually become a liberal progressive when it came to corrections issues. The dilemma was that unlike the rest of the committee, I now had experience in the jails and knew that the suggested minimums were unrealistic, given the age and condition of the county's prisons. I constantly explained to the others on the committee that most of the old decaying jails in Massachusetts just couldn't physically comply with what they were suggesting. My facilities in Salem and Lawrence didn't begin to comply with the laws that already existed.

With the election of Mike Dukakis, the politics of Massachusetts became ultra liberal in all aspects, and there seemed no stopping the movement. When the new minimum standards for county prisons became public with but one dissenting vote—my own—the other county sheriffs were up in arms. I joined them in the cry that compliance was impossible unless we built new jails. I actually preferred to renovate, but the county wouldn't even give me money for that. Now, with all this pressure on the county commissioners and state legislature, I began to see the old economic logjam starting to break down. Something had to give, and the pressure on the purse strings was intensifying.

Every new decree from the minimum standards committee came with a price tag, and there just wasn't enough money in existing budgets to cover the cost. One provision was that any inmate who served more than 90 days in jail would be given $25.00 cash when he or she was released. Sheriff Tom Eisenstadt of Suffolk County, covering Boston, calculated that it would cost his commissioners an additional $175,000 per year, just to meet this one provision. Every cell was now required to have a flush toilet, sink, and mirror, and all inmates were to have unlimited visiting rights of friends and families. This was impossible, especially for me in Salem. I pressed the legislature and the county commissioners to give me at least enough money to cover the minimum health standards. They went to work and quickly passed an order for an emergency $100,000 as a special fund to fix up whatever I saw fit. Members of the County Advisory Board, charged with keeping costs down, were steaming. The savings from their year of austerity quickly disintegrated before their eyes. The Governor's minimum standards added the needed pressure, and the money began to flow. But it just wasn't enough money to even make a dent in the changes needed.

Only three weeks after the CLUM lawsuit, a Federal Judge mandated that "the inmates must have suitable shades for their bare light bulbs in the cells." They were now using cardboard and newspapers. Also, he ruled that "the jail side inmates be allowed as much time in the recreation yard as the house side inmates. Inmates are to be provided suitable washbasins in their cells and that inmates shall have suitable showerheads on showers. Pre-trial detainees are to be allowed two more public phones for outgoing calls, and are to have access at any reasonable time to facilities in the basement of the jail, including but not limited to the single flush toilet, the single sink with running water, the showers, and the recreational facilities." I was more than willing to comply.

"And what do you need, Sheriff, more than anything else at your ancient jail?" asked the judge, as I sat on his hot-seat in Boston Superior Court.

"I need eleven correctional officers," I replied.

"Done!" he said. And we adjourned.

It was like getting a wonderful Christmas present. I had eleven jobs to fill and I was elated. I had no idea the extent to which such a grant could be fraught with political intrigue and greed. Some of my old fellow legislators who had avoided me when I was looking for votes on my bond order, now called me with names of relatives and friends who they insisted I hire as new correctional officers. I told them that we would interview any and all comers, but that I would only hire men we considered qualified to make good guards. This was a bonanza for Deputy Bethune, but he could only come up with three good men whom he had turned away earlier because of a lack of funds. One candidate sent to me by a state representative was whistled at by the inmates when he entered the jail.

"I can't hire your cousin," I told the rep over the phone after his candidate left the interview.

"Why not?" my friend asked angrily.

"The inmates whistled at him."

"So what?"

"I can't hire anyone who the inmates whistle at."

"Are you saying that my cousin is queer?"

"I don't know if he is or not—and I don't care—but the inmates apparently saw something in him that I didn't, and it sure isn't his looks that made them whistle."

Tommy McGee, Speaker of the House, called and said he was sending over a woman who he really wanted me to hire. I did need one female to transport and guard females awaiting trial overnight at the jail, or those who were being transferred to other prisons after sentencing. I told McGee that if she was good, I'd hire her, but if she's not tough enough, I wouldn't. The woman, Manya Manzi, was middle-aged and pretty. I spent almost an hour telling her how tough the job was, and that she could be called out from home on a moments notice to deliver a female felon to Framingham. She assured me that she was physically and mentally tough enough, so I hired her, and she proved to be an effective and diligent employee. My only problem was her husband, who would call me if he didn't want his wife sent in to escort a prisoner, especially after hours.

After a couple of these calls, I finally had to lay it out for him. "Sorry," I told him, "I explained to your wife before I hired her that she would be transporting prisoners at all hours to various points across the state. She must go or she will be fired."

"I will call Tommy McGee," Mr. Manzi said in a huff.

"Be my guest," I replied and hung up.   Next call, of course, was from House Speaker McGee who ruled the roost in neighboring Lynn and at the statehouse. "But no, Tommy," I told him. "Nobody is going to tell me how to run my department. Manya does her duty well, but she does it my way or she goes." Tommy wasn't happy, but he knew I wasn't going to open the door even a crack to allow local politicians—no matter how powerful—to run my department. "And if her husband calls here again on a work related matter concerning his wife, she's hitting the road." I received no more calls from   the speaker or his friend.

The most disgruntling call I received concerning my eleven new jobs was from Senator Tully's office. He was co-Chairman of the State Committee on Counties with Representative Charlie Flaherty. Their committee assistant, Jeff, called me and said that Senator Tully wanted all eleven positions—they were to be filled by him. "Senators don't like to be told what to do by judges," said the assistant, "and if you want this order passed by the Senate and the Committee on Counties, the jobs must be filled by the Senator." I was dumbfounded and I was furious.

"No way!" I shouted at the assistant and I slammed down the phone. I bolted out of my office in a rage and headed for Salem Common for a long walk. Round and round the great green expanse I walked to cool down my temper. My mind was numbed by the audacity of the Senator's assistant. I didn't know Senator Tully, but I had heard he was tough as nails. I just couldn't let him or his assistant get away with this. I decided to return to my office and call Senator Kevin Harrington, President of the Senate, and a Salem man. I had served with him in the legislature when I was a state representative. Kevin could tell by the tremor in my voice that I was greatly disturbed by the attempted hijacking of my eleven new hires. During my six years in the legislature, I hardly ever asked Kevin Harrington for a favor or for any special privilege over my fellow reps, but now I asked that he come down hard in my favor.

Kevin called me back within the half-hour and said that all was now well with the world. I would get all the funding for the new positions, and would be able to hire who I wanted, with the exception of one job "which the Senator requests" at the Lawrence Jail. I reluctantly acquiesced.

There were three old friends of mine, all in their late thirties, that I knew were good, conscientious workers who were, for one reason or another, unemployed at the time. Two of the three, Phil Hayes and Rene Caron accepted my offer to become guards. Phil was the toughest, most athletic kid I knew growing up at Forest River Park in Salem. He had played minor-league baseball and was a good sandlot football player. Rene was a little guy with a large spirit and seemed to be always filled with confidence. They both became guards on the same day. Phil Hayes asked to see me two days later. He came to me in my office, head bowed and said, "I can't remain, Bob, I feel too confined." So Phil left the job. The toughest kid on the block had claustrophobia. Rene Caron, however, remained through thick and thin and retired years later, recognized as one of the best correctional officers at the Salem Jail.

Federal Judge Walter J. Skinner, liberal and notoriously tough, came with Civil Liberties Union representatives to tour the Salem Jail. With them came newsmen and attorneys, including the commissioners, and the Essex County attorneys Barry McDonald and John Nester. We concluded that this was the Waterloo for the Salem Jail– after this there was no way we'd be allowed to remain open. Judge Skinner was silent during the hour and a half romp. He ducked his head into many cells and cubbyholes while the CLUM lawyers stayed on his heals, running a continuous commentary on the inadequacies of the old jail. When confronted by the press in the front yard after the visit, Judge Skinner said only, "I think judges should get their views in writing, and until they have done so, should keep their mouths shut."

My comment to the press was, "I will not be surprised if the judge orders the jail closed. I have taken legislators on tours over and over again. They will agree that conditions here are terrible, but no one wants to provide the money to fix up the old jails or build a new one."

Within hours of the judge's visit, came an inspection by a state health inspector, who found numerous violations of the health code. Howard Wensley, director of regional health operations for Massachusetts, concluded after his inspection, "I share Sheriff Cahill's concerns as to the costs of updating the jail, but there are certain essential minimum conditions that must be maintained in order to provide a safe and healthy environment for the incarceration of human beings." Wensley announced, "the use of chamber-pots (buckets) must be discontinued...the inmates must be tested for tuberculosis or communicable diseases before placement in the jail's general population. There is overcrowding with sometimes two to a cell, the shower stall was found to be moldy, food was uncovered in the kitchen, the kitchen floor needs repair, the refrigerator is dirty..." – and on and on he went until he had spewed forth almost every health violation imaginable. Wensley concluded by saying to the press, "My agency will try to assist Sheriff Cahill in upgrading the institution."

I didn't wait for the state's help. I called in Sam Lena, a local entrepreneur and restaurateur to come into my kitchen like gangbusters and straighten it out. "When money is needed to bring it right," I told him, "go right to Tom Duffy, the county treasurer, and have him dig into the emergency fund." Twice, the cook came to me to say Lena was overstepping his bounds in his kitchen. The poor cook almost went mad, but Sam Lena prevailed, and except for shit-buckets and overcrowding, we passed the next health inspection.

Two months later, Judge Skinner released his ultimatum to the county commissioners and the state legislators. "Either fix up the Salem Jail and House Of Correction within the next year and a half or make plans to build a new jail." If neither of these things were done, Judge Skinner said he would "order the 162-year old institution to be closed immediately and all the inmates thereof either removed or released."

The new chairman of the county commissioners, John McKean,

vehemently opposed the building of a new jail, stating that the county "cannot afford the estimated seven million dollars it would cost to build a new jail." That being said, the commissioners now had to meet the conditions spelled out by Judge Skinner, before the end of the year 1978. I wrote a letter to the county commissioners—like Judge Skinner said, "Get your views in writing first." I reminded them that the Salem Jail had been condemned by the state in 1939, and since then there were constant rumors of a new jail—that's almost forty years with no movement on a new jail. I had always been an advocate of fixing up the old jail, but now, with Judge Skinner's list of necessary improvements, and the new minimum standards due to become law in January, 1978, I recommended "that we begin the necessary steps to build a new jail and house of correction somewhere in the southern part of the county." I explained to the commissioners that although Skinner "may be willing to let the county get away with upgrading the jail, I fear some other judge in the near future might not be so cooperative. If you prefer to patch up the old facility, I will not argue. I like the old Salem Jail, and apparently most of the inmates do too, but no one likes the conditions." Even Senate President Kevin Harrington and House Leader Tom McGee came to my aid and again proposed a new jail be built at Middleton with state funds. This would mean that the state would take control of corrections from the county, but Governor Dukakis stepped into the fray and announced that, "I am unalterably opposed to the inclusion of funds for a new Essex County Jail in the state budget."

Bill Ryan and I worked through two days and nights creating a plan that I presented to the commissioners. "You have three options," I told them in a closed special meeting called to solve the jail problem. "Now that the state has backed away from paying for a new jail, we can build a new jail without state assistance—an option I know neither Chairman McKean nor Commissioner Ed Cahill like—nor would the county taxpayers for that matter. The second option would be to float a bond for $1.5 million or more to expand the Salem Jail by using land in front of the jail at Saint Peter's Street, and possibly giving the sheriff's house to the Salem Historical Committee. The city could move the house across the street to city land, thus making even more room for an expanded Salem Jail. The third option would cost approximately $1.3 million and would bring the Salem and Lawrence Jails up to at least the federal and state minimum safety and health standards."

I then broke down the costs of the third option, which Ryan and I were hoping they would agree to and pass onto the legislature—the lesser of three evils for them. The commissioners were already spending some $200,000 complying with Skinner's first Federal Court orders. After little debate, the commissioners agreed to our third option, and although there was some low grumbling in the state legislature, the $1.3 million bond order to rehabilitate our two jails passed with flying colors. The bond included provisions for: the installation of new windows, sashes, and vents, the installation of 20 new toilets, 10 showers and 20 wash basins, a new electric locking system, a new egress, new flooring, improved fire safety equipment, new automatic alarms, and an expanded wing with much bigger cells.

After four years of yelling, screaming, praying, pleading, borrowing and stealing, Bill Ryan and I were provided with the necessities we had been asking for from day one. To make the passage of the bond order even sweeter, it was my forty-third birthday. Bill Ryan and I celebrated that night by driving our cruisers to my brother Jim's house on the North River across from the Salem Jail. We trained our spotlights on his house, blaring our sirens and ordering him to come out of his house with his hands up. Jim is eight years my elder and not quite as childish as me. When he came to his door in his pajamas, he was in a fury. We trained our spotlights on his pajamas and wouldn't relent until he promised to bring us inside for a drink, which he reluctantly did. It turned out to be a wonderful night of celebration, lifting our glasses to toast the old jail across the river and the new makeover she would soon receive.

✷   ✷   ✷

It was two months later during a cold January morning that the paper headlined an Associated Press story out of Boston, "Repair Of Jail Upheld – A federal appeals court citing the state's failure to enforce minimum standards for county prisons, has upheld a lower court decision," read the article, "ordering improvements in conditions at the Essex County Jail and House of Correction in Salem...."

As I read the article and sipped my first cup of morning coffee, a pain shot up my back and then settled to the left side of my head above the ear. I winced; the pain was intense, unlike a normal headache. Then my right hand started getting cold, like I had dipped it in a snowdrift and left it there. I called to my wife.

When she came to the door I asked her, "Where's the unicorn?"

She wrinkled her brow. "What did you say?" she asked.

That's not what I was trying to say. I tried again, and out again came the word "unicorn." Sandy gave me a quizzical look. I kept trying to speak, but the wrong words were coming out. The coldness in my hand spread up my arm and the headache intensified. Sandy called my brother and asked him to get over to our house quick.

"He's either gone insane or he's having another heart attack," she told him. Living only a block away, Jim was there in a flash. He quickly decided to take me to Salem Hospital. Some words were coming out of my mouth correctly, mixed in with: "unicorn, pumpkins, bassinette and Camelot." Finally I managed to make Jim and the doctor at the hospital understand that my hand and arm were frozen, and that I needed an aspirin desperately for an excruciating headache. For the next four hours I was given a series of tests and was punctured by a variety of needles, but no one would give me an aspirin. Then my brother left, and I was put in a neurological ward into a crib-like bed. I was surrounded by people moaning and making funny noises. As much as I tried to communicate with the one available nurse, she ignored me. Because of the headache, I couldn't sleep, yet I was exhausted. In the middle of the night, a little man, wearing a red plaid Mackinaw and plaid cap, came and stood before me. He was wearing no pants, and he said nothing—he just stared at me. Finally the nurse came and took him away. They've put me in a loony bin, I concluded.

In the morning came more tests. Then my heart doctor, Chester Clarke, came for a visit. I had suffered a stroke, he told me, and that's why my right side was partially paralyzed and why I couldn't talk properly. There was also something else the doctors couldn't figure out—I had a rare blood disease. They started pumping me with penicillin, but it didn't seem to work. I spent two weeks in the hospital being fed penicillin directly into my veins every two hours, day and night, but the only thing it seemed to do was rid me of the terrible headaches. I was peeing penicillin, spitting penicillin, and it was coming out of my pores. Finally they said that the blood disease had dissipated, and they stopped pumping me with the stuff, but none of the doctors could tell me what had caused it. Had I been poisoned by an inmate? Was it the jail food that I regularly ate, against Billy Ryan's advice? Or, could it be the old witch's curse of Salem, passed on from sheriff to sheriff by the crushed Giles Corey? He had told Sheriff George Corwin in 1692 with his dying breath that he "cursed the sheriff and Salem." There was also the curse of accused witch Sarah Good to the local minister that he would "have blood to drink". He died from a blood hemorrhage soon after Sarah Good's hanging. Other high sheriffs before me had died of heart related complications, or by various infections of the blood. The previous sheriff, Roger Wells, was even at that moment slowly dying an agonizing death from sugar diabetes. Wasn't this a sweet poisoning of the blood? Some of my superstitious friends, including my mother, who loved fortunetellers, felt that my dilemma was surely due to the old witch's curse on the High Sheriffs of Essex County.

My speech, my right hand, and right arm slowly returned to near normal, but it took nearly a month of rehabilitation during which the doctors wouldn't let me out of the hospital. By this time I had so many holes in me from needles, nurses were using my thumb artery to feed me antibiotics. Doctor Clarke then informed me that he and his colleagues had discovered a greater problem. My aortic valve, the valve in the heart that closes to allow enough incoming blood to build up pressure in the aorta, then opens quickly to let the heart pump that oxygenated blood back through the body, was disintegrating and near collapse. I would have to be rushed to Boston for open-heart surgery.

Oddly enough the first question that came to my mind was whether the food at Boston's Peter-Bent Brigham Hospital was better than at Salem, for I was sick of Salem Hospital 's bland menu—the jail food was much better than hospital food. What made me realize the seriousness of the situation was the doctors telling me that I would need several pints of blood for the open-heart surgery. When my guards and deputies found out about this, they went right to work organizing a volunteer blood drive for me. That got me wondering; if I received Bill Ryan's blood, I would become more imaginative? Or with Joe Carter's blood, would I suddenly have a desire to bet on the horses? Or with Billy Cox's, would I discover a craving for scotch and soda?

Many guards and deputies tried to see me in the hospital, but only family members were allowed to visit. Adam Ricci, being an expert in sneaking into places to deliver writs, managed to get to the door of my hospital room. I saw his coke-bottle glasses peeking through the door window, and the door beginning to crack open, and then the large hand of a male nurse grabbed his collar and he was gone. The doctor wanted Deputy Larry Puleo to escort me in the ambulance from Salem to Boston, but I don't know why and neither did Larry. The food at Peter-Bent Brigham was worse than at Salem Hospital, which surprised and disappointed me greatly. If I was going to die here, I at least wanted a half decent meal before I left this world—even inmates on death-row get that. I never did mind hospitals or even the thought of dying, which is inevitable, but I did hate this hospital, which was being revamped at the time. The sound of jackhammers and saws penetrated my room. I considered that there were only two consolations to my upcoming operation. The first was that I had probably the best heart doctors in the world, including John Collins, who had already successfully performed heart transplants. The second was that at nearby Massachusetts General Hospital, my hero, John Wayne, was about to undergo the same operation I was. I had only recently seen him in the movie "Cahill - U.S. Marshall," –probably his worse film—but I liked him and I liked the title of the movie. Open-heart surgery to replace the aortic valve was new at the time, but if John Wayne wasn't scared, neither was I.

The night before the operation, after a male nurse shaved off my body hair, Doctor Collins visited my room and offered me either a plastic valve or a pig's-valve to replace my own.

"What' s John Wayne getting?"

"A pig's valve, a nice big one from a real hog."

"That's what I want."

"They only last about ten years and you'll have to renew it later."

I didn't know what to base my decision on. I was told that pig valves don't make an audible sloshing sound like plastic valves did, and I didn't want to have to listen to my ticker tick for the rest of my days. I had also found out that with a pig's valve there wouldn't be a weekly trip to the hospital to have my blood thickness checked. This information weighed against a possible replacement ten years down the road made it a difficult decision, but in the end I went with the immediate convenience and followed the lead of The Duke in choosing the pig, and swore off pork chops and bacon for the rest of my life.

"I'll stick with the pig valve and take my chances in ten years."

"Get some rest and we'll see you in the morning." When Doctor Collins left my room I pulled out a cigarette I had hidden for months in my jacket pocket, and I went into the bathroom to smoke it. I thought it might be my last cigarette. A bit dizzy, I returned to my bed. I knew my roommate wouldn't mind the smoke; he was asleep and wrapped in a plastic cast from head to toe. The nurse came in before I dozed off, went into the bathroom, and came out screaming. "Who's been smoking?" she shouted.

"I think it was him," I said pointing at my roommate. She looked at him. She didn't believe me.

"It's dangerous to smoke before an operation, you know. We may have to call it off." She snapped and stormed out of the room in a huff.

"Hell, even before they hang or shoot a guy in a firing squad, they let him have a cigarette," I shouted after her. She didn't think that was funny, and after a last look of disgust, she disappeared down the hall.

The operation went on as scheduled. I was knocked out for some five hours, and it wasn't too pleasant when I woke up. But it was March 17th, Saint Patrick's Day, one of my favorite days and I woke up to a little glass vase of green carnations on the table next to my bed. I was sore all over, with latticework stitched down the center of my chest, from collarbone to midriff. It took many days to heal, but each day I felt a little better. I had lost my 20/20 vision, and surprisingly, my hair had turned grey, but I was alive—not kicking yet, but alive. In April they moved me, not home, but back to Salem Hospital, where I informed the nurses that I would never squawk about Salem Hospital food again. I underwent further treatment and therapy in Salem, especially to bring back feeling into my right foot, which went numb during the operation. It never did completely heal, and to this day, I can't feel certain parts of my foot. Doctor Clarke warned me about returning to work. He concluded that the stroke was caused by a piece of my aortic valve breaking off and lodging in my head, thus the terrible headaches. He believed that the faulty valve was caused by on-the-job stress.

"There is no light at the end of that tunnel," said Clarke. "You have no outlet for your stress. If you continue on as sheriff, I don't think you'll live long. You must avoid further stress." He also warned me that strenuous physical activity and lifting was out of the question. This surprised me; I thought I thrived on the stress of solving the problems of prisons and prisoners, courts and court guards, but apparently it was doing me in. "The pace is just too much," concluded Doctor Clarke.

I contacted the Essex County Retirement Board and presented Tom Duffey with my dilemma. I had been in public service for eleven years: two as a city councilor, over five as a state representative, and four as high sheriff. According to Duffey, I was eligible for a disability pension. Three heart specialists hired by the state came to the hospital and examined me. They concluded that I was "unfit to continue work as the sheriff" and that I was "permanently disabled."

The first person I notified was Special Sheriff Charlie Reardon, who was holding down the fort while I was laid up. "Looks like you're next in the barrel, if you want to be," I told him. At first Charlie didn't know what I was talking about. "I'm going to ask Governor Dukakis to appoint you high sheriff," I told him, "because I have to retire." He looked shocked, but I think he was pleased. I called Mike Dukakis and explained the situation. I asked him to appoint Reardon. "Charlie has over ten years on the job," I told the governor, "plus I have a wonderful first team working here that has taken years to establish, and an open election with a bevy of candidates will split up my team and put a halt to the work we've accomplished." I knew the Governor would have to consider others for the job, so he couldn't give me an answer right away, but I also knew he was pleased with our progress in Essex County and wanted to see it continue. Hearing that I was on my way out, David Janes of Lynn, who had run against me for sheriff five years earlier, was on the phone to the Governor in hot pursuit of the job, as were three local state representatives. However, when I officially retired in August of 1978, Charlie Reardon was appointed by the governor to replace me. Charlie and I hadn't always seen eye-to-eye, and he was more conservative than I—more of a cop's cop—but I felt that he, more than any other, would keep our team together. Maybe I thought that like myself, he would become more liberal the longer he served as high sheriff.

In late April, I returned to my home in Salem, only during the day at first, returning to the hospital at night. By May 2nd I was home for good—I had been in hospitals for over four months. Ironically, on that day, I received the sad news that *Salem Evening News* Editor, Jim Shea, died. Unbeknownst to most, he had cancer, and had known for many months that death was looming. He was only in his late forties. Apparently publisher Cy Newbegin had known about the illness, which probably had something to do with his anger about my earlier offhanded remarks in the clothing store about Shea. Jim Shea, more than anyone else, taught me the lesson that the pen is mightier than the sword—I had the scars to prove it.

As I recuperated at home, I ordered additional cable television for the bedroom. The cableman, who was tall and lean, with a goatee, came to my home and started piecing the system together as I gabbed on aimlessly about the weather, happy for the company. Finally the cableman turned and stared at me with a twinkle in his eye and a whimsical half smile.

"You don't recognize me, do you, Sheriff?" he said.

I stared at him intently, scanning back through my memory. "No! I don't," I replied.

"I'm Fitzpatrick," he said, "Your favorite resident at the Salem Jail." At first, I was speechless. Then I laughed, jumped up from the bed, and shook his hand.

"Getting rehab in Arkansas really straightened me out," he said. "I was just a crazy teenaged drunk looking to have a good time when I was with you in the Salem Jail. So, your sending me out of the jail to Arkansas really got me started on the right track. Surprisingly, they have a great rehab program down there. I thank you."

"I couldn't afford to keep you any longer," I laughed, and we talked on about his two escapes. "I had you cornered good up on the Canadian border on that second escape. What made you turn around and head south?"

"Just a hunch," said Fitzy, "As I neared the border, the hair started standing up on the back of my neck. I felt something wasn't right."

"Well, you were right. We would've had you."

We reminisced for some twenty minutes, like two old pals. It did my heart good to see my most active inmate turn into a hard working, honest young man. It seemed to make all the troubles and sufferings I had just been through worthwhile. When he left my house I walked him to his truck.

"You know, we were really like Keystone Cops trying to capture you," I told him.

He laughed. "I and most of the others were just confused kids," he replied,

"Maybe we should go on stage," I suggested, shaking his hand to say goodbye. "We'd make a hell of an act, we could call it 'The Pros and Cons of Life in an Old Jailhouse'."

"We'd have them rolling in the aisles," Fitzpatrick said with a smile as he climbed into his truck and drove off down Felt Street.

As I watched him drive away, I thought of Cagney's line "top 'o the world, Ma, top o' the world." Old Fitzy had made it to the top and I felt great about that.

EPILOGUE

Soon after my retirement, Charlie Reardon called with a dilemma. The state had taken over the courts in Essex County in a coup, without warning. Charlie asked what I thought he should do.

"You have two ways to go," I replied. "Either let the state have the courts—because eventually they will take over all of county government anyway, including the jail—or you can fight back. Given that all transportation from courts to jails is done by deputy sheriffs in their own vehicles, you just have the deputies refuse to use their own cars, and that will certainly tie up things. But eventually the state will probably win any war you create. Why fight them?" I asked Charlie. "With a state takeover, all our deputies will start making good money instead of the measly money that they get now. The state will have to pay our men as much as they pay court officers in other counties. Our deputies will be happy and you'll have less worries." Charlie decided not to fight the takeover. Interestingly, Manya Manzi, House Speaker Tom McGee's candidate for court officer a couple of years back, became the Chief Court Officer under the new state system.

✳ ✳ ✳

Charlie Reardon, as the new sheriff re-appointed by Governor Mike Dukakis, didn't keep Jack Jerdan or Bill Ryan very long. Jack Jerdan went to work for the county's district attorney, and Bill Ryan went to work in state corrections and later became Mayor of Haverhill, Massachusetts, and then a state lobbyist. Warren Bethune stayed on in the system but was not re-appointed Deputy Master of the Jail by Rear-

don. Bethune, who was always threatening to retire, never did, and
remained in the sheriff's department for over forty years, dying in
1998 of sugar diabetes. Only a hand full of my old deputy sheriffs and
correctional officers still work in the Essex County Sheriff's Department.

※ ※ ※

There was a riot at the Lawrence Jail in August of 1988, and one-
third of the structure was destroyed, mostly by fire. "Officials said the
riot was caused by overcrowding and sweltering heat," reported the
Boston Globe, but my two old aficionados, Bill Ryan and Joe Carter,
who had long since left the jail, commented to me that they were
convinced that the upheaval was due to the lack of the kind of activities Joe once provided and the lack of decent food that Ryan glee-
fully procured.

On February 12, 1989, it happened again, a full-fledged riot at the
Lawrence Jail with bed sheets and toilet paper being used to set fires.
It was a knock-down battle between inmates and guards that lasted
some two hours, further destroying areas of the old structure. Harry
Cappola, Charlie Reardon's assistant and spokesman, again blamed
the riot on overcrowding. The Lawrence Jail was shut down for good.

※ ※ ※

I received an invitation from Sheriff Charlie Reardon to the ground-
breaking ceremony on a hill in Middleton, Massachusetts, for the
new Essex County Jail and House of Corrections on November 9,
1989. I didn't go. Three great and massive cement edifices were built
on that hill, with a long winding driveway leading from the highway
to of top of the hill. It looked like a fortress. It cost $53 million dol-
lars and now holds over one thousand inmates. I did eventually take
a tour of it, but wasn't impressed. It was cold and seemingly inhu-
mane, whereas the old Salem Jail, with all its faults and shortcom-
ings, had personality and warmth to it.

✳ ✳ ✳

One of the saddest days came when 184 inmates had to be transferred from the old Salem Jail to the new Middleton facility, some eight miles away. It was a cold Saturday morning in February 1991, and Saint Peter's Street was blocked to all traffic. There were buses at the gates to transfer the inmates, a bevy of police cruisers, plus a double line of twenty guards from the jail door to the buses, all wearing full riot gear: bullet-proof vests, helmets, shields, black uniforms, billy clubs. Three German Shepard dogs strained at leashes. Each inmate, with just the clothes on his back, was escorted out of the jail in handcuffs with a jail guard at each shoulder, and then shackled to a seat on the bus. Some of the inmates sang, whistled, or shouted as they reached the open air. With lights flashing, dogs yelping, and guards who looked like characters from Star Wars, it was an eerie macabre scene. Thirteen inmates refused to leave their cells, shouting that they loved the old jail and wouldn't leave it. They were forced out into daylight by the sheriff's riot squad. By the end of the day, the old jail was empty for the first time in 178 years. It was truly the end of an historic era.

✳ ✳ ✳

The inmates who had refused to go to Middleton had thrown buckets of urine at the guards, and the smell of it permeated the empty edifice. Once the inmates had left, some of the guards began acting as irresponsible as the unruly inmates. They broke nine windows in the jail, throwing things around and kicking holes in walls. "Things have been very tense for both the officers and the inmates," said Charlie Reardon when reporters confronted him about the rampage of the guards. "I do not condone their action," he responded, "but the officers involved were just releasing their tensions."

Good old Correctional Officer Ernie Comeau—of my dog-training days—was in charge of cleaning up the mess at the jail, and he was disgusted. "You can't even see the floors anymore," he reported in his French accent. "They are covered with inmates' clothing, smashed radios and televisions, pizza boxes left by the guards, and food thrown all about. It looks like a war zone."

County Commissioners hearing of the mess and damage left behind by the guards went to investigate. "It's malicious destruction, senseless vandalism," said Commissioner Kevin Leach, and he resolved to investigate further. Sheriff Reardon said he had left the jail late Sunday afternoon and was unaware of the vandalism by guards, but an article in the *Newburyport Daily News* by Associated Press reporter Bill Darmody stated that, "A former guard testified that Sheriff Reardon was present when guards tore apart the old Salem Jail." Reardon remained adamant that he wasn't there, but disciplined three officers who he discovered did participate in the trashing of the jail. Two were suspended from duty for three days and one received a letter of reprimand, and Reardon assured all that they would pay damages. I was probably the person most upset about this destruction by correctional officers. None of those professing guilt were of my old gang of deputies and guards, which gave me some consolation, but the old jail that had done its duty for so long didn't deserve such treatment.

※ ※ ※

Today, the old Salem Jail remains idle and abandoned. Some consider it a white elephant and others a precious antique of great historic value. I side with the later group. It is now owned by the City of Salem, and many people have suggested various uses for the old jail: museum, restaurant, homeless shelter, school, office building, storage facility, and the list goes on. Some think it should be torn down, which would be quite a costly chore considering the size and weight of the granite slabs and blocks that hold it together, inside and out. Whatever it becomes, it will cost a good sum of money to bring it back to life. A hotel or inn wouldn't be a bad idea, for the building is in the heart of the city within walking distance of Salem's many tourist destinations. And so I hope, one day, it returns to some distinguished glory.

The historic Sheriff's House is burned and gutted by vandals. It remains in this condition as this book goes to press. Historians and politicians debate whether to rebuild it or tear it down.

❊ ❊ ❊

Across the street from the jail, Parker Brothers Games has moved out, and their old headquarters torn down to make room for condos. The old sheriff's house next to the jail suffered a crueler fate. It was partially abandoned in 1979 after a suspicious fire exactly one year from the time of my open-heart surgery. The kitchen and attached sheds were damaged beyond repair, but Historic Salem, Inc. was interested in restoring the remaining structure. The house was com-

*The abandoned Salem Jail & House of Correction, once the oldest
working jail in America, stands damaged and decaying in
downtown Salem today. Its fate is constantly being debated in City
Hall. Is it a rare old antique of value, to be restored for some
alternative use, or is it just an old granite eyesore to be dismantled?*
(Photo by Dugie Russell)

pletely abandoned and boarded up in 1991, but fire again ruined the
remaining interior in 1999 when kids or transients who had broken
into the house from the Howard Street Cemetery set it ablaze purposely or by accident. There is still talk of restoring the house at the
time of this publication, but it is in such terrible condition, completely gutted by fire, that demolition seems most likely.

※ ※ ※

Although Cy Newbegin has departed this world, I must say something to redress our grievances and to be cordial in a way that we

weren't back in the 1970's. I did not really know the man, but some years after our quarrel, he hired my son Jimmy while still in college as a cub reporter for the *Salem Evening News*. He allowed Jimmy many feature by-lines, which is an unusual and kind gesture from a publisher to a new cub reporter. So, thanks, Cy.

✳ ✳ ✳

My two state representative pals who became sheriffs about the same time I did, died in office. My mentor, Jerry Bowes of Cape Cod, died shortly after I retired on disability, and Cliff Marshall of Norfolk County suffered a stroke in 1995, and a year later at age 58, died of a brain tumor. *The Boston Globe* praised Cliff as "an innovative corrections official." Like myself, he went into the job as a conservative politician, and because of conditions that confronted him at his jail, became an active liberal in the battle for human rights.

✳ ✳ ✳

In November of 1996, High Sheriff Charles Reardon, my old special sheriff, was arrested and charged with illegally accepting gratuities from the writ service deputies. Charlie resigned as sheriff, pleaded guilty, and was sentenced by a federal judge to a year in prison and three years probation, plus fined $30,000. He served his time in the federal penitentiary at Morgantown, Virginia. Charlie's appointed special sheriff, Harry Coppola of Lynn, went to jail as well and three other sheriff's department employees were found guilty of various corruption charges.

✳ ✳ ✳

After Reardon's resignation, Massachusetts Governor William Weld appointed Frank Cousins of Newburyport, a former state representative, as High Sheriff of Essex County. Frank is an African American and a Republican. He was later formally elected by the citizens of Essex County, beating out all Democratic opposition, and at the publishing of this book he remains high sheriff.

✹ ✹ ✹

A group of inmates sued the county and Sheriff Reardon in l984, claiming that the Salem Jail & House of Corrections provided unsafe living conditions as defined by state and federal laws. All inmates housed at the jail between July l984 and February 1991, when the old jail was closed down for good, were eligible for damages. Some 850 inmates shared the settlement of $1,395,000, provided by the State Department of Corrections, and ultimately, the taxpayers. The state fought another such suit by inmates of the Lawrence Jail in 1983 and lost; it cost the state millions of dollars with each Lawrence inmate named in the suit receiving approximately $3,200 apiece.

✹ ✹ ✹

In my short sojourn as High Sheriff of Essex County, I slowly developed from a moderate-conservative into a full-fledged liberal. The penal system in America is truly flawed. There are now new great cement fortresses of glass wall interiors, where guards watch and oversee many inmates who live in them without any privacy. Inmates are even watched while washing and going to the bathroom. In retrospect, the Salem buckets seem more humane.

Many new prisons have been built since my days as sheriff and these edifices are now filled to capacity and are overflowing. The Essex County Jail System has eight times the population today than when I took office. We once locked away people who were drunk on the streets. It was that way when I was a boy, but it didn't stop people from drinking. The drunks eventually became a burden to the system and caused overcrowding in the jails, so that policy was abandoned and the drunks were released. Now our courts and jails are crowded with those who sell or smoke marijuana. Like drinking alcohol, smoking cigarettes, or eating chocolate cookies, smoking marijuana can be addictive. Officials tried taking alcohol away from the public in the early twentieth century, but that didn't work. Those who smoked in public were punished under the laws of the seventeenth century, and we have laws against children under 18 years old smoking and that doesn't seem to work either. Have we learned nothing from our previous mistakes? If we allow pot to be smoked legally in private, almost half the populations of all the jails and prisons in America would be freed, and 90% of those freed would become hard working, law abiding citizens. Then, we could stop building these large ugly, expensive jails and prisons. I'm not talking about legalizing hard dope, but let's face it, marijuana has less effect on humans than alcohol does. We might as well banish beer and wine. How's that for liberalism?

✳ ✳ ✳

The Correctional Alternatives Center Lawrence (CAC), better known as "The Farm," is progressing stronger than ever, presently housing some 300 men on work release. It saves the county millions of dollars, and has over 100 inmates involved in community services each day, with as many repaying victims of their crimes in various forms of restitution. Also at The Farm, is a regimented boot camp for some forty offenders who undergo strict discipline and physical duties, such as cleaning up the state's highways, before being released from jail. Terry Marks and Jim St. Pierre, who initiated most of the programs at The Farm, remain on part-time duty there as consultants. John Kuczun, Don Richards, and Phil Corriveau died in their late forties, but were also instrumental in getting this successful correctional project started. The miracle farmer, Leo Lobeo, retired, but he is still farming somewhere out west.

✳ ✳ ✳

The old Newburyport Courthouse is also still in operation and was fully restored after its terrible wounds from the bombers. Recently retired were the last of my court officers who served Newburyport well: Norman "Dugie" Russell, George MacKinnon, Charlie Geary, Billy Cox, who retired in his late sixties, and Harry Healey, who recently retired at age seventy, and like MacKinnon, doesn't look a day over fifty.

✳ ✳ ✳

As for me, I keep a condo in Salem, though I prefer to spend my winter months in warmer climes. I still keep in touch with many of my old deputies and guards, and we get together now and then and laugh about our crazy escapades. I have survived five heart attacks and two open-heart surgeries. I will probably have to undergo a necessary third operation to replace my second aortic pig-valve in the near future. And so, before my time is up, just for your interest and enjoyment, I thought it important to reveal this history about the sheriffs of the "Wild East"—a bit of Americana about a recent bygone era. I hope you enjoyed it.

I recently went on an early morning boat trip from Salem to Gloucester. After docking at a Gloucester wharf, I headed up the gangplank. A group of some twelve gruff looking men were coming down the gangplank, heading for a docked fishing schooner. As I walked up the ramp, each one of them shouted loudly: "Hi, Sheriff"; "How you doing, Sheriff?"; "Nice to see ya', Sheriff." I was surprised. I smiled, waved, and shouted hellos. "Who are they?" my friend asked. I didn't recognize any of these fishermen, but I knew who they had to be—old residents of the Salem Jail who were at one time wayward youths but were now walking the straight and narrow. I am proud of them and glad that I helped them rehabilitate back into society.

THE END

ABOUT THE AUTHOR

Robert Ellis Cahill was born and raised in Salem, Massachusetts. He is a graduate of Boston University's College of Communications, and was president of his class in 1957. The following year, the U.S. Army sent him to Eritrea, East Africa where he served as a lieutenant in Security-Intelligence. He returned home to Marblehead in 1960 to become sales director for New England Divers, Inc. in Rhode Island and Connecticut, and a professional scuba diver and dive instructor. He then became Advertising Assistant for Aetna Casualty Insurance Company in Hartford, Connecticut, and two years later moved to Boston, where he spent six years as Community Relations Supervisor for John Hancock Insurance Company. Cahill continued in public relations for four more years, working as Account Executive for Culver Advertising, Inc. of Boston, and Vice-President of MacDougall Advertising of Peabody, Massachusetts.

Bob became a Salem City Councilor-at-large in 1968 and a State Representative in the Massachusetts Great and General Court for some six years. He ran for High Sheriff of Essex County in 1974, and was elected as the county's top law-enforcement officer, covering 34 cities and towns.

Bob is the author of well over 100 feature articles on various subjects, but mainly New England history and the sea, for such publications as Yankee Magazine, Boston Magazine, Pictorial Living, Ocean Industry, Skin Diver, and National Geographic. He has written 27 books, including: "Diary Of The Depths," "Lighthouse Mysteries Of The North Atlantic," "New England's Ancient Mysteries," "Haunted Happenings," and 23 others. Bob also founded and created three museums in Salem, Massachusetts and the publishing house, Old Saltbox Publishing Company, Inc of Danvers, Massachusetts.

At the publishing of this book, Bob Cahill and his wife Sandy live in Celebration, Florida, but visit Salem every year in the summer. Their four children: Keri, Danny, Jim, and Steve, now adults, live in Marblehead, San Francisco, Washington D.C., and Celebration, respectively. Bob is now working on another book about kids growing up in Salem during World War II.

Essex County was first settled by European people in 1628, and was incorporated in 1648. It is located at the northeastern corner of the state. The Atlantic Ocean is to the immediate east.

Map of Essex County MA